With A Hum

CW01084670

by

Peter Gow
aka Lewis Gates
The Autobiography

For Mum, Jacqui and Ben

INDEX

Dedication

Foreward by Richard Kelly

Men With Broken Hearts

Prologue

Epilogue

Acknowledgements

Foreword

When I first heard that my friend Pete was writing this book I had two thoughts,

1: good on you, brilliant really hope it does well for you.

2: Holy crap on a cracker, as the memories of the things we did came flooding back. Many of which I'm sure are in the following pages

Pete and I met circa 1994 when we somehow decided to join forces and our respective talents into one show. We were both going through a difficult time in our private lives , so the Lewis Gates Roadshow came to be.

At first we learnt about each other, which didn't take long as we realised that we both worked hard to make the show a 'fandabidozi' experience. On and off stage in the beginning he was Des O'Connor to my Freddie Starr, and a true friendship shortly followed as I'm glad to say still exists to this day,

In the beginning of our journey, to me Pete's confidence was a bit low because of switching to singing live from miming. But I think with the way I was ,let me explain, I am somebody that does things seriously without taking myself too serious and so a few pranks from myself which are possibly also in the following pages, I think that this is part of how we addressed this over a short length of time, Because he got his mojo [for want of a better word] going and the show went from strength to strength .

Pete had everything the looks, the voice the moves and the manorizems of the King of Rock and Roll, I had many rolls over the years and enjoyed all of them ,the result was that Pete and the show was a worldwide marketable product which he went on to prove by working world wide .

Which just goes to show that with perseverance and hard work you can succeed in this business?

I truly hope that you enjoy the stories in the following pages as I'm sure I will.

From Pete's Charlie Hodge

Richard Kelly

Prologue

The stage was pitch black in this 1100 capacity sell out theatre, my band started the 2001 Space Oddessy intro. You could feel the atmosphere building. Then Guy exploded with his drums and the band began to rock the house. The spotlight came on and I walked on stage to rapturous applause. You literally can not see anything when the follow spot is on you. As I walked from one end of the stage to the other accepting the applause, for one minute my mind took me back to where I started in the small pubs in Langley a North Manchester housing estate. I had come a long way. Memories flashed through my mind. One was my mum who never got to hear me sing live, all the famous people I had met and people that helped me along the way, Jimmy Bond, Mike & Sue and Mike Ruggiero. I was drinking in the applause, then BAM I was back in reality. I took the guitar off Jacqui smiled at my band and started singing.....

Oh See, CC Rider...... I was right where I was born to be.....

You Never Walked In That Man's Shoes,
Or Seen Things Through His Eyes,
Or Watched With Helpless Hands,
While The Heart Inside You Dies,

So Help Your Brother Along The Way,
No Matter Where He Starts,
For The Same God That Made You,
Made Him Too,
These Men With Broken Hearts.......

Elvis Presley 1970

Chapter 1

1964-1977...HOME IS WHERE THE HEART IS

My story begins at midday on Saturday 4th July 1964 at Crumpsall Hospital in North Manchester. I was born Peter Gow to my parents Brenda and Ian Gow. There were some complications leaving my mum not being able to have any more children so I would be the only child. I was born with severe eczema which nobody knew much about at the time but would cause me untold problems in the future. An hour or so later my dad left me and mum so he could go and play football for his Saturday team! Which I still can't understand, I was his only child, but more about his antics later.

My very first memory is from 1966. I was walking with my mum and granddad through the subway in Oldham. Apparently granddad was picking up a document. I found out much later he was picking up my Grans death certificate, she had died a year before I was born. I just thought it was great going through what I thought was a big tunnel.

My mum, Elizabeth Brenda Lees, was born on Andrew Street in Middleton Junction, a small village near Middleton. She lost a younger brother Andrew aged one through pneumonia. She also lost both her parents, Esther and John, and brother Dennis when she was just nineteen to tuberculosis. It left mum and her sister, Auntie Joan, her elder sister, to face the world on their own. Consequently I never got to meet my mum's parents nor her brother Dennis. My mums dad and brother Dennis were wizards with electronics and made their own televisions and countless other electrical goods. My mum always said uncle Dennis would have made me the best sound system had he lived.

My dad's dad, John Gow, was born in the Gorbals in Glasgow. A pretty rough area by all accounts. Later he lived opposite Glasgow Rangers football ground. His dad was a drunk docker that beat his wife every weekend when he got home from the pub. Consequently Granddad never touched a drop of alcohol in all his life.

He moved to Manchester after the war and got a job driving buses which he did for over forty years. He and my Gran, Gladys and dads half brother Bill settled in Blackley near Manchester. They lived in a prefab house that the government had built after the war. My granddad was in the Military Police and fought in WW2 on D-Day. Although on his second day he was blown off his motorbike by artillery fire, injured and sent back to England.

When I was one year old Mum looked through the glass panel of the front door and saw a little black puppy. She went to investigate and it was a tiny little thing. Someone had left him on our doorstep. She said you could fit him in the palm of her hand. Mum thought it would be a good idea to take him in and he could grow up with me.

He was a cross Labrador/Alsatian and was pure black. Mum named him Blacky and he would be with us for the next fourteen years. He did some really funny things over the years. One time Mum had left the roast chicken on the kitchen table and when no one was around, you guessed it he swiped it and ran out the back door. Mum was furious with him when he came back. She put him outside so she could cool down. About thirty minutes later he came back with a dead chicken in his mouth and put it down in front of Mum. She freaked out and told him to get rid of it. He had only gone over to the farmers house and got a chicken to say sorry.

He used to love going on the farmers fields and rounding all the cows up. I'm sure he thought he was a weird collie. Once one of them kicked him and I saw him go down. I watched as I thought he wouldn't get up, but after a few minutes he did the walk of shame and slowly came home.

When it was raining I used to play with my toy soldiers, I had hundreds of them all over the living room floor. Blacky would come in and walk through the soldiers missing every single one of them. When I was at school, at home-time he would sit at the back door when it was time. Mum said you could set your watch with him.

2

Going back to the mid fifties and the government built a Manchester overspill estate near Middleton called Langley. In 1962 my gran and granddad upped sticks and got a cottage flat, 16 Carrock Walk over looking farmer's fields and countryside. Everything looked rosy until 1963 my gran Gladys succumbed to clinical depression and committed suicide. So another grandparent I wouldn't get to know. By this time my mum and dad were married so they moved in with granddad to help him. Then the next year I came along and granddad and mum doted on me. On his days off he would take me and mum to different seaside resorts or to Heaton Park for the day.

Granddad would tell me stories of when he fought with Bonnie Prince Charlie, I was in awe! And when we got home Mum would sing the Sky Boat song to get me to sleep. I'm going to record it one day.

By the late sixties my Grandad met and married his second wife Marion. He moved to her house in Newton Heath. Each Sunday morning we would go see him. The house seemed huge and I was fascinated with it. I wasn't allowed to call Marion Grandma or Gran, it had to be Auntie Marion. She was an unmarried spinster in her late forties and she didn't want to feel old. Looking back I think it was very selfish of her, she never treated me like a Grandson. And she really was selfish because one of the conditions of marrying Granddad was there was to be no sex ever! So when I went to see Grandad she was just there in the background.

I wasn't allowed to play out on the fields at 5yrs old but I played on Carrock Walk and Pooley Close adjacent, with my first friend Gail Stockton. She was a bit of a tomboy really. We played on our bikes, football and cricket. We would have races around the block on our trikes. She used to have lunch with me and mum, and as time went on I think mum thought we'd end up together. As I was growing up I made other friends that lived nearby like the Catlin brothers Wayne, Rod and Daz. Daz was more my own age and we became good friends. Me, Daz, Rod and Wayne all wanted to be The Bay City Rollers for about three months, we thought we were cool miming along with broom handles in their house! Then they discovered Punk Rock and I discovered Elvis Presley and Rockabilly.. Daz ended up playing bass in a punk band at the famous Marquee Club in London. Ive not seen him for years but I hope he had a great career. Other friends included Martin Witherford and his brothers. Dennis and John Clayton, Harry Hayes, Andy Connolly and his brothers, Pete Fanning, Arthur and Dave Chatburn, Paul and Michael Hughes and of course Gail's sisters Carol, Sandra and Christine. With all these new friends I had Gail seemed to drift away doing her own things while I was playing football and cricket all day. I should have included her more. But as usual my head was in the clouds dreaming of being a professional footballer.

We used the farmer's fields as our football pitch and called it Little Wembley. Every second I had I would be on there playing football with whoever was out. Sometimes it would be twenty on each side and I would pretend to be one of my Manchester City heroes like Colin Bell or England goalkeeper Gordon Banks but most of all Man City goalkeeper Joe Corrigan, he was my real hero. We would play for hours until it went dark when our parents shouted us in. The sun seemed to shine all the time when we were young but that probably counts for everyone.

Further up the fields there were lots of trees and we used to go climbing and making dens. Mr Seal, the Farmer, didn't mind too much because we would help him when it came to hay baling time.

Further on from the fields were posh houses that faced onto Heywood road and then on to Heaton Park. At the very top of the fields you could see the whole estate sprawled out in front of you. I remember me and Dennis Clayton going apple raiding once but we strayed onto another farm. The farmer caught us and called the police. They said we had a choice of telling our parents or getting a clip round the ear. No choice there then we had a clip round the ear. If mum would have found out I'd have got the same from her as well!

We also went over to Bowlee which was a disused RAF airstrip from WW2. It still had the bomb shelters, bunkers and bomb craters and we would play our war games. There were football pitches there too so I was happy as Larry.

When I was five Daz Catlin hit me, for what reason I don't know. I was in shock so I went to tell mum. She laughed at first then told me to get back out there and hit him back. So I did and I thought I'd killed him. But he got up in the end and we had a mutual respect friendship that lasted throughout our childhood.

So in short we had five or six acres of farmland plus a disused RAF camp as a playground, I have great memories of my childhood.

Bonfire week was brilliant, we would go collecting wood from anywhere we could find it. We would have our bonfire just off the road on the fields. One time we went and confiscated a full wooden telephone pole that had been left by BT the night before, we used it as our centre pole it was huge and took six of us to carry it. When it was dark we would sneak over to Bowlee where the official Bonfire was and carry back as much as wood as we could carry. We had some huge bonfires over the years! We couldn't find a centre pole one year so we built the wood around the lamp post, it was brilliant when it went bang! We would take turns guarding our wood against other gangs that were after nicking ours. Uncle Pete, Gail's dad, used to bring home pieces of sets from Granada, he worked at the place that made them. We had some hilarious bonfires with Hilda Ogden's mural and parts of the Rovers Return. He even brought us parts from a castle one year. We had a turret as the look out post, it was unbelievable when I think back at what we got up to.

Mums sister, Auntie Joan and Uncle Bill had three kids, my cousins Christine, Jackie and Ian. Me and mum used to see them regularly and I felt like I was another brother rather than a cousin. They lived in Blackley so we would walk to Heaton Park from Langley and meet them there. I've got happy memories of sunny days, ice cream and going on the swings etc. We would then go back to Auntie Joan's house and have tea. Then my dad arrived at about 7pm after his shift to take us home.

On my dads side there was his half brother Uncle Bill and Auntie Marian with there three girls Lynn, Gillian and Janet. We only saw them on Christmas day when we had to go to there house at about 2pm for Christmas day dinner. It was awful! Not only did I have to leave my brand new toys behind, they were really posh! In fact Auntie Marion thought she was the Queen in the clothes she wore and her persona. Talk about pretentious, she never knew how ridiculous she sounded. Looking back it was hilarious but at the time I didn't like it one bit. There was very little food on the table and I felt really awkward taking more than I should, it was embarrassing. They had their own house in Chadderton near Oldham. I just didn't feel comfortable at all. Granddad and his new wife Marian usually made an appearance about 7pm so I felt better then. I didn't have anything in common with these cousins and so it proved later on when I never saw them again even to this day! Not even attending my mum's funeral which I was disgusted about. Mum had made all their wedding dresses and they couldn't be bothered to pay their respects!

When it was school holidays mum took me with her to the local shops on Bowness road. On the way back we used to call in and see her friends Cath and Albert Pole for a brew. They had a large family and I thought it was cool, all these grown up sons and daughters with their different characters. Mum made some wedding dresses for young Cath and Irene. It seemed like there was laughter all the time. They were truly comical and genuine warm people.

She had other great friends, Carol and Tommy Price, son David and daughter Susan, they lived three doors down. Carol would call at our house all the time for a brew and became my mums best friend. On New Years Eve we would have a party at our house and we would dance to my Elvis songs. Later when my mum was ill Carol and Tommy were a huge help. And later still they became Ben's Godparents. Without doubt the most honest people Ive ever met.

My mum was an extremely talented dressmaker, making many wedding dresses for far too little payment, but she loved the creativity. She also made dresses and clothes for lots of people. She would also make the outfits for the confirmation day at St Mary's. She learnt from her Auntie Lizzie who had a dressmaking shop in Middleton Junction. Auntie Lizzie took over the mother role when my mum's parents died. Mum was very close to her and Uncle Herbert. He fought in WW1 in the battle of the Somme. He had half of his stomach blown away and was sick most his life. Understandably he was extremely quiet but he always had a smile for me when we visited, and that made me feel special. They lived on Victoria Avenue in Blackley.

I started school when I was five at St. Mary's Catholic School on Langley. Don't remember much about my two years there. Apart from the teachers making us eat semolina pudding and me throwing up. Needless to say mum was really angry and tore a strip out of the teacher. I never had semolina again and I still can't stand it today.

My dad had a job at the local cigarette factory and my mum would supplement the money he gave her each week by making clothes for people. She also used to work for Vernon's Pools every Thursday. I would go with her most weeks till I got older.

My dad would play football every weekend and I wanted to go with him. I was proud he was such a good player and had about twenty trophies on display in our living room. I used to polish them and I was so proud of him. But I was only allowed to go watch him occasionally, which I could never understand. Later on I would understand why!

I moved up to St Mary's junior school when I was seven. Ive got special memories of this. Made some great friends such as Chris Mannion, Ged Philbin and Mick Barker. At dinner times we all played football in the school yard. Even the local priest Father John joined in sometimes. With my father being a goalkeeper everyone assumed I would be one for the school team. But I never got a look in because Ged Philbin was far too good. I didn't mind, Ged was a good friend.

7

The headmistress was a nun the same as in the infants. Sister Barbara was very firm but mostly fair. When it was confirmation time at this catholic school, my mum was asked to make all the outfits and the confirmation Queens dress. I was asked to be one of six train carriers. I think it was only because mum was making the outfits for free. Good old St Mary's Catholic School. But we'll come back to Sister Barbara later.

I was around nine or ten when we were all called into assembly for an announcement. One of my friends Steven Slattery had passed away. We all knew he wasn't well, he had to where a wig because of the cancer. In any case we were all in shock. He had only been playing with us a matter of weeks earlier. The whole school attended his funeral and it was pretty surreal, it took a long time afterwards for it to sink in. He was a lovely lad, God Bless you Steven.

I passed my eleven plus exam in the final year and got a choice of high school. Mum wanted me to go to the posh school Cardinal Langley but I chose Bishop Marshall's where most of my friends were going.

On the first day at Bishops I made a life long friend in Stephen McKay. I would call for him on the way to school; his mum and dad were so nice. We ended up in the same class and played for the school football team. Again they presumed I would be a goalkeeper, so I was. The headmaster was an ex-pro footballer from Wolverhampton Wanderers so everything was geared towards football, I was in heaven.

In his younger days dad was a semi-pro footballer for Oldham and Rochdale, even playing against a sixteen year old George Best who scored four goals against him. He was now playing for good amateur teems such as Langley Villa, Hollang and Langley Rangers. I would go and watch him whenever I could, I was really proud of this great goalkeeper. But it always seemed as though he didn't want me there as if I was a nuisance and in the way. I didn't understand this at such an early stage but it all added up later on.

When I was twelve in that hot summer of 1976 my dad gave me his old Elvis records. Out of curiosity I put one on the turntable in my room, Hound Dog and boom this voice screamed at me and sent a bolt of electric from my feet to my head, I physically felt it! I was stunned, I'd never heard of this guy Elvis but I knew there and then he would play a huge part in my life. Never in my wildest dreams did I ever think I would sing his songs for a living! Let alone travel the world singing his songs!

When I was ten or eleven my Mum shouted me in from outside and told me we were going out. All three of us got in the car and drove to the solicitors office on Lakeland Court. Mum explained to me that I was to sign some documents that would mean I would be entitled to half of the house if she died. So I signed and went back playing football. In hindsight she was very astute, she knew my Dad wouldn't want to live with me and so it was her way of helping me financially at some point in the future. I can honestly say that at that time a forgot about it until years later when Mum was proven right but more about that later....

I loved it at Bishop Marshall's School and made a lot of friends especially through the football team, Steve McKay, Paul Bravender, Chris Paul, Kevin Bagshaw, John Horsefield, Terry Edhouse, Paul Booth, Mike Dargue, Bobby Burns, Anthony Collins, Malcolm Thorburn, Stuart Fannon, Alan Casey, Eddie Atkin, Wayne Lomas, Jimmy Harding, Robert Patron, Caroline Bilal, Carole Slack, Deb Dillon, Ann Morley, Nicola Morris, Berni Moynahan. Lorraine Crawford, Julie Patriarco and many more. If I've missed anyone, my sincere apologies.

I got a bit of mickey taking about my eczema but I got used to it and ignored it. Then one day it seemed pretty bad, I can't remember who it was but Chris Paul stood up for me and told them to back off or else. I was a bit overwhelmed but very thankful for him making a stand. It's something I've never forgot. After that I got treated just like everyone else. Chris went on to serve in the army fighting overseas so that we could live in peace.

9

If your reading this Chris I've got nothing but thanks and huge respect for what you did and what you did for our country!

One of our sports teachers was Mr Goode and one day we were playing against one of our rival teams. The referee didn't turn up so Mr Goode decided he would be ref. Every decision he gave was against us and we lost. So we decided to teach him a lesson. When we were taking the nets down after the match we tied him to the goalposts with the nets and we all went and got a shower. Don't know who set him free but we were all in the Headmasters office on Monday morning and we all got the cane. The pain was worth it though and Mr Goode refused to teach us again. I think he learnt his lesson!

The next match we played I was really buzzing because my dad was coming to watch. I had broken into the school team as goalkeeper. There was a through ball and I came out and dived at the striker's feet. I ended up with a gashed knee, which afterwards left me with fourteen stitches. I was out of action and off school for three months. All my dad said was that I shouldn't have got injured. He looked at me with contempt. He took me home afterwards, left me with mum and Granddad and promptly left to play his own match on the Saturday afternoon. I was gutted; I thought he would have been proud that I had carried on playing (which caused an infection because of the dirt in my knee). My mum was going bananas and got granddad to take us to the hospital. I felt my dad was embarrassed. I was fourteen!

I remember me, Steve McKay and Malcolm Thorburn being in mostly the same classes and we got up to no good. One of the teacher's chairs was on its last legs. So me, Steve and Malcolm took it apart and put it together again using sellotape! When Miss came in and sat down it just collapsed completely, we were all in stitches.

I used to enjoy engineering drawing and got my only O'Level in it. The teacher was Martin Lynott, Phil Lynott's cousin (Thin Lizzy).

One subject I was keenly interested in was music with Mr Sowerby. I was so impressed with how if you played the right notes it would sound good. But he didn't really let any of us have a go on any of the instruments, he just asked each of us to copy him singing and do the scales. Alas as unbelievable as this sounds I was kicked out of music and told I was tone deaf! I was gutted and it affected my confidence for quite a while. However in hindsight I think I might just have proved Mr Sowerby wrong.......

In the last year our school was taken over by the bigger Cardinal Langley School and run mainly by priests from Cardinal Langley School. When we broke up for Christmas Steve and i thought we'd buy some cans of beer and drink them at dinner time. I put them in my sports bag but one of the priests checked all our bags and we were caught red handed. They confiscated my bag but nothing happened because they weren't really bothered about our school. However when I went to retrieve my bag after Christmas the unopened cans had disappeared? Talk about catholic priests being hypocrites.

By now Grandad had settled into his new home with Auntie Marion. He lived in one of the high rise flats on Victoria Avenue East in Blackley. For the first couple of years Grandad and Auntie Marion would come and see me on Christmas morning but she soon put a stop to that. I was his only Grandson what was she thinking? She was very selfish. It upset me quite a bit because I looked forward to seeing him on Christmas morning. But we still visited him on Sundays and I would go see him midweek sometimes, on my racing bike when I got older. He was on the fourth floor and I thought it was great going up in the lift and then seeing the views across to Alkrington. I used to go up to the fifteenth floor to see Auntie Jenny and Uncle George (Marion's sister). They had no children of their own so they used to spoil me. Aunty Jenny was the opposite of Marion and Uncle George was a massive Man City fan so we got along really well. Next door to Grandads lived Bert and Jean, they were so sweet and had lots of time for me. I used to call and see them every time I was there. Grandad seemed content so I was happy for him. It was just very hard putting up with Auntie Marion when I could tell she was false. This was proven true later when he passed away but more on that later.

It was around this time that John Clayton introduced me to his sister and brother in law Jimmy and Marian Bond. Jimmy was a big Elvis fan and we used to spend hours at his house listening to Elvis albums and drinking home made beer that he had made. Mum would have killed me had she known. Marian was great as well to put up with us, she would make bacon butties and laugh at Jimmy's dry sense of humour. They had four kids, Jimmy Jr, Gary, Phillip and Anne that added to the atmosphere of chaos. They were happy carefree days that I will always treasure.

But my life was about to change forever......

Chapter 2

1977-1984... IF I CAN DREAM

They say that everyone remembers where they were when Elvis died; I remember exactly where I was. I was thirteen years old and in Blackpool on our holidays. We stayed in a flat and I clearly remember Reginald Bosenquet announce it on the ITV news at 10pm, it was unconfirmed though and very sketchy. I was allowed to stay up and I kept switching channels to BBC1 and ITV. Still no firm confirmation. Then midnight came and normally on the BBC they would play the national anthem at midnight before it closed down for the night, but this time they played Love Me Tender with a picture of Elvis on the screen and confirmed the worst possible news. The King, Elvis Presley had died of a heart attack aged 42 at his home Graceland in Memphis, Tennessee!

It didn't hit me really, how one man had touched millions of lives. I was only thirteen, talk about unlucky. The next day we walked down the prom and it was as though nothing had happened, kids with their ice creams playing on the beach, it was surreal. Then I saw a newspaper stand and every paper had the headline about Elvis passing. I wanted to buy all of them but my dad said just the one.

The following day as we walked through the town it seemed like everyone was selling Elvis memorabilia. My mum was wise enough to let me buy quite a lot of Elvis stuff. The highlight of my holiday was the trip to the indoor market where there was an Elvis stall selling hundreds of Elvis records, LPs, 45s, and lots of bootleg albums. It was run by two Jewish men and they really looked after me. They were there to make money but you could tell they were really big Elvis fans themselves. They had been to see him in Las Vegas the previous year and were now distraught at the terrible news from Memphis. It was like being in an Aladdin's cave! I'd bought a couple of Elvis budget albums in the last year. But today I couldn't contain myself. Amongst other

13

vinyl I bought was a gold coloured 45rpm of Little Darlin'. I thought I was really cool!

So I was thirteen and I was obsessed with everything Elvis. Me and Jimmy Bond would try and get as many albums and singles that we could afford and then play them back at his house during the day. I was off school on crutches after I got injured at football but I still got around to his house most days. Then the summer came, I was crutch free and we would go to HMV in Manchester to try to get any new Elvis releases.

Jimmy, John Clayton and I went on a camping trip to Blackpool. It was hilarious, me and John didn't have a clue how to put up the tent so Jimmy took control. We got the bus into Blackpool and went to the Elvis shop. We bought some stuff and left it there to pick up after we had been to the Funhouse. First time I'd been to the Funhouse at Blackpool Pleasure Beach. It was great and we had a ball. We picked up our Elvis albums from the Elvis shop and headed back to the camp. Three lads in a two man tent is a tight fit, we were crunched up but didn't care. Now what you've got to remember is John was obsessed with the Elvis song Tiger Man, when I did my little bit at Jimmy's party's he got control of the single living room light and switched it on and off really fast when I moved around. So it was pitch black and me and Jimmy were trying to get to sleep and John starts singing Tiger Man and switching the torch on and off rapid. God knows what everyone else thought, we thought he was daft as a brush. Next thing he heard some girls passing by so he stuck his head out at the bottom with his torch under his chin trying to get the girls to join us. Needless to say they didn't, they must have thought he was completely crazy. I've got great memories of our weekend away in Blackpool.

I was fourteen or fifteen when we went to our first Elvis convention at the Free Trade Hall in Manchester. It was an all dayer and we got to meet Elvis' tour manager Diamond Joe Esposito. And then we saw Leyton Summers and we had our photo with him. He was one of the first Elvis impersonators in the UK and I instantly knew I wanted to be just like him. I had

14

no idea how, with my ginger hair, or as my mum called it strawberry blonde, I'm strawberry white nowadays!!

After the convention I met Dennis Williams and his wife Sandra. He was the branch leader of the Elvis fan club of Great Britain run by Todd Slaughter. I used to go over to Denis' house in Rusholme and watch lots of Elvis videos that you couldn't buy in the shops, it was brilliant. I would get the last bus home from Manchester.

Dennis used to organise mini bus trips to other Elvis conventions such as Leicester, Leeds and London. I was in my element watching shows and meeting members of Elvis' Memphis Mafia who were guests of honour. It always ended with an Elvis disco and we were all on the dance floor copying Elvis moves while the music was very loud. I suppose we all looked pretty strange really but we were happy and not harming anyone. On one trip to Leeds it took us four hours to get there instead of forty five minutes. The snow was three feet deep but Dennis still got us there and back. Needless to say we got lost a few times on the way back home. On the way back from Leicester once we nearly ended up in Scotland, it was hilarious! I didn't think it could get any better than this and Dennis has proven to be one of my long time close friends.

Dennis also took a coach load of us to London a few times. The first time was an all day Elvis Convention and George Klein, Elvis close friend, he was the main headliner. There was Elvis movies on a large screen, Elvis mime competition and live bands. George Klein was on at around 7pm I thought it was great to hear all these stories of him and Elvis. When he finished a live band started and George came and sat down right next to me, I thought it was a bit surreal, I cant remember what we spoke about but I was on a real high.

Our next visit to London was to Wembley Arena. Again it was an all dayer with similar things going on. The star headline this time was Freddie Starr who was on at about 8pm with his band and full orchestra. But just before he came on Todd Slaughter introduced and I quote "a very special Elvis fan" Billy Fury! The

15

audience went bananas. The hairs on the back of my neck stood up, the atmosphere in the Arena was electric. He couldn't perform he said he was sorry but his health wasn't good. Two weeks later Billy Fury died! What a star to come and be with fellow Elvis fans when he was clearly very ill.

It was at this event that the famous book burning took place. Albert Goldman had published a derogatory book about Elvis. It painted him in a very bad light about his prescribed drug addiction. Of course this was long before we all learned about how much our hero was addicted. Todd Slaughter walked on stage and promptly burned the book to rapturous applause. Although some of the book was true the majority of it had been made up for publicity. In years to come Mr Goldman admitted this but by then he had made his money!

Freddie Starr came on stage and was of course fantastic with his hour long Elvis show. The only night of his career that he never did an encore, Apparently after he finished the last song "American Trilogy" he walked off stage and collapsed with pure emotion. What an entertainer!

Another fan club event was in Leicester to see Charlie Hodge, Elvis' long time friend and musician. He was the only friend of Elvis' that had his own room at Graceland.. He was there to unveil a life size bronze statue and a Q&A session. He was so funny, I could see why Elvis loved him.

A few months later and we were off to De Montfort Hall in Leicester for a full day convention. The hall seemed huge. Again the usual events took place and Dennis and his son entered the mime competition. I was far too shy at that time. Heading the bill that night were 70's rock'n'roll band Les Grays MUD. They were awesome, even changing the lyrics of their songs to Elvis lyrics..

One strange trip was to Gloucester to attend Diane and Ray's Elvis event. Dennis knew Diane and Ray and arranged for us to go meet them at their house. When we walked in I couldn't believe what I was seeing. The house was resplendent with Elvis memorabilia all over the walls and ceiling. And when you could see a space they had clearly put up Elvis wallpaper. I had never seen anything like it, this couple were true Elvis fans and nice people to boot.

When Dennis could see I was getting serious about collecting Elvis records etc. He introduced me to a man called Harry. He lived in a pretty colourful part of Manchester called Collyhurst. Harry bought and sold Elvis bootleg vinyl albums and 45s. So Dennis took me and WOW I'd never seen so many Elvis albums, all of them not available to the general public. I remember I bought an album called "The Last Farewell" Elvis very last concert (and still not available to buy legally). It blew my mind! He must have had thousands of bootlegs and all I had on me was £20 so I settled for the one album. Harry's probably dead by now but he was a real character with his knowledge of what Elvis did and where. It's no wonder people travelled to his house from all over the world.

While my mates at School were into 80s music I had also discovered Rockabilly and Doowop. I had my hair cut short like the Rockabilly's had it. I got myself a blue drape jacket, pink socks and even blue suede shoes! I made friends with Syd Edhouse and Mark Nuttall. Syd was a teddy boy but Mark was a Rockabilly through and through. He opened my eyes to the really early beginnings of rock'n'roll pre 1956. I thought Mark was cool in his appearance and I tried to style myself the same. My mum hated it; she thought I'd end up in trouble. But we were just in it for the music and the style and we all thought we looked cool. Along with Martin Witherford they had motorbikes at one time or another. I was too young to have one but they taught me how to ride and when Martin was away on holiday I got to lend it for the week. I was only fifteen and he told me to stay local which I did. It was exhilarating riding around Middleton.

I remember at this time we all went to Preston to see Bill Haley's last ever UK show. It was electric when he came on stage and all the teds and teddy-girls were in the aisles dancing. It was like being back in the 50s. Mark also introduced me to other Rockabilly legends like Charlie Gracie, Ray Campi, Johnny Burnette, Sonny Burgess, Billy Lee Riley, Gene Vincent and our own Welsh legends Crazy Cavan & The Rhythm Rockers who I

17

got to see live and they were fantastic. I also got to see Shakin Stevens before he made it big. He was with The Sunsets then and played at The Midland pub in Manchester. He was terrific but later on he sold his soul to showbiz and made millions so I can't say I blame him.

I left school at fifteen mainly because another school, Cardinal Langley, had taken over ours. The teachers were all priests which didn't go down well at all. We were left with no teachers for lessons because priority was for Cardinal Langley. So we didn't attend for the most part of our last year. Although some of us took our exams and I'm proud to say I got my one and only O'level in Engineering Drawing.

I went for an interview at British Aerospace for an apprenticeship. My Uncle Bill knew the top brass and I was told I would get the placement. I passed the entrance test but was told I was too young, and to come back next year.

I was fifteen, carefree and wanted money in my pocket. So I went for a job as drivers mate delivering furniture for the co-op. I sat down for my interview with a very strange Scottish man who asked me questions about.... food? Talk about being confused! I decided I would take the job which was in a posh part of Middleton called Alkrington. I was on a work experience scheme and I was paid £23.50 a week and I had to give mum £10 for my keep at home. I got £13.50 for myself, a pint of beer only cost about 30p then so I could go out on a Saturday night, get chippy supper on the way home all for less than a fiver. I thought it was brilliant!

I made some really good friends when I worked at the Co-op. Miss Webster was the manageress and she taught me how to man manage people, get them working with you rather than for you. Anne Armstrong was the fruit and veg manager, she was great she took me under her wing and we had a great laugh in the process. Steve was the main butcher and he taught me everything he knew. In the end I became a qualified butcher. Finally Rose was the main till girl. She was probably only five years older than me and she was so fast on the till.

As I said it was a posh area and we had some celebrity customers come in like Bernard Manning's mum who I became friends with, I always looked after her making sure Bernard got the best beef etc. Frank "Foo Foo" Lamar was another customer; he was really down to earth.

Miss Webster asked me if I wanted to go on a management course one evening a week at Rochdale College. So I went straight after work on Tuesdays. The course was OK but I wasn't keen on Rochdale at all. The others on the course seemed to know each other. They included me sometimes but I never felt comfortable it was a clique. I passed the course and got my B-Tech Business and Management Degree. I was glad when it was over.

It was around this time when I was sixteen that I had my first crush. I was training to be a butcher and working on the front counter. She was called Stella Bolland and she used to come into the co-op every Saturday morning. I would make sure I was at the counter to serve her and her mum. She was the same age as me and it was obvious there was a spark, she had beautiful brown eyes. Eventually I got up enough courage to ask her out. The only thing was I only ever saw her with her mum. Her mum just shot me down straight away. I was gutted. Her mum thought I wasn't good enough for her daughter, being a simple trainee butcher. I also had a crush on Cheryl who lived above the shop but I didn't have enough courage to ask her out after the Stella Borland thing. I didn't know what life had held in store for me then. But somehow i knew I would be alright.

So I had money in my pockets and I was out most weekends in the pubs in Middleton. Pie and chips on the way home. I also started playing open age football at weekends. Saturday afternoons I played for Dave Hughes at Royton YFC. I didn't tell him I was a goalkeeper so I played in defence. Eventually Dave found out so I played the odd game in goal if they were short. But I really enjoyed playing outfield. I was with them for about five years and I think I played in every position. I even played against my school teacher Mr Niles. It was funny because he thought I would be in goal but I played in defence and I had to mark him. Which I'm proud to say I did really well. Although he wouldn't speak to me afterwards which I thought was a bit sad. My dad came to see me playing for Royton. The last time he had come to see me was when I got injured playing for the school team. I played in defence and thought id had a good game. After the match when I asked him what he thought he said nothing then came out with "you would be better off as a goalkeeper"? I actually got man of the match and my own dad was putting me down! I could see a pattern developing?

One Saturday afternoon we played against a team from Oldham and our captain told me to man mark that young kid on the other team. I thought no problem I can do that, he only looked tiny. How wrong was I, the kid tore us apart and we got beat 5 – 0, the kid scored three of them. I went over to him after the match and asked his name. He replied David Platt (the future England and Arsenal star) so nowadays I don't feel to bad that he ripped us apart. Although I've got to say I've never run around so much in my life!!

Once when Dave put me in midfield he took me off after thirty minutes. He said he subbed me before I got myself sent off! I did like a strong tackle! Dave got me trials with some professional clubs like Blackburn, Bolton, Bury and Rochdale but I got injured the week of the trial. He said he would put me forward the next year but I had already started my Elvis show and would be retired from football, I was twenty one. And yes I do regret not staying another season to see how I would have done. I played my last game one Saturday afternoon in Oldham. The next day I was booked to appear at The Nowster pub in Middleton. All my football mates had ribbed me every weekend about me doing my Elvis show. My God the whole squad turned up at The Nowster to give me a fantastic send off. They swamped the pub completely, it was tremendous and I got a bit emotional. Much alcohol was consumed!

I also played for a few Sunday morning teams like Heber's WMC, Gardner's Arms (Sandy lane), Woodside WMC and

Middleton Gas. At Middleton Gas they played me as a striker. I said yes without thinking, I just wanted to play. I played twelve games for them scoring fourteen goals in the Middleton Sunday league. I felt on top of the world, fearless! Then their regular striker came back from his injury and I was dropped. I didn't hang around I was off to newer pastures.

I had lots of energy back then, I would work six days a week at the Co-op 7am till 5pm, football training at night time with Royton twice a week. Then playing two or sometimes three matches over the weekend.

I broke my nose once when I was playing as goalkeeper on Bowlee Playing Fields. The opposition had Mick Pollard as their centre forward. I knew Mick from School, he was in the year above me, he was huge at school but now he was a colossus. There's me at 5'9 trying to jump for the ball as he was careering in on goal. I beat him a couple of times then he must have got miffed. He jumped up to challenge me and elbowed me right in the face. That's all I could remember till the smelling salts brought me around. I was so glad that there manager took him off he probably felt sorry for me.

My life was pretty full on with work, football and parties at Jimmy and Marian Bonds house. It was at one of those weekend parties that the spark ignited. I've got two left feet when I'm dancing but Jimmy put some Elvis songs on and I was transformed into moving like the king. So much so that Jimmy reckoned I was good enough to do it professionally. I thought he was joking but the following week he persuaded me to give it a go, he seemed very confident. My mum had always said I couldn't sing and I believed her. So Jimmy said he'd help me set up a mime act. We made two forty five minute sets straight off our vinyl records of Elvis concerts so it gave the illusion of being live. I would use his bird cage stand as a microphone stand and Jimmy Jr would use the light switch as a strobe! I kid you not; it was hilarious and frightening at the same time. Marion was very patient with us. But I had ginger hair? Jimmy told me not to worry about that as soon as an audience would see me it would be OK. So I started to grow my hair long.

He persuaded me to try it out at the next party in a few weeks time. My mum made me my first Elvis suit, it was brown and gold and I was ready to go!

The reaction was fantastic. I know they were all friends but they seemed genuinely impressed. Me and Jimmy were ecstatic. Then he dropped the bombshell. He said he knew it would be a success and that he'd got me a booking at Langley Labour Club on Easter Sunday night. In just two weeks! I didn't know what to say, for once I was speechless!

We agreed I needed a stage name; everyone in the business seemed to have one back then. I came up with Louis because I thought it sounded regal (French) and yet American sounding. Jimmy suggested a few second names, Louis Chambers, Louis Grant but we decided on Louis Gates. Gates being Elvis' surname from his movie Blue Hawaii. I would change the spelling of Louis to Lewis later on but that's how I originally became Louis Gates. It did feel a bit strange at first though.

It was the first and only time I would ever be nervous. To be precise I was a nervous wreck. Along with myself and Jimmy I took some friends of ours for moral support, Mark Ward, Darren Lyons and Harry Hayes. They kept me occupied, joking around etc. Then suddenly it was Showtime. Jimmy had sorted the sound out; we had a microphone placed in front of a guitar amp connected to the house speakers. 2001 Space Odyssey started. I thought if I don't do this now I may never get another chance. As I walked on stage I felt all the nerves leave my body, I felt alive and this was where I was meant to be. The audience didn't know what to make of me. But when I started miming and copying Elvis' moves they started cheering. Afterwards Jimmy said that some of them thought I was actually singing, my miming had been that good and the moves were all spot on. Don't know about that but I must have been doing something right. If I got a reaction like that with ginger hair I had to get black hair and sideburns! All five of us were elated after the show and I knew then that I wanted more and this would change my life forever.

I got paid £10 and promptly split it five ways!!

I was nineteen when the Co-op moved me to the bigger superstore in Middleton called Domus. They were training me up as assistant manager.

On my very first day at Domus I was walking through the warehouse when I stopped still in my tracks. I was stunned with her beauty. It was love at first sight for both of us, I couldn't believe it. All I could do was ask her had she worked there long, six times in a row! I was on cloud nine. Cathy Gilbody was the same age as me she had beautiful blue smiling eyes and long flowing blonde hair. Everything was in the right place if you know what I mean. I didn't stand a chance. I couldn't believe she would be interested in me but after a few weeks I asked her out for a drink. I picked her up from her parent's house where she lived. I was so nervous when I knocked on the door. Her mum asked me in; oh my God I was meeting her parents! They were very nice though and put me at my ease. The first pub we went in I spilled my drink all over her I was that nervous. My first date, I thought I'd blown it but she didn't seem to mind. Phew I had a second chance. We went in a few more pubs and I walked her home although I didn't get a kiss goodnight I asked her if she wanted to come watch me play football the following day and she said she would love to.

The following day, Sunday, I was on the pitch when all of a sudden everyone was wolf whistling. I turned around and it was Cathy. Nobody would believe she was my girlfriend. After the match she walked home with me, I was covered in mud as usual. When we got home I walked in and introduced her to my mum and dad and then went and had a bath (well she dropped her parents on me the night before). I walked her home later and she kissed me, my first ever kiss, I was nineteen, mesmerised and head over heels!

Meanwhile I had asked Jimmy Bond to be my manager (you couldn't make this up, James Bond was Elvis' manager!) and he was tirelessly trying to get me some bookings. We got a re-booking at Langley Labour Club on August Bank Holiday Sunday afternoon. I walked on stage at about 2pm and was going down well when at 2.15pm the Concert Secretary walked on stage and told me I'll need to cut it short because there was a more professional act coming on. I couldn't believe it! Jimmy sorted the tape deck out and I finished. I was in shock and upset that this old man would do such a horrible thing. I swore I would never go back there again and I never did, despite several phone calls off them when I was more established.

Jimmy arranged for us to rehearse at Demesne Community Center on Wednesday nights. Me and John Clayton would push these huge speakers and amps etc. in one of those big old prams that we had borrowed off his mum Mrs Clayton. We must have looked like Laurel and Hardy but hey you gotta start somewhere and all the while I dreamed of having a live band!

I invested in my first black wig and sideburns at the grand sum of £25. I wasn't allowed to dye my hair because of my eczema. I say sideburns, they were actually two black pieces of carpet cut to shape and stuck on with double sided tape. It was comical because the only wig I could afford looked like Adolf Hitler. Picture that, Adolf Hitler with tiny sideburns doing Elvis! I thought it was great!!

Jimmy bond got me bookings at the local pubs like The Falcon, The Gay Gordon, The Cardinals Hat and The New Broom. I was working during the week, playing football at weekends and doing shows at weekend evenings. Cath would always come and support me and i felt indestructible!

I can't remember how I got a booking at Pontin's. But me and John Clayton went on the coach to Southport. The show went well but we were treated absolutely awful by the management and the staff. We had been given one of the chalets for the night. So in the morning when we were about to leave I'm ashamed to say we filled all the cups and bowls etc. with water and put them back in the cupboards. Not exactly rock 'n' roll trashing the hotel room but it felt great at the time. Of course looking back it was all a bit silly. We never got a re-booking at Pontin's.

I was a bit shy about singing live over the top of Elvis' voice on the tape so I sang into a dummy microphone. I was even

24

miming to Elvis talking in-between the songs. It felt right and my timing was good because of listening countless hours to the Kings concerts. I felt better as well, as if I was giving the audience my 100%. Unbeknown to me it would prove to be extremely lucrative in the future but for now the audience would hear just Elvis' voice!

It was at The Gay Gordon pub that I met Mike & Sue Smith. They worked behind the bar and Mike was a huge Elvis fan, we hit it off straight away and have been friends ever since. On some Saturdays when I didn't have a show Cath and I would go out with Mike and Sue to the Woodside Club or The Dyers and Polishers Club in Middleton. We would watch all the entertainers and I would pick up a few things to make me more professional. Mike even got me a booking at The Dyers and Polishers Club. I thought it was brilliant! I had a proper stage and a full audience. So word was spreading about me even the local newspaper did a spread on me. This led to a booking at The Woodside Club in Middleton. It was a charity night and I got to meet Bill Tarmey (Jack Duckworth from Coronation Street). He was great and sang a few cracking songs, he was a good singer in his own right.

Not long after this I met John Clews and Steve Grayson who came to see my show and offered to manage me. I didn't want to leave Jimmy Bond. He had done so much for me and he had been like a big brother to me. But he said I should try it and see what happens. Eventually he persuaded me to go with John and Steve after much ale was drank. It would be a small step up the ladder. Reluctantly I agreed. However that wasn't the end of Jimmy Bond in this story, more about my good friend later.

John had been a professional drummer with the well known Hillsiders Country Band in the seventies. So he had a real good grip on what it takes to perform. He also had the gift of the gab being a Liverpudlian. In fact he could have sold sand to the Arabs. He suggested we have a rehearsal he had a few ideas to improve the show. So I was rehearsing every Wednesday evening at Demesne. Straight away he introduced different coloured lighting and proper strobes etc. I bought a lighting desk which he would operate with several spotlights. With my show being a visual mime act I needed more gimmicks, so I decided to ask my mum if she would make some scarves to throw into the audience. Slowly but surely the show became more slick. I Learned pretty early on to try and emulate Elvis. She agreed and that started the mammoth task of sewing twenty scarves per show. It went down a storm, audiences couldn't get enough of them and we always ran out of them each show.

John and Steve got me bookings outside of Middleton like Heywood, Blackley, Charlestown and Manchester. At one venue in Manchester called The Sir Henry Royce John had arranged a ticketed show, £2 on the door. I agreed to it but when I got there the place was empty. Then at about 8.30pm all these Rastafarians walked in and paid their £2. I panicked; I couldn't understand how I was going to do the show. John said not to panic and just do what im good at. He was right they loved it and were up on the dance floor all night. It was a bit surreal though! Then he booked me into The Pomona Hotel in Manchester. Big Jim White had been regularly booked into the venue. with his well known Forever Elvis Show. I just went along with it. So I'm halfway through the first set and this feminine man came up to the stage playing around and pretending to stroke the bottom of my leg, so I played along like Freddie Starr would i.e. blowing kisses in jest. John came running up to the stage and shouted at me " it's a gay pub now stop it". Oh no! I had no idea. I ran off stage at the interval and went directly to my dressing room hoping to catch John and have it out with him. He wasn't there, he'd legged it, I guess I looked angry.

Another time John asked me to get suited and booted we had a meeting at Middleton Civic Hall. He told me to leave the talking to him so I did. It was a production of Bye Bye Birdie and at the interval we went into the managers office not only did he tell the manager he had a similar production on at Liverpool Empire he also told the guy I had my own band? I was lost for words. When we got outside I asked him about it and he just said don't worry that manager wouldn't know and we had to look at getting a band together. I told him there was one small problem I couldn't sing and that's why I mimed. He said we'll get a way around don't worry. I was speechless, literally!

Yes John could definitely sell snow to the Eskimo's.

Steve introduced me to his brother in law Tony Chiappori who offered to drive for me. He had one of those huge Granada's, he would put a white sheet on the back seat and I would get ready at home and was driven to the venue and I felt just like the real Elvis. I thought I was living the dream. My mate Mark Ward would travel with us and act as security! We must have looked insane, all five of us turning up at pubs like the Memphis Mafia. I was on fees of £40-£50 by now but by the time I had paid all the entourage I was left with about £10. How stupid I was back then I didn't realise they were just on the gravy train!

But I had a dream of having a full live band to play in theatres etc. So I bit my tongue and carried on.

I was nineteen in February 1984 and feeling on top of the world. So one evening at my house I proposed to Cath. It was very romantic and she said yes. I think she was a bit shocked but it felt right. The following day at work everybody was saying congratulations the ring is gorgeous. This confused me until I found Cath when she showed me the ring she had gone out and bought. Now we all know that's not the way to do it, I just went along with it to see how things panned out. But it did make me think something wasn't right.

We got a flat together just round the corner from my mums. She moved in full time and the idea was for me to stay at weekends and eventually move in full time somewhere down the line. It didn't work out like that, she kept pushing for me to move in straight away and I didn't like being told what to do. We had my mate Steve McKay and his girlfriend stop over after a night out. In the morning Cath was making bacon butties for them and told me I'd have to make my own. In fact I don't think she ever cooked a meal for me ever! It was the beginning of the end for me and this beautiful woman. It all seemed to go down hill pretty fast, I was feeling heartbroken but clung on in hope things would get better.

27

I had been having problems with my right eye. When I was a goalkeeper I always had problems judging the distance of a cross ball and coming out to catch it, even as far back as school.

One thing Cath did urge me to do was get my eyes tested which I did. I was referred to Manchester Royal Eye Hospital and they checked me out. The outcome was that I had a scratch on my cornea blocking my full vision. Cath and I waited patiently for the specialist to talk to us about treatment. He said there was only two options, one was to leave it as it is until a later date, or to stitch my eye up and wear an eye patch. I couldn't believe it. I thought they would operate on me but as they explained they didn't have the technology at the time. I spoke with Cath and we both agreed I should leave it and hope for some new technology in the future. Can you imagine me walking on stage with my eye stitched up, probably would have scared off all the people in the audience!

I also decided not to tell my mum she had enough problems on her plate with my Dads infidelities and I didn't want to be another one. In fact my Mum went to her grave not knowing about my eye problem.

May Bank holiday 1984 Sunday night I was doing a show at The Gay Gordon pub on Langley. It was crammed full, you couldn't have gotten any more in if you tried. The show was about a quarter the way through when I saw this girl in the audience. I thought she had a look of a very young Priscilla Presley and it looked like there was a halo of light all around her, like some sort of sign. Then it happened, I fell in love at first sight again. What was wrong with the universe, love at first sight can only happen once in a lifetime can't it? I must have been losing my mind! It turned out that she was Tony Chiappori's youngest daughter Donna and I was totally smitten. Nothing happened that night but I made an excuse with Tony to send her with some equipment round to my house the following day. The doorbell went and when I answered it she stood there with that halo around her again. Instantly I knew we were meant to be together. I took the equipment off her and she stepped forward and kissed me. I was in dreamland. We made arrangements to meet again the following day. The next day came and I was at Donna's house and her two older sisters Lesley and Tracey made it very clear that they wanted to be my girlfriend as well. Especially Tracey who gave Donna a hard time for many years to come.

But what about Cath? I still loved her, I always would. But she had her own ideas and ways and they were not mine, I decided to end it that night. The following day at work she couldn't accept that we were over. It was one of the hardest things I've ever had to do. On the way out through the warehouse she grabbed me and was begging me not to finish it. I tried to keep walking when she was hanging on to my leg it was so embarrassing and heartbreaking. This happened the full length of the warehouse and onto the shop floor. Some of the till girls held her back so I could leave. I still loved her and I was crying but I knew my future was with Donna. As I walked away my heart was breaking but I knew I dare not look back. At the next show at The Charlestown pub Cath turned up and I had to sing Unchained Melody. She was right on the front row with tears in her eyes, that was as hard as it gets!

John and Steve did get me up the ladder a bit by getting me bookings further afield. It was March 1984 and they had gone down to North Wales to try getting me summer bookings in Towyn, Rhyl, Kinmel Bay and Prestatyn. They came back and told me they had only been able to secure one date at The Harbour Hotel in Kinmel Bay. Which I could understand, it was very difficult trying to sell a straight mime act. Comedy mime acts sold all the time but people just didn't think an Elvis mime act was for them. I gave Steve £10 petrol money but he said he would need £30 because they'd had drinks in each venue. The first seeds of doubt were planted with regards their honesty. But I gave them the full amount hoping they would get some more bookings. And after all I had my first booking at the seaside in July at The Harbour Hotel in Kinmel Bay, Rhyl.

The next few months I would do shows all over the North West of Manchester. I would be driven to the show all dressed up to go on stage and I thought it was brilliant. I had also got a small following that would travel in a minibus to watch me. One night that stands out was at Jack Cassidy's (the wrestler) pub in Manchester. The show was going great, when one by one the power sockets we were using slowly died. It seemed like one by one my followers left and my roadies seemed to leave as well. The audience was stunned. And remember I didn't have a live microphone as I was miming. The last two that remained was me on stage and John Clews who was bent over backwards with his hand on the only socket that worked! Talk about 'the show must go on' it was comical!

John also booked me into a place in Whitefield near Bury. The thing was he had booked me in as a live act with my own band! Needless to say when we sound checked the landlord wasn't best pleased. John calmed him down and promised the punters would enjoy it when we started. I got through the first forty five minutes and the place was slowly emptying. The landlord told John to pack up and leave. I wouldn't have minded being paid off but he didn't even give us any fee at all.

More and more expenses were asked for and then John turned up and said the lighting desk needed fixing and it would cost £70. My mum paid it against her better judgement. It turned out that John had sold the lighting desk and used mum's money to pay off some loan shark.

It's all a bit hazy from here on but my mum decided to step in and manage me. She knew nothing about showbiz but at least I knew I could trust her.

John and Steve didn't take this well and visited my mum and dad. Of all people John Ward came and pleaded their case. I still don't know why he had to come and plead their innocence. But mum was having none of it and that was it I washed my hands of them they were fired.

That was on the Saturday. On the Sunday afternoon we all used to meet up and have a game of football. I couldn't believe it when John and Steve turned up, it made my blood boil, they had ripped me off Mum had calculated at somewhere in the region of £700 in total which was a lot of money back then, and I thought they were my friends! The first tackle I went in on Steve and I whacked him in the air. Still don't know how I did that he was about twenty stone! John saw this and very quickly retreated and went in goal, as if I couldn't get at him there. I crunched him and he went off home.

Donna had come to watch me play football, something Cath only ever did the one time, and for the first time in twelve months I felt like my life and career was back on track.

But there were to be more bumps along the way......

Chapter 3

1984-1988....GIRLS, GIRLS, GIRLS

My mum threw herself into managing my career. She knew nothing about showbusness but she learnt very quickly about all the shark agents out there. I had some dates in the diary that Steve and John had booked. However when we turned up at the first one there was another artiste already set up? Mum went to see the manager of this small club in Rhodes, Middleton. He told her that John Clews had cancelled Louis Gates and put this other act on instead. Talk about sour grapes. Mum never made the same mistake again. The following morning she phoned all the venues that were booked and confirmed every single one of them.

She also phoned The Harbour Hotel in North Wales that John and Steve had booked me into. She had a good conversation with Hilary the owner and the date in July was left secure.

July came around and with the chance of a summer season at The Harbour I was so excited. Mike and Sue from The Gay Gordon pub arranged a fifty seater coach to support me. I was a bit overwhelmed but when I walked on stage it was like being home at The Gay Gordon pub in Middleton. The show went extremely well and Hilary offered my mum a return booking for two weeks time. After another knockout show Hilary offered me a contract to appear every other week for Fridays and Saturdays throughout the year at the princely sum of £37.50 per night plus free accommodation for me, mum, dad and Tony, Donna's dad. Not bad for a mime act and I thought I'd made it! Eventually I did but I was just a big fish in a tiny pond. I was still dreaming of having my own live band but for now it was just a pipe dream.

I was totally in love with Donna even though she was just sixteen. We became very close very quickly and I had found someone that actually understood me and my dreams.

Understandably she was naïve in some thing's, but I helped her with advice as best I could and we became soul mates.

32

Out of loyalty to her I kept her dad on as a Charlie Hodge figure handing me the scarves on stage and security etc.. Some roadie he only had one hand through an accident years ago but he was good company and had my best interests at heart, or so I thought.

I took Donna to see Freddie Starr at The Palace Theatre in Manchester. It was her first time in a theatre and she loved it. I bought two of Freddie's LP Vinyl albums and after the show we waited at the backstage door to try and get them signed. After thirty minutes or so Freddie came out and signed the albums for me, shook my hand and kissed Donna. He was the total opposite to his stage persona, he was very quiet and laid back. I think I impressed Donna that night, I just wanted her to see what it was like at the top level of the business and what I wanted to achieve with my dreams.

Manchester's Elvis...Big Jim White's promoter was called Scotch Ian (yes he was very dodgy) and he approached my mum with view to filling in for Big Jim on any dates Jim couldn't do. She didn't trust him but realised it might get me seen more. He was a funny looking man about 5ft and fifteen stone a bit like Eddie Large the comedian. He got me gigs at places like The Bank of England pub and New Cross Labour Club both in Ancoats. The Labour club was fantastic, it was huge! It even had a balcony and I thought I could get used to this; the audiences went wild, it was crazy!

The next gig that Big Jim pulled out of was a large round pub in Sale, can't remember the name of it. They had partitioned a small part of the pub off as my dressing room so I could walk straight on stage. Scotch Ian was on the door cramming people in. I'm sure fire and safety would have closed it down there must have been over three hundred people in a room that probably held about a hundred and fifty!

So I walked out on stage to rapturous applause and started the show. About halfway through the first set I was singing Love Me Tender when I could feel my left sideburn start to peel off. I put my hand to it hoping no one would notice. But it came loose again. I told Tony and he went to the curtained dressing room and called me over. So with half my head in the dressing room and the other half on stage he replaced the sideburn's tape! The crazy thing was that nobody noticed because the atmosphere was electric. I decided I needed proper sideburns after that.

It was at this show that I met Christine Roberts and her friends from Sale. I would become very close with Christine and her family a few years later.

I started performing at The Harbour Hotel in Rhyl every other weekend and the reactions i got were phenomenal. Very quickly I found myself a big fish in a very small pond. Donna couldn't come all the time because of her work so while the cats away? I felt like the real Elvis with lots of attention from the girls. I know it was wrong but I hadn't had a girlfriend until I was nineteen and after all it was Rock 'n' Roll! The stumbling block was Donna's dad. However we found out he was still implicitly involved with John Clews and Steve Grayson in trying to derail my career. I didn't want anything to do with my ex-managers so I fired him which left the coast clear.

That weekend I was performing at The Harbour Hotel and it was the first time without Tony which was really strange. But I knew it was the right decision to fire him. When we got home on the Sunday afternoon, we walked into our house and realised we had been burgled! Although nothing was taken which was weird? As you can imagine Mum was quite upset and I was determined to find out who did it. The Police were a waste of time as usual so I put some feelers out. But no one knew anything. I had an inkling it had something to do with the people I had fired but I had no proof. So Dad put locks on all the internal doors thinking if they got in again they wouldn't be able to go in the other rooms.

Two weeks later I was back at The Harbour for two nights. Mum got a call off her friend Carol Price saying all the lights were on in the house. We did the shows and went home. All the lights had been left on as Carol had said. It was as if they were sending a message saying we can still get in if we want to. Again nothing had been taken. Mum felt intimidated. I found out later it was a guy called Barry Collins who admitted to the break-in to the police. He admitted to several break-ins and was trying to get a lighter sentence by owning up. A few weeks later Donna found out that Barry Collins was a friend of her Dads so its not rocket science to realise who ordered the break-ins. My Dad got a company to fit a burglar alarm system, he didn't want to spend any money but Mum made him. At last we had peace of mind. But talk about sour grapes because they had been kicked off the gravy train, unbelievable!

One girl I dated at The Harbour was Tracey; she came to the shows each night with her mum Olive and little sister Becky. We went out after the shows to nightclubs and other late night venues. She was a lot of fun, honest and easy going. I dated her for about three months and thought it might go somewhere. However I realised I was only seeing her because she reminded me of Cath. Tracy was really nice but it wasn't fair on her or me so I ended it. I'm pleased to say i still speak to her on Facebook.

I saw my Granddad pretty regularly back then. I even took Cath to meet him once; Auntie Marion wasn't best pleased because Cath had got married to my mate Mark Ward at that time. I couldn't have cared less; she couldn't treat me like a Grandson so it had nothing to do with her. Granddad thought Cath was lovely which was all that mattered to me. Granddad thought we were made for each other. However it was a bit risky seeing Donna, Cath and whoever else in Wales, at the time I just thought it was a game. I can see now how selfish I was back then.

We had a deal at The Harbour which gave me, Mum and Dad accommodation and an evening meal each night so it made it fairly viable. I did Christmas there too from Boxing Night through to New Years Day! I was in heaven with lots of, as Elvis would say, girls, girls, girls and more girls. It was a great Christmas that year.

When I was home I would see Donna all the time and we would make plans for the future. Even though I wasn't being true I knew she was the one I wanted to marry. She still lived at home with her parents and it grated with her dad that he had been cut loose from the gravy train.

Then one day she was at our house and we got a phone call from the local newspaper The Middleton Guardian. They had previously done some positive articles about the local lad that had done good. Anyway my mum dealt with business calls and when she sat down I could tell something was wrong. Then she told us what had been said. Apparently Donna's dad had informed The Guardian that Louis Gates girlfriend had had an abortion two years ago. Obviously this caused much upset, Donna was devastated and so were we. When I walked her home she opened up to me and explained what had happened. I was stuck for words but admired her honesty. I decided that it was before I came along and it wasn't going to pull us apart. After all that is what the phone call had intended to do. What kind of Father would set is own daughter up to be ridiculed by the press? Donna left home the following week and got a council flat nearby.

In January 1985 Hilary the owner of The Harbour Hotel offered my mum a contract for me to appear every night during summer season which lasted twenty two weeks. It meant doing 154 consecutive shows! i was a bit shocked but also over the moon. Things were really taking off for me. My dad moaned about his shift work but mum just told him he would have to travel back and forward to Manchester each day. She knew this was too good a deal to turn down. I paid his petrol but it didn't stop him moaning.

By now my mum had made many friends at The Harbour including Olive (Tracy's mum), Beau, Eddie and Maureen and of course all the staff. One of the staff was a chambermaid called Edith she came across a bit odd at times but she had a heart of gold. She would often say to my mum that she heard me singing in the bath when she passed my room and that it was the same as Elvis'. Mum just brushed it away saying she had heard me singing and that I was tone deaf?

Later on Donna and I visited Edith's house. This was after my mum had died. She did card readings and was a psychic. She never charged anyone she just had the gift. She told me many things that only me and mum knew. She also saw what the future held for us. I was sceptical before we went to see her but afterwards I was converted into a believer in the afterlife.

I realised that to keep the audiences interested i had to make it feel like I was completely live. Especially if I was appearing every night. I already had my microphone with the lead cut to make it look like a radio mic but I needed something else. So I got myself seven tapes and recorded off my Elvis live albums like Aloha from Hawaii and Madison Square Garden, seven different shows. I even put in as much of Elvis talking in between songs as I could, and learnt everything off by heart. I also put clap along songs in the set. So along with Elvis' hits I put "Yellow Rose Of Texas", we had the room bouncing with that one, "I Love Only One Girl", "Didja Ever" and "Drums Of The Islands". All these songs along with the Elvis hits meant I went down a storm so I had found a winning formula. I would tweak it sometimes but always I was miming to Elvis' talking in between songs. I would also use other singers songs such as Freddie Starr " Great Balls Of Fire " and Shakin Stevens " Tallahassee Lassie ", it was bonkers they loved it. Audiences would come in every night because they knew it would be a completely different show. Despite all of this I was still dreaming of having my own band and performing in theatres. I didn't know how it would work but it was a burning desire!

That spring I was given the opportunity to play football with my dad's works team at Hyde United's ground, it was a friendly match. I jumped at the idea but he wasn't over keen I could tell. I ended up playing at centre back and had a good game, we won. Dad was in goal behind me but all he did was criticise all through the game and afterwards. It was a dream come true for me to play on the same side as my dad. Every son wants their Dad to be proud of him. He told me they only asked me because they were one man short, thanks for that Dad. I knew this wasn't true because most of the players were congratulating me on a good game afterwards. They were interested in me playing for them permanently but I had retired from football early, I didn't want to get injured and it to conflict with my Elvis show.

My dad was at the end of his career at forty three and I was gutted about his reaction!

I was now twenty and as fit as a fiddle. I would even go and do weights at the gym with my mate Rob Walker. He was a grave digger at Blackley Cemetery and had muscles everywhere like the movie "Rocky". One Friday night we went out to a nightclub called Smokies and got chatting to these two gorgeous blondes. We were doing alright till they asked us what we did for a living when Rob said he was a grave digger and I said I impersonate Elvis: I've never seen two ladies dart for the exit so fast, it was hilarious!

I never saw my dad get violent with my mum, only the once and I stood in between and told him he'd have to get through me first. I was ready to knock him out if necessary. He didn't dare as I was much bigger, stronger and younger than him. He backed down and I kept an eye on things. Even more envious dirty looks would come my way from him. By this time I couldn't care less it was obvious he didn't. I knew he was jealous of me and mums closeness. It was something he could never get used to and it would show itself even more later on.

Dennis Williams from the Elvis fan club got me a charity gig at The International Club in Manchester. It was on a Monday night and I was on the bill with lots of other clubland artistes. I was buzzing when I got there and my name was in big bold letters, I was the headline act! The first time ever I'd been top of the bill. It was a huge place. The capacity was about fifteen hundred and the dressing rooms were beneath the stage. Denis came up to me and asked if h could see the dressing rooms behind the curtain? I walked over and pulled back the curtain to reveal a brick wall. We both laughed our socks off, then I took him downstairs to show him the real dressing rooms. We got there in the afternoon and I was shocked to find Prefab Sprout rehearsing on stage. They hadn't had their big break by then but you could tell they would at some point they were very, very good.

The show was going down well and we had raised a substantial amount of money for the children's home. Mum and Dad were sat at the back when I came on. Halfway through my set a very drunk man sat next to Mum and offered a recording contract for me and wanted to manage me. Mum told him I was miming but he didn't believe her. He kept on at her until she told him to get lost. How could a mime act get a recording contract? Anyway the guy turned out to be Paul McCartney's Brother Mike, from the band Scaffold. No wonder he wanted to manage me I had one hell of a voice coming out of those speaker's!!

Donna had a job as a secretary in legal firm. And seeing as she had some money of her own for the first time, she decided to buy me my first ring. It was only a small signet ring but I was overjoyed. I would shower her with presents too when I was home. Then on my birthday she bought me a solid silver, Onyx and Zirconia set TCB ring. An exact replica to Elvis' famous ring, I was in shock! she knew I wanted one but I never dreamt I would ever own one. She had saved up for months, it cost her £120 which back in the eighties was a huge amount of money. Of course Elvis' TCB ring was made of solid gold and diamonds but I didn't care one bit. I wore it with pride at the next show and everyone was asking about it. You can buy replica Elvis jewellery online nowadays but back then there was nothing. She had had it personally hand made which made it all the more special.

We got a gig off Scotch Ian, it was a nightclub in Manchester can't remember the name but it's actually the Manchester Roadhouse now. Anyway when we got there the manager said I was on between the female strippers!
Well that's a first one for me and I was looking forward to it until I got on stage and discovered they would be male strippers and the toilets were directly behind where I was playing. When I started there was a stampede of women coming at me. I didn't know what to do. When they all charged passed me towards the toilets where the strippers were getting changed. My God I felt like a skittle at the bowling alley. I didn't even have a live microphone it was a dummy remember made to look like a radio

microphone. It was unbelievable. I just got the gig done, got paid and left very quickly.

Scotch Ian got me a gig with some drag acts along the way. They were all really nice to me giving me advice on how to handle an audience. One night in Newton Heath I was on with a double drag act similar to Hinge and Bracket, older readers might remember them. They were two of the nicest genuine showbiz people I've ever met and very funny.

I was beginning to get a reputation in the Manchester area playing at pubs and clubs. Even Big Jim White had sent a message through Scotch Ian that he wanted my mum to make him an Elvis jumpsuit. Mum turned him down flat, said she only made suits for her son. By this time she had made me a white suit and a pale blue suit, together with my brown suit and later a red suit. I could swap and change between sets. You must remember there was no "Stars in their Eyes" as yet and only about half a dozen Elvis

impersonators in the whole country. The ones I can remember were Big Jim White, Billy Dean, Steve Preston and John E Prescott. I went to see them all and they were all good in their own ways but I knew I was straggling behind because of the miming. I knew that one day eventually I would need to go live.

I did a show once at The Atlantic Club in Altrincham, Cheshire. The first set went down really well and in the interval quite a few people had come for requests and autographs. I went backstage to get ready for the second set and the Concert Secretary followed me. I couldn't believe what I was hearing. He was paying me off because I didn't sound anything like Elvis? I told him he was told it was a mime act when it was booked, but he just said I wasn't going down well and sounded nothing like Elvis? I said to him you've paid me so why don't you give me a chance to entertain the audience. He wouldn't have it so I went out front to take the gear down and there was nearly a riot. They all charged to the front to demand why I was leaving. When I told them what had happened they couldn't believe it either. I told them to go ask the concert secretary stood at the bar. About twenty women mobbed him. We got the gear down and in the car and left before anything kicked off.

A similar thing happened at a pub called The Lively Lobster in Sale. Again the first set went down really well then the landlord came up with the same thing, I didn't sound like Elvis, I pleaded with him to let me carry on, after all he had paid the fee already, but he was determined to stop the show. We left as quickly as we could because not only is it embarrassing, I could tell the audience were getting wound up and having a go at the landlord. I found out two weeks later the landlord had committed suicide. So I felt sorry for him and less sorry for me. He clearly had other problems greater than mine.

I was doing summer season at The Harbour Hotel when I met the Henderson family, Mum Avril and daughters Jacqui, Michelle and the youngest Pamela. Avril used to bring Pamela to the show most nights, she was only eight. Avril was a single parent and didn't much care for Elvis but Pamela did. Avril always said she personally didn't care much for Louis Gates but Peter was lovely. Jacqui and Michelle came to the show occasionally and I was really attracted to Jacqui but she was married and in my book that was out of bounds. So I adopted all three as my little sisters!

As the summer progressed I really felt part of their family. We would go to the Marina Hotel after the show at The Harbour and play pool and just hang out. Sometimes ending up back at their house trying to make sense of my sudden success. Suddenly I had three little sisters! Avril became my sounding board for things that i didn't understand. Although my Mum said to be careful as there was something she wasn't sure about her. She just couldn't put her finger on what it was. We would find out down the line what it was but back then I thought it was great to have an adult who understood my thought processes.

Eventually Avril became what they call in Rock n Roll as my head-hunter. In other words when I was on stage I would scan the girls in the audience and let Avril know which one I'd like to take out after the show. It sounds really conceited now but back then it was a different world. I'm not classing myself as good looking as Elvis was, probably the opposite really. But in the mid eighties that's what it was like performing as Elvis. I was like a kid in a candy store. From not having a girlfriend until I was nineteen to being twenty one and having four or five dates a week. When I look back know I'm amazed I had the energy! The summer season consisted of 154 consecutive shows each year for five years. I had to blow off steam somehow and that was how I did it.

I had two 21st's, one at home in Middleton at The School House restaurant. All the so called family came and my pretentious Auntie Marion asked me when I was going to get a proper job! Unbelievable! But I was happy I had Donna by my side. I announced at that meal that I was turning professional. I think there was only my mum and granddad that was pleased for me. The rest of the so called family thought I was being silly. I was earning £50-60 a night, two or three nights a week in the winter as well as every night in the summer season for 154 consecutive nights. I only earned £60 a week working at the Co-op. It was a no brainer and I never looked back!

The second 21st party was after the show at The Harbour. I had no idea about it, it was a surprise. After the show Hilary brought out this huge cake like the American flag and everyone sang happy birthday. Hilary also put on a huge buffet for everyone which I really appreciated. I was happy, I had Tracey by my side and I enjoyed The Harbour's 21st, they were more my people much better than the 21st back in Middleton. In fact I've had hardly any contact with blood relatives over the years, they all seem very self centered and never took my show seriously, ' When will you be getting a proper job?'. Almost forty years later and they probably would still be saying the same thing. I feel blessed and lucky that I've had a fantastic career and seen the world, I've been able to make a good living at performing. I've always said that I've got my Lewis Gates family, people that I have met through the show and become very close to. I've now got several "Little Sisters" around the country and I love them as a brother all the same.

I had ended it with Tracey and then one night during the Summer Season along came Julia! Oh my God she was a stunner. Blonde hair, laughing blue eyes and a great figure. After the show Avril knew who I wanted to see, she said the Blonde on the middle table. Apparently she said there was an incredible spark between us while I was performing. She was from Cleator Moor in Cumbria and was on holiday with her parents. She was the same age as me and I dated her until the end of her holiday. By now word had got round that if any girls wanted to date me they should approach Avril. Avril made many excuses for me that week I was totally smitten with Julia. We stayed at my friend Billy's caravan. I was in heaven.

We exchanged numbers and she said she would call me. Her holiday ended and she went home to Cumbria. One week passed then two and still no call so I called her. Her mum answered and told me not to call again it was just a holiday romance. I thought it was more than that but obviously she didn't. I was gutted, it was the first time I had been ditched and it hurt, I suppose it was karma.

It was 1985 and I was twenty one and selling out every night at The Harbour Hotel. I performed every night from April through to October.

I was introduced to Colin Barber by his parents who used to come see the show every night when they were in Wales. Mrs Barber was a real Elvis fan, Mr Barber not as much but he liked my show. Colin spoke with me after a show one night. He said he could supply a full Elvis merchandise table for the foyer in the hotel. I was impressed with his honesty and humility. We were both on the same page, he knew I was doing a true tribute to the King. He offered to supply Lewis Gates t-shirts for sale in the foyer on his merchandise table all through the summer. I couldn't believe it, my very own Lewis Gates t-shirts and I didn't have to pay a penny! Colin Barber is one of the nice guys, we keep in touch even today although he is very poorly right now.

The Harbour was situated on the Kinmel Bay side of the famous blue bridge. Opposite was a pub called The Ferry and to let off steam me and head barman Dave would have a few beers after the show. The Landlord was called Arthur Rose. It was usually dead quiet when I was on over the road but he was cool with us going in after hours. His daughter, Lynn who was very pretty and about my age, would come into the Harbour with her friends to see the show frequently. Anyway one thing leads to another and I ended up at her house after the show. I thought she was lovely and I'll leave rest to your imagination.

Everyone in Rhyl knew who Lewis Gates was by this time so Hilary asked me would I do my show on a float for the Rhyl Festival. I didn't know what it entailed but I agreed to it. She had hired a huge flatbed truck and she dressed it up promoting The Harbour Hotel. I put a small sound system on it and I performed as we drove down the promenade and through the streets. It was brilliant I really enjoyed it. We ended up parking in the car park at the side of the fun fair. Lots of other floats were there as well as many young dance troupes. As we pulled into the car park with my music blasting, all the dance troupes started following me. It was like the Pied Piper, it must have been a sight to see and my mums face was bursting with pride. I ended up doing about an hours show until the judges came along and asked us to stop so they could speak to the crowd. We didn't win, we came second but I had a ball performing outside on a moving truck!

I was also asked to do many private parties in the local area after I had done my show at The Harbour. One night when Avril was passing me the scarves when I was doing Love Me Tender, she was asked if I would do Roy Kellett's birthday party at his private house in Dyserth. She didn't know what price to quote so knowing my mum wouldn't want to do a private party at midnight thirty minutes away up in the hills. She just blurted out £250 thinking he wouldn't agree. He promptly pulled out a wad of fifty pound notes and gave her five of them. She was in shock and so was i. She said he must have had a few grand in the wad he pulled out.

Roy Kellet owned a caravan sales company and I knew he was loaded so I was curious to see his house. House......it was a huge mansion! So Avril and I went in to see where I would be performing. Roy was really nice and showed us around, telling us to use whatever we needed including his own swimming pool, I cant swim but it was nice to be offered. I did my seventy five minute show in the TV room and there was around fifty to sixty in this large room. It went down extremely well and Roy gave me a fifty pound tip. What a top man he was.

Towards the end of the summer season I started dating one of the waitresses, Natalie Davies. She was beautiful inside and out, and had a sweet sense of humour. It went as far as me meeting her parents and I stayed at her house a few times. She even came up to Manchester on the train and my mum made us tea. My mum really liked her and you could tell she was hoping I would settle down with Natalie. Her train back to Rhyl was at 5pm which was great for me because Donna would be home from work at 6pm. But this particular time Natalie got really upset about going back and I felt so sorry for her. So I jumped on the train and went back with her to Rhyl. I phoned my mum and said to make an excuse for when Donna came round. Obviously mum wasn't best pleased but she really liked Natalie so she did it for me. I can't remember the excuse but I got away with it that time, phew! I was running the gauntlet but i felt like no one could touch me!

I met Brian and Pauline Fellows and their family that year. They would become very close and dear to me. They would get me bookings in their home town of Dudley in the West Midlands and then promptly arrange a minibus for everyone to go to see my show. Salt of the earth people. They all came to both my weddings and I've sang at various parties they have had. Ive also sang at Brian and Pauline's funerals which was extremely hard. Debbie would become another of my little sisters and I am her son Daniel's godfather.

During that winter I got a call do a show at Irlam Social Club one Friday night. I was to be support act for The Houghton Weavers, they were well known throughout the north and even had their own TV sow. They were a folk band and had a big following. So the club was full to capacity about 250 with all

45

their fans, I thought there was only one thing to do and that was to just do my show. Well I had them all clapping along and cheering then at the end they were stood up cheering for more. I did a couple more and got the same reaction, As I went backstage their lead singer pulled me to one side. He said " son you've got a brilliant show, i've never seen anything like it. But we can't have you on with us again, your too good to be a support act". He meant it in a nice way of course and I understood how he felt, they had to go on after me with the audience canting for Elvis. Like the professionals they were they went on and calmed the audience down for their calmer music.

As 1986 dawned I was performing at some nice venues like The Candlelight Nightclub in Oldham. Where I'd been to watch Raving Rupert's Elvis show the year before. He was only 5ft 4' but I thought he was great. I did well at the Candlelight; I had Mike and Sue's daughter Tracey as a miming backing singer. I went to see the manager the week after to secure another booking. But he wasn't having any of it and said my backing singer was smoking on stage. That was ludicrous as Tracey has never smoked in her life. I think he didn't like admitting that an Elvis mime act had gone down better than the live one, Raving Rupert. If he would have just said he didn't want a mime act again it wouldn't have been a problem. I came across this a few times at venues. Why cant people just be honest I've got thick skin.

Another funny one was at Holywell Comrades club in North Wales. We went in to set up and asked the old guy on the door where the dressing room was, he pointed to the chairman's room. I noticed my poster up on the wall but it had my fee written on it, £60. I couldn't believe it, I asked the old guy about it and he just said "I hope your worth it lad". Talk about Wheel Tappers and Shunter's club! I went and got changed and stood in my Elvis suit and wig etc. in the foyer waiting for the 2001 theme to start. The old guy is there and he comes out with "its £1.50 to get in and see the act" I thought he was joking so I laughed, but he was deadly serious. He said the act has got ginger hair I spoke to him before. Unbelievable! Anyway my entrance music started so I made a bee line for the concert room. The old guy is now chasing me and shouting for his £1.50. I thought he was going to rugby tackle me. I finally got to the stage and put my guitar on and he turns up all out of breath still asking for my ticket money. I couldn't talk to him because if you remember I was using a dummy microphone, so I just carried on and tried to ignore him. He must have stood there for about two songs before it finally clicked with him. The audience were in stitches. Brilliant!

While doing summer season at The Harbour I got to know a Merseyside couple, John and Norma and their family and they got me a booking at the 911 Social Club in Kirby, Liverpool. When we got there they had two doormen wearing long coats like gangsters. They treated me like royalty and said they would look after me. As one of them turned around I saw a sawn off shotgun under his coat! Oh my God what was I getting into here! The show went down a storm; two hundred scouser's going bananas it was fantastic. Avril had come to this show because my mum was poorly. So she was side stage giving me my scarves etc. The dance floor was full and it came to a part of a song where I usually jumped in the air and landing like Shakin' Stevens was famous for. Avril looked at me and mouthed 'don't even think of doing it'. Red rag to a bull; I dived off the stage into the air, but I misjudged the height of the stage. I must have been about ten feet in the air I thought I was never going to land. I landed amongst the dancers who went even more bananas. My knees took another battering but I didn't care, you don't when your young do you. Avril tried in vain to disentangle me but gave up in the end. That was one of a number of gigs in Kirby and every one of them was a huge success.

Back at The Harbour in August mum had been approached by two theatre promoters. I had just finished the 16th August Anniversary show and I saw these two guys watching intently at my performance. After the show mum introduced me to them and told me they were interested in putting me into the theatre show ' Forever Elvis ' starring Big Jim White. I said it would be brilliant to work alongside Big Jim but they said no and that I would be replacing him! I was in shock. At this point my mum told me to leave and let her discuss it. I was over the moon; I didn't think things could get better than this. Apparently they had been extremely complimentary about my little show and they would get around the miming somehow. The fee would be £100 per night which was roughly three times what I was earning at The Harbour. However the conclusion my mum came to was that I wasn't ready to take such a big step so soon, she reckoned it was the wrong time. They left the offer on the table in case mum changed her mind and then they left. I was devastated and we argued about it at length. I respected my mum one hundred per cent but I thought she was wrong about this one and I feel the same to this day. I think the bottom line was she wasn't ready to let go of her only son which I understand but in essence it would have furthered my career. She loved me unconditionally, and I her, so I don't blame her. It was just a great shame.

By this time Cath had married and divorced one of my best mates Mark Ward. She had two girls with him which broke my heart because she had always said she would never ever have kids. That was one of the main reasons I had ended it with her!

Anyway I saw her one day at the local shopping centre and it felt like we had never been apart. I started seeing her again. I would get a taxi and pick her up from her mum's house and we would go to the Whitegate pub in Chadderton, Oldham in secret for lunch.

Like I've said earlier i hadn't had a girlfriend until I was nineteen and now at twenty one I had three at the same time. I thought I was indestructible! What a fool!

I was booked in to Spibs Nightclub in Heywood. I had played there before and it had always been a sell out crowd. However this time as you might have guessed all three girlfriends turned up at the venue, Cath, Donna and Natalie. I didn't have a clue what to do. Avril had travelled up to help mum with the show and she suggested staying backstage and then after the show she would have the car running and I should go straight into the car and away. I'm ashamed to say that this Elvis, really did leave the building! Really fast!

New Years Eve was a blast at The Harbour Hotel that year. Never seen so many people crammed into one room. I had to literally stand still I couldn't move. It was great I was on top of the world. Even the welsh police loved me. I would be staggering back to the hotel at about four or five in the morning, sometimes they would stop and when they realised it was me it was fine. They even gave me a lift back to the hotel a few times. One time after the show we all went up the promenade to The Marina Hotel, it had a 3am licence. Me and the gang were all drunk when Avril suggested we called it a night. So I said on one condition that I could car surf down the prom! So there I was on top of Avril's car singing the Hawaii 5'0 song pretending to surf in my lemon coloured box suit – the full length of the prom. A police car passed us so I waved and they realised it was me, waved back and just carried on. Avril told me off for that one. I suppose it was pushing it a bit. But God bless the Welsh Constabulary!

As 1987 dawned Mum was hard at work pushing my career forward. We seemed to have three quarters of the diary filled with gigs at The Harbour. But she kept on approaching venues in the North West.

We did four shows at The Harbour at Easter. Then summer season started in late April through to the last week in October, 186 consecutive shows, much more than the year before and no day off! With every Friday and Saturday in December along with Boxing Day through to New Years Eve at The Harbour it was a bit chaotic but I was enjoying every second. And what's more with all the shows came more girls, girls and girls! During the rest of the year we had shows booked in to Liverpool, Heywood, Manchester, Bury, Warrington, Birmingham, Sale, Stoke, Stockport, Tameside, Cheshire and all over Yorkshire. At the Liverpool show, a pub on the notorious London Road, my mum saw someone attempting to pull my wig off when I was entering the small stage. She promptly pulled this idiots arm behind his back and threw him out. This got a huge cheer and the audience was completely on my side and we had a great show. Another one was at Fitzroy Social Club in Stalybridge. I had to do three thirty minute sets and I was told not to worry in my third set if the room empties, which it literally did and I was left performing to the Concert Secretary who told me if I didn't finish the show I wouldn't get paid! I did it, got paid and vowed to never do three thirty minute sets ever again and I never did. I also played at a workingmens club in the same area. Cant remember its name. The concert room was nearly empty when I came on and after three songs the concert secretary came over and told me to turn the volume down which I did. He came over again and again until the volume was almost at zero. I walked off. You cant give the illusion of being live if the jukebox was louder than the artiste! I guess it was all in the learning process.

The best one of 87' was at The Clough Hotel in Blackley, just over the road from where Grandad lived. Mum invited him and Auntie Marion because they had not seen my show before. It was one of the proudest nights of my career. It went really well and Granddad couldn't get over how his shy little Peter could be so different on stage. That was something mum could never get used to either.

It was around this time that mums friends Carol and Tommy told her they had seen Dad with another woman, he was having an affair! I didn't know about this for a few months. But Mum took it in her stride and when she told me I was ready to knock him out! I was so angry. How dare he do this to my Mum! I was so sorry for her. Apparently it was someone from the factory where he worked. And twenty years older than him, she must have been in her sixties. What a sad character he was. I told Mum to kick him out but she wouldn't, I guess she was too old school. However it would come to a head the following year with a dramatic outcome!

Early in the summer season there were two men in the audience filming the show. Mum went straight over and stopped them and they told her it was just for private use. That was on the Friday; on the Sunday night somebody came to see the show and said they had seen me on the big screen that afternoon at a nightclub in Greenfield, up the coast. They were charging the public £5 on a Sunday afternoon to watch my show that they had filmed. I've never seen mum so angry. On Monday dinnertime she went to the nightclub and tore them apart and confiscated the video. Talk about cheek, I know I was only small time but they should have asked permission or paid a small fee. Once again mum saved the day as she always did!

August that year brought the tenth anniversary of Elvis death. The Harbour pulled out all the stops and made it so special. There were hundreds of balloons in a net on the ceiling. On the crescendo in An American Trilogy they were released onto the audience. Not sure how many was in that night but I'm sure we exceeded the fire limit. It was standing room only and one of the best shows I had done so far.

So 1987 was a truly remarkable year for me, I was on top of my game and felt untouchable! However1988 would bring me down and smash my life into a million pieces......

Chapter 4

1988......MAMA LIKED THE ROSES

1988 started much the same as the previous year. A brilliant New Years Eve at The Harbour Hotel then pretty quiet in January, just one show a week. But it would be the year that would change my life completely.

January was time to recharge my batteries. The diary from February onwards was full with one nighter bookings, and I felt like I knew where my career was heading. Donna and I seemed solid. She had moved into her own flat to get away from her toxic family. She was employed as a secretary and we were enjoying life to the full.

Towards the end of January my mum had a funny turn, she seemed confused and dizzy but refused to go to the doctors. About a week later she had another episode but much worse. My dad was on nights and refused to get out of bed to take her to the doctors! I phoned for a taxi and took her to our doctors. The Receptionist said I needed an appointment and to sit at the back and wait. I wasn't having that so I stormed into Doctor Manchester's room. He wasn't with a patient and I told him she needed to see a specialist. He was so good and understanding. He checked her over and told me I was right she did need to see a specialist but it might be expensive. I told him money didn't matter and so he made the call and got us in to see a private doctor on John Street in Manchester the following day! All the top specialists in the North West work out of John Street so I knew we would be in good hands. I thanked Dr Manchester for his professionalism and we went home in a taxi.

We got home and told my dad what had happened. His response was "well I'm in work so I can't take you tomorrow". Unbelievable! I told him I would take mum in a taxi and it shamed him enough to agree to take us. We entered the doctors and he checked mum over and then diagnosed her with emphysema. He said if we would have left it another two or three weeks she would have died. The cause of it was smoking and the thick Manchester smog from the nineteen fifties. He told her she would have to stop smoking straight away which she did. She would have to see him every week at his surgery at North Manchester General Hospital. We wouldn't need to pay for this as it was the NHS. We got up to leave and the doctor's secretary handed my dad the bill for the hour's consultation. The look on his face said it all so I said give it to me and I'll pay it. His fee was £50 for the hour consultation. I only had £65 on me but I was willing to pay it if it was going to save my mum, He must have felt ashamed again so he went and paid it, giving me a very dirty look. These dirty looks were becoming regular but it was like water off a ducks back. He just seemed oblivious that Mum was seriously ill.

Mum also had to use an oxygen mask and tank and countless tablets. Her independence was slowly ebbing away from her and it affected her mental health at times. Her friends Carol and Tommy were so supportive at this time; I could never thank them enough.

One night Carol told me again that my dad had been seen entering another woman's house in Middleton on several occasions. I was livid! Carol said best to not tell mum this time until she was feeling a bit better, I agreed totally.

With the help of the oxygen and medication Mum seemed to get better quicker than we thought she would. So one day when my dad was at work I sat there while Carol told her about this other woman. She didn't seem surprised but was understandably very upset.

The following day I had a long conversation with mum and the outcome we agreed on was she wanted to leave dad and move to Rhyl permanently with me and Donna. I was earning enough to look after us. And obviously Donna would get a job as well.

So it was agreed we would go to The Harbour in Rhyl at Easter for the four shows and send dad back on his own. I had spoken to Hilary at The Harbour and she said we could stay as long as we wanted till we found a place of our own which gave us some breathing space. I had also arranged for one of my friends to bring all our belongings down to Rhyl in his Luton van.

Everything was looking great until Donna got word of me seeing someone in Rhyl. Ironically I wasn't seeing anyone this time but I was guilty many times in the past. She called our relationship off and I was devastated. I didn't know what to do I loved her so much but I guess it was payback for my infidelities in the past few years. Yet somehow I knew we would be together again someday.

As devastated as I was I tried to concentrate on my shows. We had three sell out shows in Kirkby, Liverpool that went down incredibly well. Shows in Warrington, Manchester and Stockport also went down really well. Avril, Jacqui and her husband Tim came to do the shows with me around this time, Mum was in no state at all. I made Dad take time off work to look after her. At the 125 club I got completely mobbed again, Avril had to drag me back on stage I was loving it. We did a wedding reception at The Rudyard Lake Hotel in Leek, it was very posh and I thought to myself that I could get used to this kind of venue. Jacqui did my make up and sideburns etc. which meant she was very up close. I really wanted to kiss her but she was married to Tim and I was raised in Middleton and that was out of bounds. But there was a spark there that would ignite years later

Donna and I had been apart for about three months when she realised we were meant to be together. We got back together and all my Christmases seemed to come at once, I was over the moon. Then came the bombshell, she had gone out with this lad for about two months and she was now pregnant! Talk about sucker punch. Mum seemed more like her own self so I spoke with her at length about it. I told her I couldn't bring up another man's child. I know lots of men do it now but I was very young and definitely very selfish. Then my mum came up with something I never thought I would here her say. She said if Donna really was the girl for me she would pay for an abortion! Mum was schooled by nuns and was very Catholic so it came as a shock to hear her say this, but it was the answer to my problem. Donna was in agreement, so the clinic in Leeds was booked for the following day. Mum said there was only one condition which was not to tell my dad and he doesn't know to this day. It was an emotional time for me, Donna and Mum but we got through it and tried to look to the future.

I did four shows at Easter at The Harbour as usual and they all went well. In May I did lots of one nighter's all over the North West. And then I was back at The Harbour for the summer season. I did every night from mid-April to the end of October again. My Dad wasn't happy. He had to drive back and forth to Manchester from Rhyl everyday. I looked after Mum during the day and she seemed to be getting better. Dad was off at weekends and he would take Mum to Pensarn beach just up the road from the hotel. When they got back my mum seemed to have slipped backwards, I have no idea what went on but she definitely relapsed.

The way the show worked was my dad and Avril would go downstairs to the cabaret room and check the stage, sound and lights etc. while I was getting ready upstairs. This one night I will never forget as long as I live. I had come out of the bathroom and to my horror my mum was trying to end it all by jumping from the window! I ran across the room and stopped her just in time. I got her sat down and sat next to her. She kept talking to me as if I was a five year old; obviously the tablets had affected her in a negative way. She knew who I was but she thought I was a lttle boy again. She kept trying to trick me into leaving the room so she could jump. When she realised I wouldn't leave, she kept on saying to me that it would be ok if I let her jump and I wouldn't get told off from Dad. It was now five minutes to showtime and Avril and Dad came back to let me know everything was ok and to bring me downstairs. When I told them what had happened they were both shocked especially Dad because his mum had done the same thing years ago. I didn't want to do the show, how could I?

I had just pulled my Mum back from the window ledge. Avril and Dad said there were a hundred and fifty people downstairs that had come just to see me and I didn't exactly have a choice.

55

Reluctantly I agreed, Dad stayed with Mum and Avril did fantastic doing Dads job on the sound and lights. I can't remember much about that night apart from wanting it over so I could be with Mum. Afterwards I didn't go partying as normal; I sat with Mum upstairs in her room. I still had my Elvis suit on two hours later when she seemed to come back to normal. She kept apologising to me for what had happened, I just consoled her and said it didn't matter. For the first time in my life I was scared!

On the Tuesday after Easter Granddad and Auntie Marion visited me and mum, Dad was at work. Granddad had not been to our house for ages so it was great to see him. For the first time he looked very old, he was 73 and as I waved them goodbye I wondered when would be the next time I would see him again. He had stopped driving years ago but they both had free bus passes. I went inside to see to mum and about ten minutes later I got a frantic knock on the door, it was Paul Hughes. He said to hurry up my Granddad had slumped to the floor at the bus stop on Windermere road.. I got Carol to sit with mum and I legged it to the bust stop. They weren't there they must have got in an ambulance already. I sprinted back home and told Carol that I was getting a taxi to Crumpsall Hospital. We didn't tell mum, it would have been all too much for her. I got to the A&E at Crumpsall and Auntie Marion was all confused. A nurse led us to one of the private waiting rooms. Then about five minutes later she came and told us the sad news that Granddad had passed away it was a big heart attack. I was in shock and didn't know what to do; Auntie Marion was quietly weeping.

Soon the nurse came and asked if we wanted to see him so I said yes. When I saw him he seemed so at peace and yet it cut me like a knife to my very core. We went back to the room and I told Auntie Marion I was going to call home and relay the bad news. When I got through it was my dad, Carol had called his work to get him home, I said to him "Dad, Granddad didn't make it" there was a long silence when he told me he would see me when I got home. My Dads half brother Uncle Bill picked up Auntie Marion, he never said a word, he could have offered me a lift as well but that just shows what a strange lot they are. They left and I went back inside to pick up Granddads belongings. I stood outside A&E with a black bin bag of Granddad's clothes, I felt totally empty and lost and felt like life wouldn't be the same again. The taxi came and I went home.

The funeral the following week was a strange affair. Granddad lived in the high rise flats on Victoria Avenue and when we got there there were so many faces I didn't recognise from Scotland. They all said "you must be Peter the Elvis man" Granddad must have been telling everyone about me, I was humbled. But it was a bit too much for me so I went next door to see Bert and Jean. They were devastated as well but they comforted me. They were normal down to earth people and I cared for them dearly.

Then it was time for the funeral procession. I thought me and Dad would have been in the first limousine but no? Dad said we were going in our car at the back of the line. I was livid; him and I was the only bloodline Granddad had, Uncle Bill being Grandads stepson. But Uncle Bill and my cousins got to ride in the three limousines at the front.

Because Granddad had been a bus driver and had been the brother-in-law of the ex Chief of Police for Manchester, Uncle Tom Cotton, they closed all the roads and intersections. Being last in the cortage we were also at the back of the church, I was furious Dad tried to calm me down but failed miserably like everything else he had attempted to do with me over the years.

It was a cremation so after the service we went home I didn't want to be around all my false relatives I wanted a hug off mum. But when we got home she was oblivious of Granddad's funeral she was in a world of her own because of the medication. So I just gave her a big hug anyway and told her I loved her. It took a long time for me to get my head around losing Granddad.

Back on the work front I was taking bookings further a field like The Kentish Town Hotel in London. Jacqui's husband Tim drove Donna and me to London for two gigs. Then I did The Boulevard Nightclub in Essex. Mum made Dad drive Donna and me down there. I couldn't believe it I was to be on stage at 11pm for twenty minutes and they paid me the princely sum of £300, a long way from the Langley Labour Clubs fee! I thought it was fantastic, Dad was less pleased.

It was now the start of May and the summer season would begin the following week. My Mum really wasn't well and I spoke with her, I wanted to cancel the whole season and start back again when she was better. She wouldn't' have any of it and was determined it would go ahead. There was no convincing her she was so strong headed. We spoke all afternoon but it was all in vain. I was told I was doing it, she reckoned the money I would earn would give me, her and Donna a new start in Rhyl. Reluctantly I had to agree with her. The season started off well. Usually Avril or Michelle would sit with Mum at the back of the room where it was less noisy. I was so surprised that she felt comfortable with Michelle. She was, as Elvis would say, "Nutty as a fruitcake" in a lovely way. Mum liked her and that's all that mattered to me. Things were calming down thanks to my little sister Michelle.

Al and Julie Lucas were market traders in Rhyl. They made and sold gnomes for the garden. They were based in the Wellington Road Market. I had become friends with them the year before when they and their friends used to come to the show at The Harbour.

They were both Liverpudlians and always upbeat and straightforward which I liked. The day after I finished the summer season they had booked me to do a private house party. They lived in a huge house on the outskirts of Rhyl and Al had made a small stage for me in the living room. Avril and Jacqui couldn't help out on this show so Michelle came to do the show with me. My mum really took to Michelle when she had done some shows with us at The Harbour. Mum and Dad were there but Mum was increasingly not liking crowds so she sat with Michelle who gave me the scarves and water.

The show at Al and Julie's house went down really well, there were about thirty people there and Al and his family were made up. Later on Al would become my manager for a short time. But that's for later……

That summer season was turning out to be the best ever. It was full every night and people were lined up outside at the windows trying to get a glimpse. And of course there were girls and more girls every week.

My Dad had taken sickness leave to look after Mum while we were Rhyl. But I think it had more to do with not wanting to drive back and forth to Middleton everyday.. During the day he would take her to Pensarn beach. She seemed to like it there probably because it was quiet. It must have been hard for her at night time at the show which of course was very loud. But she was determined to be there. She also got to have a conversation with Hilary about the possibilities of me, her and Donna moving into The Harbour after the season. Hilary was ok with that although a little surprised that Mum was going to leave Dad and make a life of our own in Wales.

As the season progressed Mum seemed to deteriorate on a daily basis. So much so that I wanted to just take her home to rest. But she was having none of it. She was looking forward to moving to Wales and finishing the season off. I spoke with Hilary and she agreed to cut the season short ending in early September instead of late October. She told mum she was refurbishing and to move into the hotel whenever it was convenient. Of course she wasn't doing a refurb it was a ruse to give Mum a rest before the upheaval of moving to Wales. I'll never forget that loving gesture.

So I was back home in Middleton in early September which in itself felt strange. Donna was living in her flat to get away from her demanding and unscrupulous family. The flat was awful though. I told Mum about it and she knew where the flat was. She insisted that Donna move into our house and we could save up for a deposit for a mortgage for somewhere in Rhyl when the three of us were ready to move. Typical of Mum, she sent Dad out to get a double bed, wardrobes and sets of drawers. They would have all come in handy for when Mum was feeling better and the three of us would move to Wales.

Everything seemed to be going alright. Mum seemed to be getting a lot better even asking Donna to call her Mum. Donna was only eighteen but she was in a well paid secretarial job and we were looking forward to our future.

I'm ashamed to say this but on September 30th I had a row with Mum. I can't even remember what it was about but I stormed off to the pub in a huff. When I got back two hours later Mum being Mum forgave me. With what was about to happen I've had to live with the guilt ever since. I know she forgave me but I shouldn't have rowed with her.....

Chapter 5

1988-1989....LONG BLACK LIMOUSINE

Monday 3rd October 1988, a day etched on my soul. It started off like any other day. Donna went to work at 8am; Dad was already in work on a six-two shift. So it was just me and Mum. I made her lunch and generally was just being there for her, Dad got home at 2.30pm and later Donna got home at 6pm. I made our teas and settled down to watch TV for the night. At about 9.20pm Mum complained of her eyesight being all fuzzy then all of a sudden her body just lunged backwards on the sofa, I saw the whites of her eyes and her tongue had flopped out. I jumped up to help but to my amazement my Dad pulled her onto the floor quickly and started CPR. Instantly I shot to the phone and dialled 999.

At the same time I told Donna to go fetch Carol and Tommy. The ambulance seemed to take an eternity to arrive, meanwhile Carol and Tommy had got there and was trying to help my Dad. Eventually the medics arrived and got Mum into the ambulance. My Dad was dithering whether to get in or not so I just jumped in and shouted to him to get in.

The siren was blaring away and we were moving really fast. The medics worked furiously, I was sat where I could see what was happening and I could tell she was gone. The flat line happened as we were passing Victoria Avenue in Blackley which was kind of ironic. I was distraught and just stared at her! Her head flopped backwards with her hair falling down. My Mum who I had looked up to and deeply loved all my life had died.

They turned the sirens off and we slowed down. We got to Crumpsall Hospital and jumped out of the ambulance thinking they were going to bring Mum out and into A+E but they said they couldn't as she had died on route they had to take her to the morgue. I wanted to see her but the hospital wouldn't let me. They led us to a small room where I put my arm around Dad to console him. I thought that maybe now he might want to be close for the first time. I knew I was the adult now but he just refused my love. Mum had always said that if anything happened to her I would have to be the adult because Dad was incapable. I didn't have the words to call Donna, Carol and Tommy, I wasn't capable of telling them so I called a taxi and we went home.

Home without Mum, it was unimaginable! I walked through the door and they could tell by my face she had gone. I collapsed into Donna's arms I was in massive shock and felt like my whole life had stop breathing. There was a stunned silence; we couldn't believe what had happened!

Tommy and Carol were brilliant with my Dad, good job really because he didn't want to know me. He showed his true colours, even at one point telling me to get out of his sight, i'd said nothing I was just sat there. I got the impression he would rather be me that had died. Eventually Donna and I went to bed but I knew I wouldn't sleep. For all her eighteen years Donna was so good just holding me and consoling me.

About an hour or so later we heard Tommy and Carol leaving and our home was silent and almost grieving with us. Mum was such a huge part of my life I honestly didn't know what I was going to do. I had worked my socks off that year to save as much money as possible to help Mum, Donna and I to go and live in Wales and leave the monster behind. Everything I was doing was for Mum but it was all for nothing, she was gone and I've never felt so alone in my life.

I didn't sleep a wink that night and when me and Donna got up Dad was sat in his chair in his own little world. Donna asked him if wanted some breakfast and he replied no in a really off handed way, we put it down to grieving. I couldn't eat anything either which was a first for me, I just felt numb. Carol and Tommy came at noon and the atmosphere eased slightly but looking back it was obvious he didn't want me or Donna there whatsoever. He was obsessed with registering mums death so Tommy went with him to do it.

I couldn't eat anything all day, Donna kept on at me that I needed to eat but I just couldn't face anything. She got me an appointment to see Dr Manchester the following day to see if he could give me anything to help me sleep. He gave me some sleeping tablets, enough for two weeks and to go back to him if they didn't work. They did work that night and I felt back in the real world the following day. However I was at the lowest part of my life. One night I just thought there was no point to everything without Mum, I wanted to be with her. So I sat on the edge of our bed when Donna was asleep and proceeded to take all the sleeping tablets. However Donna wasn't asleep and got me to be sick to bring the tablets up. I was just out of it as she held me for a long time, she saved my life. My dad was oblivious to what happened to me but that was no surprise.

Mum was to have a post mortem and then moved to Wellens Funeral home in Middleton. We went to see her straight away, she looked so peaceful and young like the photos of her when she was in her 20's. Dad left after twenty minutes I said I would get a taxi back home. Donna was quite frightened; she had never seen a dead body before. I just sat with Mum holding her hand for about an hour until they said we had to leave.

Every morning I would wash the pots from the previous evening, much to Dads annoyance. He thought I should have done them after he got home from work at 10.45pm. He went back to work three days after she died, I was in disbelief about that. Anyway on the Wednesday morning a pure white dove came and landed on the kitchen window sill. This was strange; we only ever got sparrows and small birds on our estate. I looked at it and it looked straight at me for a few minutes. It seemed to say everything would be alright. I told Donna and we just put it down to grief. It came back on the Thursday and again on Friday. It stayed a little longer each time and seemed to radiate love each time. I looked forward to seeing it again but that was the last I saw the dove. Perhaps Mum was trying to send me a message. She always called me "a doubting Thomas" because I had always questioned the bible and religion. I don't know but it gave me a great sense of calmness and peacefulness knowing Mum was in a better place and in no more pain.

Donna had booked a week off work because this was the week all three of us were supposed to leave Dad and move to Rhyl, how ironic that we had to bury her instead. I was so glad Donna was off work; I couldn't have gone through it without her. That night my cousin Christine came to cook us a meal which was really nice of her, I always thought of here as an older sister. I wanted her to stay but she gave me a big hug as she was leaving and told me to ring her if I needed anything which was nice, but nothing was registering with me I was still numb. Auntie Maisie came to see if there was anything she could do, so I asked if Gail would come see me. She gave me Gail's address. I was shocked; she was living and working as a nanny in New York. I decided to write her a letter and tell her about Mum, don't forget there was no internet or mobile phones back then. I told her about Mum and how distraught I was and said I could do with a hug from my best friend. I mailed it and continued to get on with this terrible week. I went back to see Mum every day that week including the day of the funeral, despite Dad not wanting me to. To my amazement the day before the funeral Gail came to see me. She had got the next available flight, I couldn't believe it! I was sat on our front steps when she came with one of her nieces. Pathetically I had gone into Lewis Gates mode, the big star and I was blasé about the situation. Deep down I wanted a hug, I spoke with her it was no wonder she didn't stay long. She had flown all the way back from New York to see me. Looking back now I was horrible and I've had to live with it since then, i've never seen her since. I was on some really strong sleeping tablets by then but that was no excuse, I was a self consuming idiot.

Monday 10th October 1988, the day of the funeral. Our little house was full of so called family that we had not seen for years. I recognised my cousin Ian who I was pretty close with and I appreciated him being there. I got dressed into my only suit and faced up to the day. I looked outside onto the lawn and it was completely full of flowers, the side garden was too. Eventually the limousines came and we all exited the house. I asked my Dad would I be sitting in the front car and he said "yes in the front seat" because Granddads Auntie Marion and Auntie Joan were sitting in the back with him. I couldn't believe what he had said.

Anyway as I walked up to the car I saw Mums coffin in the hearse. Everybody was on the street paying their respects; I was trying to hold it together so I didn't see them all apart from Gail and her sisters, I nearly broke down. I got into the car and I sat faced behind the hearse. I couldn't believe my Dad would do this to me, my heart was breaking! It was the worst journey of my life!

We arrived at the church on Wood Street at 11am and they took Mum in. I sat on the front row with Donna, Dad, Auntie Joan and Auntie Marion. I had wanted certain gospel songs played but Mums sister, Auntie Joan wouldn't allow it. Days beforehand when I had asked Dad about it he said that Auntie Joan was more knowledgeable about Catholic masses. So I sat there with tears rolling down my face Donna holding my hand all the way through. As we followed Mum out of the church Dad physically pushed me forward so I was walking directly behind Mum. I could see she was a popular woman, the church was packed full of people. We got into the cars and headed to Blackley Crematorium. When we got there one of the few things I registered was it was ice cold and overcast. When we got to the grave the priest started talking about Mum as if he knew her, what a joke, where was the Catholic Church when Mum was ill. Not one of the Nuns came to see her, Mum had sewn lots of things for them over the years for free and now they didn't want to know! Typical Catholics.

As Mum was lowered into the grave I could actually feel a part of me dying. I looked down to where she was lying and Donna threw a rose onto the coffin, roses were Mums favourites. I noticed Cath, Barbara and Irene Pole were there, Mum would have been pleased. After a while everyone dispersed, my legs buckled so Mick and Sue helped me back to the car.

Dad had booked The School House restaurant for a cheap lunch of Quiche or jacket potato. This was where I had my 21st nice one dad! I didn't know how to act amongst all the horrid family so I put my show face on and mingled like I would after a show in Lewis Gates mode. After everyone had eaten they all drifted away and we went home. I invited Mick and Sue they had always been there for me. We had a few drinks and later me, Donna Mick and Sue went to the Falcon pub.

The following day we went back to the grave and there were lots of flowers still there. When we got home Dad asked me to go and get the death certificate from Wellens Funeral directors but not to open it? Donna and I went and got it and I wanted to open it but Dad totally refused, why I don't know. And to date I've never seen it. I asked Avril and she said it was probably an aneurysm and Mum wouldn't have felt a thing, it would have happened so fast. So I've had that little comfort over the years.

The following Friday and Saturday I had bookings at St Mary's Club in Liverpool and The Dyers and Polishers club in Middleton respectively. Obviously I didn't feel up to it at that point and Dad just plain refused to do the shows. So I phoned and explained what had happened and the both understood.

We went back to the cemetery every day and I saw my mate Rob Walker who was a gravedigger at Blackley Cemetery. He said he would look after Mums grave which gave me some comfort. The following week we were booked in at the Harbour Hotel for two nights. I still didn't want to do any shows just yet. In fact I wasn't sure if I wanted to do shows ever again! But Dad, after refusing the week before, insisted we had to do The Harbour. Donna and I argued with him all week but he was adamant and had got Tommy and Carol to speak with me about it. I felt cornered and eventually agreed to go to Wales and do the shows.

On the way to Wales Dad put on all of Mums favourite songs on the tape. I sat there with tears rolling down my face. We got there and Dad went into show mode unloading and setting up the equipment. It felt like a bad dream!
I did the show but I couldn't remember anything about it. Apparently it was a full house, all the locals showing their support for me and Mum. I just hope my mouth moved at the right time, being a mime act it would have looked silly if it didn't.

Hilary, Lorraine and all their staff were magnificent from what I can recall.

December brought the Christmas shows at The Harbour. I was booked in for every Thursday, Friday and Saturday. Along with Christmas Eve, Boxing Day and New Years Eve. I couldn't help but see my Mum at my side giving me scarves, water and her proud smile. I knew it would take years before I recovered. Every night was packed with firms Christmas parties; it was chaotic but helped me grow a little stronger each show. New Years Eve was poignant at midnight. I was still on stage and led the Auld Lang Syne celebrations but I felt empty inside and tears just kept rolling down my face, I couldn't breathe. As the party died down I went upstairs to get changed. I sat on the bed and I was inconsolable, Donna was there for me but I was just distraught.

I wondered what life had in store for me now. But I could never have predicted what would happen next......

Age 5 months on Carrock Walk

Mum on her wedding day with
Uncle Herbert who had fought in WW1

My Grandad   Above aged 18 months with Grandad

Below my playground

Above age 4

Aged 8   Aged 10

Bishop Marshall School

Bishop Marshalls Uniform
Age 12

Mum and Blacky

Age 15

Mum & Me age 17

Mum, Cath & Me 1984

Me and my mate Rob Walker
The Gravedigger

Jimmy Bond and me in Blackpool

At a party age 19

Mum made me my first
ever Elvis suit in brown

First publicity shot 1984
& second suit made by Mum

At The Harbour 1985 with Mum
Following me with scarves

At The Harbour Hotel with Mum 1984

Harbour Hotel Circa 1985

Mike & Sue after the show

At The Gay Gordon, Langley 1984

Donna caught me just after the show

Mums first business card

Middleton Guardian 1984

The
Harbour
Hotel
1985 –
1986

Mum
Behind
Me
In
White
Top

Hilary, Mum & Me at my 2nd 21st at The Harbour

Elvis lookalike is a hit

On The Harbours Float in Rhyl Carnival 1985
I felt like the pied piper

ELVIS PRESLEY fans might be forgiven for thinking the King himself has re-appeared in Kinmel Bay.

For, every Friday and Saturday night at the Harbour Hotel in Kinmel Bay, Louis Gates puts on his costume and combs his hair and looks every inch like the real thing.

Although he only mimes to Elvis tapes and records his act has become so polished that customers are often fooled.

Manager Miss Hilary Brereton said: "Some people start shouting out requests not realising he is miming and that it is all on tape.

"Since Louis first appeared here in February, he has been very popular and we invited him back just after Easter. He has been coming here on a Friday and Saturday night ever since.

"I hope he will keep on coming back, and I would also like to see an Elvis music club or something formed here so people who enjoy

his music will have somewhere to go."

She added: "I think he has only been miming to Elvis records for about 12 months but he has got it off to a fine art and he also has all his movements."

Louis Grant is from Middleton, near Manchester, and works at the local Co-op during the day. At night he is transformed into his hero.

Miss Brereton said his mother Brenda makes all his costumes and they too were very realistic.

"Over the Summer, we have been packing people in to the Harbour Hotel to hear him and I think a lot of local people have also started to come in.

"The music is free and I am sure this different act will carry on proving very popular," she added.

Louis Gates will be appearing at the Harbour Hotel this Friday and Saturday evening, September 27 and 28, but don't worry if you can't make it — he will be back in a fortnight.

...s Presley lookalike, Louis Gates, ...o will be appearing at the Harbour Hotel, Kinmel Bay, this weekend.

Rhyl Journal 1984

My biggest fan Becky she came to
to the show every night all year round

74

Cath

Girlfriends

Donna

Natalie

Tracey

Mums last Summer Season
Just 6 weeks before she died

Final show at The Harbour 1989

Great friends Brian & Pauline Fellows
I would later sing at both their funerals

With Colin Barber my good friend
and Merchandise Manager

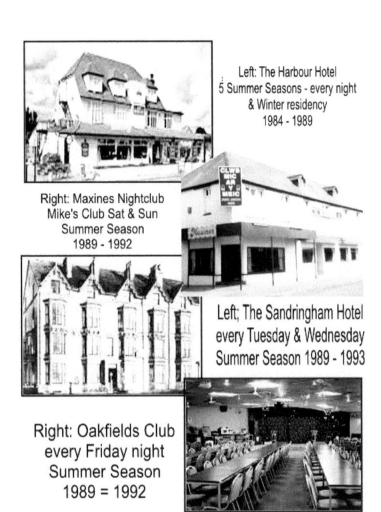

Left: The Harbour Hotel
5 Summer Seasons - every night
& Winter residency
1984 - 1989

Right: Maxines Nightclub
Mike's Club Sat & Sun
Summer Season
1989 - 1992

Left; The Sandringham Hotel
every Tuesday & Wednesday
Summer Season 1989 - 1993

Right: Oakfields Club
every Friday night
Summer Season
1989 = 1992

Chapter 6

1989......ALL SHOOK UP

It was a quiet month in January 89' I only had a couple of shows booked. They went down well but in truth I still wasn't with it at all it had only been three months since my world had collapsed. I'd had my wings clipped and I was just going through the motions. It was Donna's birthday 10th January and I completely forgot all about it. She understood and I made up for it the day after. She tried to cook meals for us, but Dad just kept saying "its not like Brenda's cooking" and pushed it to one side. Donna was just nineteen, how cruel was he. She made an attempt at making buttercream cake, she knew it was my favourite. But when it was baking, the oven made a big bang. We all went in to see the oven blown up with smoke everywhere and the cake ruined. Dad went ballistic with her saying it was Brenda's oven and she wasn't to use it again. I think he would have given her a slap if I wasn't there. I had a big stand up row with him then he just walked away.

I was told in March that Donna had been having an affair with Jacqui's husband Tim. He had been doing some driving for me while my Mum was poorly. When I confronted her she didn't deny anything, in fact she told me everything. How they had kissed one night at Tims house and also backstage when I was on stage in Kentish Town. The worst time was when they had kissed at Mums funeral when we had got back home after the funeral. I went into a storm I had just lost my Mum and now I was losing my girlfriend. She turned on the water works and pleaded that she wanted to be with me not him. That was easy to say now she had been caught out. I was really finding all this too much I felt like my head was going to explode. Eventually I calmed down, I went into Mums bedroom and sat on her bed crying and hoping I would get some kind of advice or decision on what I should do. In the end I decided that I loved Donna but she would have to prove to me she loved me and wanted to be with me. I told her to phone Tim and tell him so. I was on the other phone so I could hear the conversation. When it was done I spoke and told him if he came anywhere near my family again I would kill him, I wasn't joking! I then told Donna to have a bath and I humiliated her by washing her with the sponge. It sounds awful now but it was how I had to handle the situation to let her know how serious I was. I cried myself to sleep that night, she tried to comfort me without success I was heartbroken for the second time in under three months. I wondered what was the next awful thing to happen to me!

By the time we got to April I knew Dad didn't want us living there let alone doing the shows with me. He had told Carol and Tommy how he felt. With the best of intentions they told me to try and handle Dad with kid gloves. I told Carol it was him who was causing all the friction, she didn't believe me at that time.

Saturday 15th April and I was booked into huge bingo hall in Wavertree, Liverpool. At dinnertime we all watched the Hillsborough disaster unfold. Liverpool were playing Nottingham Forest in the semi final of the F.A. Cup. There was a sudden surge in one of the stands where the Liverpool fans were. People were getting crushed to death at the front section of the high railings. Most of you know what the outcome was with ninety six people losing their lives, it was horrendous!

I just assumed the show in Liverpool that night would be cancelled out of respect. I called the agent and he agreed, he said he would call the venue to confirm. To my utter horror they told him they wanted to carry on with the gig. I couldn't believe it! So we went to Liverpool and set up my speakers etc. The manager came to me and said the show was going ahead in memoriam to the Liverpool fans that had lost their lives. His only request was that I finish off with "You'll Never Walk Alone" which I did and it was extremely poignant.

From the end of April into May bookings picked up I was doing two shows a week in places like: Liverpool, Manchester, Warrington and Stoke. But still I was working on autopilot. At the end of May I was booked into Kirkby Liberal Club in Liverpool. I had quite a big following by then in Kirkby.

Dad got home from work at 2pm that Friday afternoon and declared he'd had enough and I would have to get someone else to do the shows with. Donna and I were speechless. This was at 2pm and I would need to set off for Kirkby at 5pm to set up before doors opened at 7pm. I had half expected this but I didn't think he would let me down on the day of a show. He must have known all week what he was going to do but this was low even for him. He let me down big time and he knew it. It was just plain nasty!

I desperately tried to get in touch with the club but I couldn't get through. Finally I spoke with the Entertainments Secretary just after 6pm. I told him my situation and that if we could re-arrange the show I would do it for free, I was so embarrassed. He went into a rant saying two hundred and fifty people had bought tickets and they were totally sold out. I apologised profusely and asked again if we could put another date in the diary free of charge, I didn't want to lose my fans on Merseyside. He was just horrible to me which I could understand, but there was no way I could get to Kirkby. He cancelled the show and hung up on me. I felt terrible for the two hundred and fifty people that had bought tickets, Donna calmed me down but I was fuming with Dad. He went out somewhere probably to his fancy woman, good job he did because I was ready to knock him out. Again Donna was brilliant in calming me down.

I knew then that I would need to move away from my childhood home for my own sanity. I was twenty four so it probably was time. However I didn't want to do it like this. Donna and I were saving up for a deposit and that was the route I wanted to go down. However you have to play the cards your dealt with and I decided I would move to Rhyl and stay at Avril's house. She had told me many times if it got too much I should go live with my adopted family in Rhyl.

That weekend was awful with the tension he caused but we got through it and on Monday I packed a bag and got a train to North Wales. Donna was to follow me on the Friday after she'd worked her weeks notice.

80

I found out at a later date off Carol Price that she had told my Dad to sit down and as she told him about me leaving and that I had left for good. Apparently it was as if he hadn't heard her. He quickly said he'd had a wonderful time at Heaton Park with Ann, his new girlfriend! So that's why he wanted me and Donna out of the way. I really wouldn't have expected him to be on his own for the rest of his life but Ann was well known for being a bit of a gold digger on the estate. She had already fleeced her previous husband and she was onto her next victim, my Dad. After the way he had treated me over the years i think he probably deserved her!

Nevertheless we were on a new adventure that I wouldn't have missed for the world.

I landed at Avril's house and the first thing she said was "what do you want to eat for tea". The happy atmosphere was amazing. It was like having a huge weight lifted off my shoulders and I felt like I had a warm blanket wrapped around me. I phoned Donna at work and explained what had happened. She wasn't keen on spending another week at my Dads so she just stayed that night and the following day came down to Rhyl. After we had eaten I began to tell Avril what had happened over the last six months. It felt good to unburden my problems to someone else other than Donna. I got the my little sister Pamela's room room and I collapsed into bed exhausted, I was asleep in minutes.

The following day I went into the Harbour and spoke with Hilary about the situation. She said I could come and stay at the hotel for as long as I wanted. I decided to stay for two weeks at Avril's then move into the hotel. I was that comfortable at Avril's the two weeks stretched to three. I kind of liked be spoilt by Avril, Michelle, Jacqui and Pamela. My little sisters. I could never repay their kindness.

Eventually me and Donna moved into the Harbour Hotel, Hilary gave us a suite on the top floor. Through a stroke of luck all my equipment had been stored at the hotel, often we would leave it there if I didn't have any gigs the following weekend.

The week after that all we had to do was put the gear up rather than loading and unloading.

Of course there wasn't any mobile phones back then so I used the hotels pay phone or the phone box outside. I called Carol and Tommy to see if they were ok, tell them Donna and I was alright and to see if the situation was any different. Carol told me that they had been shocked by how my Dad had treated them. Up until I had left he had gone to visit Carol and Tommy every night. Since I had left he hadn't been once and when they had seen him in the street he had been very curt with them. It had broken their hearts because they genuinely cared for him and Mum. Carol apologised to me for when she had thought it was me causing all the tension and arguments. We both came to the conclusion that he was a very selfish, self centred horrible man. I told Carol I hoped this new woman took him to the cleaners.

We moved into the Harbour just in time for the summer season. All the locals had sympathy with me, some of them offering to help with the show. They were really wonderful and every single one of them said they thought Dad was a bit strange and they never said anything for Mums sake. Of course they all loved and missed Mum.

With Donna working on the show, all those one nighters with different ladies, had to stop! I didn't mind I was still too upset over Mum to be bothered with that scene. Besides me and Donna had become closer, eventually we became soul mates.

The shows went really well. Although it was difficult signing autographs and talking with the audience after the shows. Some people had been and seen the show for the past four years. They wanted to know where my Mum and Dad were. So I had to go through everything every single night, it was mentally very hard but i got through it.

In the last week of summer season Al Lucas offered to be my manager. He seemed really clued up, but they all do don't they. I agreed for a six month trial. The only downside was he was a scouser. Al also offered me a day job at the market selling cheap watches for £90 a week. Julie also had a stall selling garden gnomes. Getting to the market for 8.30am and working till about 3.30pm when Donna would take over for the last two hours after doing a couple of shifts at The Harbour as a waitress. I would go back to the hotel to have a bath and rest up for 8.30pm for the show. Do the show and collapse into bed at midnight then up at 7.30am and do the whole thing again. Having said all that the extra wages from the market came in handy on top of the low wages at The Harbour.

During the season a few people approached me about going to perform at their venues. The first one was Mike Ruggiero from Maxine's Nightclub near the fairground. He said if I ever wanted to come and be resident at Maxine's to give him a call, he offered me £100 a night. The second was Les Hughes from The Sandringham Hotel on the promenade. He told me to name my price to leave the Harbour and be resident at his hotel. I had also heard that Oakfield's Caravan park were interested in booking me on a regular basis. All this money was turning my head, probably in a good way. At The Harbour I was only paid £75 for two nights. Mum had negotiated extra meals and drinks but I hadn't had a raise since I first started there. So I thought I would ask Hilary and Lorraine for a rise. I really didn't want to move from the harbour I had a lot of memories and friends there. From the profits of me appearing in summer season they had even built an extension to fit more people in so it surely would be in their interests to try and keep me there. All I was asking was £100 for the two nights, £50 per night was still less than the going rate. I was earning £60-80 for one nighters! Alas they were not interested, I was surprised. I thought I was being reasonable. Its true they said we could stay at the hotel free of charge and have free meals. And yet Donna had to work as a waitress free of charge for this. But we wanted to live in our own flat and be independent and the wage at The Harbour wouldn't be enough to do that. I told them this but they just looked at me as if I was deserting them. It would be a huge move for me, I had earn't my apprenticeship at The Harbour, my mum thought I wouldn't be as successful anywhere else. I had done five years at The Harbour and stayed loyal to them, I didn't perform anywhere else in the area. I expected at least the respect of negotiations, the only reply I got was "we cant afford it". I couldn't believe it! The venue was the busiest cabaret venue in Rhyl and Towyn and yet I was still on just £37.50 a night.

I discussed it with Donna and we decided we had no choice but to leave The Harbour for good. We went straight to Mike at Maxine's Club. He said he would put my show on every other Saturday and Sunday night throughout the year at £100 per show. I couldn't believe how highly I was regarded. Then I paid a visit see Arthur Sheridan the manager at The Sandringham Hotel. He told me he would put my show on Tuesdays and Wednesdays for the summer season and the odd weekend in winter. It was the same fee as Maxine's Club £100 per show. Next call was to Oakfields Caravan Park in Towyn. The manager, a lovely man called Stan said he would put me on every Friday night, April through to the end of October. Again at £100 per show. I was in dreamland, it meant during summer season I would be doing just five shows per week and getting paid £500. I would have to do about fourteen shows at The Harbour for this amount. I felt like going back into the Harbour and showing them how much people appreciated me. I didn't because I felt I was more professional than that and besides karma played a part with Hilary and Lorraine at a later date!

We both moved out of The Harbour. The final show was very emotional for me. This was where my mum felt most comfortable and I had lots of good memories. It felt like leaving my home all over again.

We moved back into Avril's house and a week later I moved in to Al and Julies house, Jacqui staying at Avril's till we could find our own place. I had to share a big room with their son Tony who was about my age. With the income of £500 a week we could easily find our own place pretty quick. I couldn't buy a house yet as I was self-employed and Donna resigning from her waitress job at The Harbour, hadn't got another job.

I went to see Les Hughes and he offered to lend me a Luton van and a driver to go get the rest of my things from my Mums.

He never charged me a penny. He had a reputation of being tight with his money but you speak as you find and I shall never forget his generosity. Its true I would make him a lot of money in the future at his Sandringham Hotel. But he treated me with total respect as did his manager Arthur he was a true gentleman.

It was surreal when we got to my Mums. It was my family home for twenty four years and saying goodbye to it was very emotional. I had lived and breathed the fields in front of our house and now I was saying goodbye to my youth. Carol and Tommy helped load the van with us and I think they felt for me, I know I did them. Salt of the earth people, I would miss them immensely. The only thing I took that belonged to Mum was a framed padded Mothers Day card I got her one year. It was on the wall and I took it down.

As we pulled off I wondered if I would ever see my home again.

When we got back to Rhyl Al Lucas said I could store most of my stuff at his house. I stayed at Al's for a few months.

Eventually we moved into an attic flat on Princes street right in the centre of Rhyl.

We both felt fantastic being independent and looking forward to the future. Talk about an emotional roller-coaster. I just knew in my heart there would be better times ahead!

Chapter 7

1989-1991......Mystery Train

We woke up that first morning in our little attic flat, opened the window and breathed in the sea air. I always had this strong feeling that everything would be alright for us.

No sooner had we moved into our flat and the summer season was upon us. My first booking away from The Harbour was at Maxine's Club near the fairground. The owner Mike Ruggiero was just the sort of person I needed, a total professional with lots of talent and humility. He knew I would be a little wary on my first night and he put me right at ease straight away. It was like I had worked for him for years. The club was jam packed, he had put posters of me all around the club and the night was a huge success. I performed on the dance floor with seats in front of me. I did the first set and when I walked out for the second set I stopped dead in my tracks. My Mum was sat on the front row with a huge proud smile on her face. I was frozen, I think it was her way of saying I would be alright with Mike and being away from The Harbour Hotel that she loved, we had argued about it countless times.

So I was doing the second set and after about three songs she was gone! It was really hard to finish the set because of seeing her but I did, the audience were going crazy but I was desperately looking around for her. It would be the only time I would see her proudly smiling at me ever again and she was gone in a flash.

Mike was so pleased he had took the gamble on me. We all had a great time after the show, Mike played guitar we all sang and much alcohol was consumed.

One day Mike suggested I leave my equipment upstairs at Maxine's club, there was loads of space and it made sense I didnt fancy lugging it all up three flights of stairs to our flat. So that's what we did and each time I worked away from his club I would pick it up and drop it off after the show. I was unloading the gear one night and he helped us. I had a huge touring case with amps and lights in it, it took two people to carry it, Mike just threw onto his shoulder and marched off upstairs. Me and Donna were dumbstruck I'd never seen anything like that before......what a character!

We had Monday off and then it was onto the next venue, The Sandringham Hotel, right on the front of the promenade. We went to set up the gear at 5pm. We walked in and the place was jam packed. I went to the bar and asked this chap that had a big welcoming smile, are your Arthur? He said no he was Jock the bar manager and he would go and get Arthur. He told us to set up where ever we wanted so we set up in the corner. Arthur appeared and I couldn't believe it, he was all of five foot tall, grey hair with glasses. I didn't know what to expect, he greeted us with a big smile and a warm welcome. He really took care of us. Having said that Les Hughes (the owner) had been trying to persuade my mum to let him book me at his hotel for years. The Tuesday and Wednesday nights shows were a huge success. The lounge doors opened out to the promenade, I think there was just as many people outside watching me as there were inside. Arthur said he'd never seen anything like it. I never paid for a drink that night.

We had Thursday night off, I was shattered. Then on Friday we arrived and Oakfield's Caravan Park in Towyn. It was quite a large room similar to a working mens club. I had done lots of these venues before back in Manchester so I wasn't daunted. A tall Liverpudlian called Stan greeted us and explained how the night would run. Because I was booked on Fridays it meant that it would be the last night for most of the audience before they went home on the Saturday. I thought this was just the challenge I needed and that first night I truly delivered, I went down exceedingly well, getting several standing ovations. Afterwards everybody wanted a signed picture and I stood for about forty five minutes signing autograph's for everyone.

So that's how my first summer season away from The Harbour went. I was earning £500 a week for five shows and let me tell you £500 was a lot of money back in the eighties, most peoples weekly wage back then were around £150 per week. Everything just felt right, three very different venues full every night, I was over the moon.

I would do the odd one nighter in Manchester or Liverpool during the winter months and my manager Al Lucas would take me in his van if he could. But I noticed a distinct change in him. Ever since we moved into our own flat he became strange. Looking back now I think he was the controlling type. I paid him his commission for the gigs he got me, but he wanted commission off the summer season shows which I had negotiated prior to him managing me. I agreed to pay him 10% to keep him sweet. Then he started asking for me to pay his phone bill, he reckoned he had done a lot of calls. That was the final straw, I phoned him and fired him. I didn't need someone to manage me let alone another dubious Scouser!

He came to our flat one night buzzing the bell for a long time, but I just ignored him. As far as I was concerned he was fired and that was that. Funny how people are nice until there's an argument about money. I never saw him again thank God!

I had a lot of fans/friends that originally saw my show at The Harbour migrate to Maxine's Club and The Sandringham Hotel. Friends like May and Lynn from Stoke, Brian and Pauline from the Midlands, John and Norma from Liverpool and Debbie Fellows and her family from the Midlands. They all agreed that it wasn't like the Harbour but I told them I was spreading my wings and getting ready to fly!

Then there was Ralph who would bring his seven year old daughter to see my show at The Sandringham Hotel and Maxine's Club. I don't know what had happened to her but she couldn't communicate very well, but she loved my show and it seemed to bring her out of her shell a little bit. Ralph told me she called me "shaky legs" which was nice. Ralph worked on Rhyl's fairground and we became friends. When Christine and her kids came to

Rhyl for the week Ralph would let them on all the rides for free. I got to know a few of the fairground lads as well, they would shout "Hiya Elvis" if they saw me in the street. One day one of them knocked on my door and told me some terrible news that Ralph had passed away at home, he was only thirty four. I was gutted and wondered what would happen to his daughter. Mike asked if Donna and I would travel to Salford and attend the funeral on behalf of Maxine's Nightclub. It was so sad his daughter was in tears at the church. We were invited back to Ralph's favourite snooker club for the wake. We didn't know anybody so we decided to pay our respects to his ex-wife and his daughter. Before we could, his daughter had pulled her mum over to us and said "shaky legs" mum. For once I was stuck for words it was heartbreaking.

We became close friends with Mick from Maxine's. He was probably the most honest person I've ever met. He kept giving me help and advice about handling an audience. I wondered what he was on about, I was a mime act. He said Pete, I've heard you singing along with Elvis into that dummy microphone, you have a great voice and you should try going live. The thought frightened me to death. Apparently when he had introduced me, he would sit behind his disco console on stage and he said I was reaching all the high notes of Elvis' songs with ease. He also said I should spread my wings and perform nationwide. He was cutting his own throat saying that because Maxine's club was absolutely rammed every weekend, you couldn't get a seat! But that was Mick......totally selfless. If I said Mick was kind and generous it would be the understatement of the century!

Mick was just totally crazy too. When I was on stage he would approach the stage dressed in those inflated costumes like Batman and The Hulk. One night he asked to look at my set list so I showed him. I knew he was up to something and when I came to perform Don't Cry Daddy he came out and sat on the stage holding my hand dressed in giant baby dress resplendent with a huge red dummy! I couldn't contain myself, he kept baby talking me not to cry daddy. He was crazy and I learnt so much off him especially that nothing was off limits on stage as long as I stayed in control of the show. The guy was a genius.

He was always coming up with idea's, one of them was to do a show in the car park adjacent to the club. He built a small stage and would start the show with some songs and then he would do a disco whilst roaming around the Sunday market, just a hundred yards away with his radio microphone. He would come back to the car park/stage with twenty/thirty people he had invited to the show, he was like the pied piper!

So he sang one more song then started the audience participatience "if we cheer loudly I bet Elvis Presley will appear on our the roof" so after a few cheers I appeared on the flat roof via the fire escape and everyone cheered louder and I made my entrance onto the stage. Something so simple and maybe old school but we pulled it off every Sunday, the crowd loved it and then came back at the night time to see the show again, it was really cool.

He lent us his car once it was an allegro. Donna and I went to Liverpool shopping in it. On the way back about thirty minutes from Rhyl, Donna screamed. The car listed to one side and I kid you not the back wheel came flying past us! That was quite surreal! We got hold of Mick and he came and rescued us, he said "it does that sometimes" he forgot to tell us, it was so funny I was in tears of laughter.

He used to have guest singers at the club and one of them was a lady singer whose name I can't recall, anyhow she had a great voice and she sang my mums song "The Rose". It shook me to my my very core and I wept quietly. She apologised afterwards but I told her to carry on singing it, she interpreted the song with so much emotion.

Another guest singer was a guy called Brian, he was a country singer and he was alright. I decided with the help from my friend May Whitby to put a show on at Kidsgrove Town Hall in Stoke. I asked Brian to be support act and he agreed. May and I put posters up all around town and May sold the tickets. It wasn't a great attendance and when Brian refused to come off after his forty five minute set, I wanted the ground to eat me up. He actually thought he'd made the big time because it was a huge stage!

Mick also entered me and my backing singers into a talent competition in Coventry. He drove us all the way there and back. We didn't come close to winning anything but it was a great experience.

Then there was the time Mick arranged for me, him and other singers from the club to appear in a charity concert at the Theatre Clwyd in Mold, North Wales. We all had to do sound checks and of course I was still a miming, so they played my funny version of Hound Dog. Now the celebrity compère's were Sinbad from Brookside and Paul O'grady as Lily Savage. When I started miming to the funny bit Sinbad almost lost his cup of tea and Paul O'grady was laughing his socks off. That was so funny. On the way back Mick took us all to the White House Restaurant (very posh) for our Sunday tea. When we all finished he flatly refused to take any money off any one of the fifteen of us......this guy was truly has a heart of gold!

He was so generous, he used to lend money to staff and friends if they were in need. Hardly any of them paid him back.

One day he called me to come and have a look at some speakers that somebody was selling. They would be a huge upgrade to mine. Mike said "do you like them" I said yes but I couldn't afford them. He said"ok they're yours and you can pay me back weekly. I was dumbfounded when I found out they were £800 and in the early 1990s that was a lot of money. Yet again I was gobsmacked with his generosity.

So that's what we did, he was paying me £200 every Saturday and Sunday so we just worked four weeks for free and it was paid off. I think we were the only people that ever paid him back what he was owed.

One Friday night at Oakfields was funny. Donna had put the tape into the tape deck and pressed play. The show was going well and I was walking through the audience singing Love Me Tender and giving scarves to the ladies. And then the glitch, halfway through Love Me Tender the tape switched to Blue Christmas. Everyone was in stitches, I just carried on and mimed to Blue Christmas, there was nothing I could do but hope the tape had more Elvis songs on it. Which it did thank God! The audience were in fits of laughter.

Blue Christmas in July, cant believe I got away with that one!

And then came the floods! I was late getting up on the Monday morning, well it was my day off. We had done a great show the night before at Mick's Maxine's club. I turned the TV on and couldn't believe what I was watching. All of Towyn, Kinmel Bay and Rhyl was flooded. The sea walls had not stopped the big waves. I thought wow at least were on the top floor and not been affected. Then I heard Mick shouting up from the street/river. I opened the window looked down and there he was in a canoe! He said he was just checking everyone was alright and was off to the next of his staff's houses. He his truly a one of a kind. The floods were terrible they destroyed all ground floor properties including the downstairs at Maxines club, Oakfields club and Avril's house in Kimnel Bay. It took a long time until everything was put straight again, in some cases it never was.

I had become a big fish in a little pond in Rhyl and Towyn in the nineties and I felt on top of the world. Like most performers I am my own worst critic but even I was surprised with how the shows were going. Afterwards the queues for autographs were unbelievable and I was a bit overawed. I would sign about seventy to eight autographs every night.

One Thursday morning there was a knock on the door. It was Mick asking if I would do him a great favour that afternoon. Before he had explained I immediately said yes! Somebody from a nursing home in Rhos-on-Sea had been in touch with him saying the artiste had let them down for that afternoons garden fete, could he find someone. I couldn't refuse him after everything he had done for us. He arranged it all and I just had to turn up dressed in my Elvis jumpsuit. The sun was shining and when we got there Mick decided to do a bit of an oldies disco. But Mick never just did disco, he was Mr Entertainment. Walking around all the old folks talking with them on his microphone. He had told me on the way that I would know my cue to come out and do my show. So when I heard him shouting "I think Elvis Presley is in the building – come on people shout We Want Elvis – I'm sure he'll appear ". And so I did and all the old men and women were made up, they thoroughly enjoyed the afternoon.

We finished the day by having ice creams on the promenade. I didn't have my normal clothes on i still had my jumpsuit on. People passing kept giving us double looks. Mick was acting like it was normal to be having ice cream with Elvis on the promenade. He kept shouting to people "Saturday and Sunday nights at Maxine's Club in Rhyl come and see this guy he's fantastic!"

Sometime around this period I met Rob Banks. He was a fellow Mancunian and we hit it off straight away. He would come to all the shows and eventually I offered him a job as a roadie. Donna wasn't too pleased, it would mean paying him £10/15 per show and she just couldn't understand it. As time went on she finally realised it was a good move. There was literally not much that Rob wouldn't do to help the show. He even spray painted the van we had at the time.

In November we did a one nighter at The Criterion Pub in Heywood, back in Manchester. The fee wasn't great but we needed the money to pay the rent. So we travelled back to Manchester that Saturday night and about halfway we heard a huge bang. I thought it was the van back firing but Rob knew straight away it was the crank shaft that had gone. We were up the creek without a paddle and desperately needed to do the gig. Rob said to leave it to him, he really knew his engines. We were in the AA so Rob called them out and told Donna exactly what to say. They towed us to Heywood and we arrived at the venue on the back of an AA truck with all its lights flashing. The landlord thought it was a brilliant effect! So i thought great but how do we get home. Rob had the answer again. He said after the show load the van and push it a hundred yards down the road and call the AA again. They were obligated to pick us up and tow us back to Rhyl. Was there no ends to Robs know how.

We got to pay our rent and my new mate saved the day.

We don't see much of him nowadays but we stay in touch on Facebook and he came to see me and the band a while back, it was great to see him again.

Hilary from The Harbour passed on a letter she had received from my dad, I had no idea what it was. I opened it and it was an appointment from the eye hospital in Manchester. They must have sent it to him. I discussed it with Donna and we made an appointment at St. Asaph Hospital, the nearest eye specialist to us. Come the day of the appointment I was a bit nervous but I shouldn't have been, the doctor told me that technology had moved on and I would be able to have a cornea transplant should the day arise. I did a huge sigh of relief. So he said just carry on day to day, I may never need a transplant. However on the negative side I might wake up one day in excruciate pain and would need the transplant straight away. But more about that later......

It was now 1990 and we had moved from the attic flat in Princes Street to Grange Road, opposite The Grange Hotel, the sister hotel to The Harbour Hotel. It was a ground floor apartment so no more stairs everyday. However we were broke in December and had to go three days without food, it was awful and not recommended. It came to Christmas week Donna said she would call her dad and ask for a loan. I said absolutely not but it turned out later that she had asked him for some money and he had refused. He told her she could go and spend Christmas with them but I wasn't welcome!

So Christmas day that year we had chicken flavoured crisp sandwiches and orange cordial. But we had each other and that's what counted.

The apartment was ideally situated just off the promenade so I would go jogging the full length of the promenade every time I could, I knew I had to keep my stamina up for the amount of shows I was doing. It was great with all that sea air.

Because of our financial position I wasn't able to go see my mum on the 1st Anniversary of her passing. I blamed my Dad for this, if he hadn't mentally abused me and forced me out, maybe I wouldn't have been in that situation and been able to go see mum.

Then I got the wanderlust again. I started seeing Rachel (Natalies younger sister) she was so nice but too young. I needed to lay down some roots. I felt awful on Rachel I think she had like me for a long time. It was just bad timing. So I decided I wanted to see Cath again and I told Donna I wasn't sure if it was her or Cath I wanted to be with. She was devastated and I felt awful but I had to be true to myself. I remember getting on a Manchester bound train that would get me in at Victoria station at about 9pm. I rushed to get a taxi to Cath's house, I arrived at 9.30pm. I knocked on her door and as she opened it her face was a picture. She told me I could stay the night but only on the sofa which was fair enough. We spoke at length about what we both wanted.

I woke up in the morning with two lovely kids looking at me, Cath's girls Rachael and Stacey. They were about eight or nine and wondered who this strange man was on their sofa. Cath came downstairs and explained who I was. Bless them they were two great kids. I realised it would be hard, she had been a single parent for a long time and she was set in her ways. I went back to Rhyl two days later not knowing what I wanted. I did some shows, Rob Banks helped me out, don't know what I would have done without him.

On the Monday I went back to see Cath and I stayed for three days but not on the sofa thank heavens. Cath said the girls were looking forward to see me again. I had a lovely mid-week with Cath and the girls but I started having my doubts about my future with them. Don't get me wrong I could have easily stepped in as a step-dad to Rachael and Stacey but it was Cath that was stuck in her own world. Nothing wrong with that, she had made her life as a single parent. It was just that it didn't really include me, I was very high maintenance with my ego and that was my fault. I think she realised that as well. So as I was getting ready to leave for the train, we had a full and frank conversation. There was tears on both our cheeks as I said goodbye.

I got to the station and went to McDonald's for a burger. I sat down and just across the way Bill Roach (Ken Barlow) from Coronation Street was sat with his wife and children. I felt I needed a family of my own. I stood on the train platform not knowing what I wanted, It was a pivitol moment in my life and then it hit me right between the eyes. It was definitely Donna I needed. But i had messed her around so much I didn't know if she wanted me back? I got off the train in Rhyl and got a taxi straight to where I knew she was staying. I laid it all straight to her and promised I would be true to her. We had got engaged about a two months ago and I had asked her to marry me. I asked her where her engagement ring was. She said she had thrown into the sea. Some lucky person would find it, it cost me £250 a lot of money back then. I said it didn't matter and I would buy her another one. Slowly she started to warm to me and after talking for an hour we were back together again. I couldn't believe how lucky I was. I never cheated on her from that day on.

We only stayed at the apartment on Grange road for six months which was a shame because I really liked it. We were on the move again. We moved into a flat right on the promenade. It seemed ok at first and then all the holiday makers started staring in the big bay fronted windows. You could actually hear some saying that's where Louis Gates lives! Donna put up some lace nets and we closed the curtains most days.

Donna took a phone call while we lived on the promenade. It was Granada Television. She handed me the phone and it was actually the popular TV show "Stars In their Eyes". They explained they were doing an Elvis special and would I be interested in being one of the twelve Elvis performers? I told them I was a mime act and wasn't sure if it could be done. They responded with they would get around it somehow, they just desperately wanted me on the show. Then I was an idiot, I asked them for a fee. They refused and pointed out how much exposure

I would get form being on television. I told them I had enough exposure where I lived in North Wales. So the conversation ended. Donna blew her top at me saying I was stupid, But I didn't seemed bothered at all. Looking back now I can see it was the medication I was on. Every day I was high then low.

What a fool I was, I could have accelerated my career big time. Instead I stayed a big fish in a tiny pond for a wile longer.

It was while we were in our promenade flat that I remembered my Mum had put my name on the deeds to the family home on Langley. Her intension being it would help give me a start in life. I sent my dad a letter and heard nothing back. I sent another letter and the same thing. So knowing my Father wouldn't release any money, I instructed a solicitor to contact him. Four letters and twelve months later he eventually replied saying he would give me a third of what the house was worth. Now I may be wrong but I think he should have offered me half seeing as my mum wasn't here anymore. However I didn't make any ruffles and accepted his offer of £7,500. The cheeky man based it on what it was worth twenty years ago. Of course he should have based it on what it was worth at that point of time.

It took about three months before I got the money my mum wanted me to have. I got a call from my solicitors and when I got there I signed some documents, he opened his safe and pulled out £7,500 in cash. We were shocked I thought we were picking up a cheque. We walked the hundred yards to the bank and deposited it as quick as we could!

Compared to the previous Christmas of crisp sandwiches, we really pushed the boat out. It was great, I bought all the presents that I knew Donna wanted. It was a festive Christmas that year....

Chapter 8

1991-1992.....CHANGE OF HABIT

Its 1991 and we were living in a lovely flat on Rhyl's promenade, life seemed good. Or at least I thought it was. Donna had took me to the doctors to sort out my depression. She said later on that I had just been staring out the window for months. I knew what the depression was, of course it was losing my mother. I had bottled everything up since she had died three years ago. The doctor prescribed anti-depressants which seemed to make things worse. Donna said I was getting better day by day. I wasn't sure, in truth there was twelve months that I couldn't account for.

Donna also got me to see the dermatologist specialist at Bodelwyddan hospital to try and sort out my eczema. It had started to flare up. I saw a lady called Dr Elmslea and she prescribed different creams, bath lotion and oil of primrose tablets. Within three weeks it had subsided. She told me it would and to keep on with the medicine she had prescribed, if I didn't it might flare up again.

Two weeks later I went to bed in our flat. I couldn't settle, I tried reading my book but still no good. Then wham! I could hardly breathe. I made some noises and Donna came running to help me, I was panicking for air. An ambulance medic came and gave me an injection and an oxygen mask. He told me I was having an asthma attack. The oxygen and injection made it easier to breath. I thought I was going to hospital but the medic told me to keep the oxygen mask on all night and that I would be alright. He made an appointment for me to see the asthma specialist the following day. Which I did and he prescribed me inhalers and antihistamine tablets. It was to become a permanent way of life for me.

Then right out of the blue and just prior to the summer season Donna told me I was going to be a Father. I was over the moon.

I decided to brake the cycle my dad had created and shower this child with love and guidance. I'd had no real Father figure in my life but I was determined to get it right.

We had a few one nighters to do before the season and I told Donna I would get Rob Banks to drive me to the shows. She wouldn't have it, she was being really stubborn. I tried to reason with her saying Rob would be there anyway and it made sense. But no, not a chance. Then at about 11am one morning Donna shouted me, I was still in bed. I phoned for an ambulance, she was losing the baby.

We got to St Asaph Hospital and I was told to wait in the waiting room. Thirty minutes later a nurse told me I could see Donna. I asked the nurse was the baby alright, she just shrugged her shoulders and walked away.

I walked into the ward and found Donna in tears, it was then I knew we had lost the baby. I consoled her for a long time, but I noticed a black bin bag about ten yards away at the nurses station. I asked Donna if our baby was in that bag and she said yes! I couldn't believe it, how insensitive was that. I hit the roof and marched down the corridor to where all the nurses were stood. Some of them dispersed when the saw me coming. I asked the senior nurse what the hell was going, my wife had lost the baby and you leave him in a bag within Donna's eyesight. All she did was apologise profusely and walked back to the ward with me. She picked up the bag with our dead baby inside and walked out. Words failed me, even today Im astonished by the treatment. I wondered what could have been. One of the nurses called me back as I was leaving the hospital. She said the baby would have been a boy and she was so sorry. We were both stunned and traumatized!

The following day I went in a taxi to pick Donna up to come home. She was still in tears so I consoled her as best as I could. She told me there were new mothers on the same ward as her with their babies. Could it get any worse, I just got all her things together and we left as quickly as we could. I was getting ready to hit someone.

On the drive back we held hands but didn't speak. I looked out of the window and I saw something that gave us great comfort. It was the clouds that had split and it looked as if there was a kind of stairway in the sky. It sounds strange but what we saw told us our baby boy had gone to heaven. No doubt my mum and Grandad had picked him up.

In the days after, we were inconsolable. Then someone suggested we go to the Spiritualist Church. We decided to give it a go. There was probably only ten people in this small room and the man that was officiating was from Llandudno. He contacted some spirits for some of the others then he said there was a small man holding a baby.

He described my grandad very specifically, even saying to tell Peter that he drove buses in Manchester! Donna and I were stunned he continued saying things that only me and my Grandad knew. Then he said don't cry for the baby he's doing alright he's with me.

A great big wave of emotion swamped us both, it made our relationship stronger.

We made friends with Chris and Ivy who owned a small hotel a few doors down from us. Ivy would come and see the shows sometimes and we would end up back at there hotel for drinks. I don't think Chris came to see the show, he was a computer geek, there wasn't anything he didn't know about computers. That was my first taste of the internet I was twenty seven and green behind the ears.

We tried to get on with our lives but it was so hard, I'm sure there are people that have been in that position have felt exactly the same.

In an effort to lift our moods we decided to make plans to get married, I was twenty seven and Donna was twenty one. It felt like we had lived through the worst together already and it just felt right.

I don't know how she found out but Donna's sister Leslie was banging on our door one Sunday morning demanding to know why they were not invited to our wedding. Donna sent her away and told her not to bother us again. I had already told her Dad Tony that is daughter didn't want any of them there, this was backstage in a social club in Sale. I was about to go on stage! He kept saying it was me that had made the decision, I told him neither of us wanted them at the wedding. Donna genuinely didn't want them to attend and that was final as far as she was concerned. He just made a fool of himself ranting and threatening all sorts, I told he had to leave in no uncertain terms, finally he left and we got on with my show. What a bunch of controlling clowns!

Chris and Ivy said we could have the reception at there hotel for free which was very generous of them. Ivy was a bridesmaid and Chris was my best man. Looking back I should have asked Steve McKay to be my best man but I had no idea where he was living. Someone told me he had moved abroad but that's all I knew, and don't forget computers were in their infancy back then and it was a struggle contacting people once you had lost touch with them. I also should have asked Mick from Maxine's, But my head wasn't in the right place and I just went along with flow.

My stag night was brutal, we went on a pub crawl and I was drinking pints of Southern Comfort with lemonade. It's a wonder I could stand up. At the end of the night they tied me to the front of the hotel where Donna was staying. Apparently she went ballistic. My friend Colin Barber, my merchandise guy, rescued me and made sure I got back to our flat alright. He also got me up on the wedding day and got me to the Registry Office on time. God bless him perhaps he should have been my best man, he was a true friend.

When Donna walked down the small isle she looked beautiful. She wore a traditional white wedding dress and she looked stunning, my heart was ready to burst. The ceremony was lovely and I was proud to see all our friends from different parts of the UK that had come along. It was amazing they had travelled from Birmingham, Liverpool, Stoke, Warrington, Cumbria and of course Manchester. In the group picture of us outside there was no family there whatsoever. Donna didn't want her family there which I was pleased about, they would have just cause trouble and ruined it all. In my heart these people from every corner of the country were part of my Louis Gates family!

We went back to Chris and Ivy's hotel and had a fantastic party! There was no family arguments that you get at normal wedding receptions, there was no family there! I had given Ivy the money that she needed to buy the food. She did Chilli and rice, my favourite and different salads for Donna, and the usual sausage roll and pork pies etc.

It was brilliant! I just wished that my Mum could have been there, maybe she was.

Not long after our wedding we met Christine Roberts and her family, I had met her mum and dad, Millie and Joe at the harbour a few years back. Joe was a typical Scotsman and Millie was a lovely little lady you would be proud to call your grandma. After my mum had died she told me that she would look after me as a son. An absolutely lovely couple and they treated me like family.

So Christine and her kids Lisa, Ellen and Matthew came into The Sandringham one night and it was like we had known each other for years. Christine became one of my Little Sisters, even if she was older than me. I was lost and Christine and Millie welcomed me and Donna with open arms into their family. For the first time since mum died I felt safe and part of a family.

She invited us to Sunday dinner at her house in Sale, Manchester. When we got there the house was full with her family mainly her sister Linda and her kids. It was just what we needed to feel wanted. We went a few times during that summer, eventually going every Sunday.

I threw myself into the shows and changed the whole feel and format. It had always been an ambition to play the young Elvis. So with this in mind I arranged the first thirty minutes as 1956 Elvis pink jacket, black baggy trousers and white shoes. The next thirty minutes as 1960s GI Elvis, I found an authentic US Army outfit complete with Sergeant stripes. After the break the final part would be 1970s Las Vegas Elvis for forty five minutes. It went down a storm, better than I could have ever wished for, I should have done it years ago. I put dialogue from an Elvis story album in-between my costume changes and the audiences went crazy. At long last I was doing my theatre show albeit in small venues, but it was a start!

1991 was my final summer season in Rhyl. Mick had told me to get out there and spread my wings and perform nationwide and that way I would grow as an artist. He would lose a lot of customers if I wasn't there but he was more concerned about me as an artiste. When I look back I can see it was the most unselfish advice anyone could have given me. He was a larger than life character with a huge heart and I would miss him greatly. Of course it was the best decision we would make. And besides I was getting homesick and we both decided to look at moving back home to Manchester. It was more central for being on the road.

I spoke with Arthur at The Sandringham and he was pleased for me. We agreed that I would still do Tuesdays and Wednesdays at his place and he even re-negotiated my fee so that I wouldn't lose out with the extra petrol etc.

Stan at Oakfields couldn't budge on my fee which I understood, Id been the highest earner there for the past few years. I did a show at Easter for him and said our goodbyes which was a bit emotional. Stan was a lovely man and I'll never forget his kindness.

Mick at Maxine's left it up to me whenever I wanted to do the odd gig. I did a few shows over Easter and then made arrangements to move back to Manchester. I knew it was the right thing to do but I really didn't want to leave Mick.

I went to get my wages from The Sandringham for the week. I told Arthur we had found a flat in Crumpsall, North Manchester. He asked how I was going to get all my stuff moved from Rhyl. I said I was going to rent a van. He said wait there a minute. He phoned Les Hughes (the owner) and told him what the situation was. He hung up and said Les is going to let you have one of his vans and a driver for free, as long I would still do Tuesdays and Wednesdays at The Sandringham. It was a no brainer, I was over the moon. I bought Arthur a drink then went back and told Donna what had just happened. She couldn't believe it either. What wonderful people I was working for.

We arrived at our flat in Manchester, it was raining as usual. But we didn't care we were looking forward to the next chapter of our lives. We were only there a few weeks and we got burgled, in broad daylight! We had gone to do some shopping got back and the front door had been kicked in. They only took our TV we didn't own very much at that time. Donna was freaked out and insisted we get on the council housing list for something in a better area.

I had to let Rob Banks go at this time. He wasn't happy but I couldn't afford his wages and petrol for him to travel from Liverpool where he was now living. He said he would pay the petrol himself and work for nothing! But I couldn't have him do that. He was a true friend and it hurt to let him go. Took me a while to get used to not having him around. He's one of the good guys and I miss him.

We would continue our friendship with Christine and her family and staying for Sunday dinner. Soon she introduced us to her friends on the darts team. They were so funny with their antics and for the first time Mum left I had a genuine smile on my face. We had a minibus I used for work and when the darts team were playing we would pick up Christine and everyone from their homes in Sale. At 2am one night the police pulled us over wanting to know why we were out so late. Of course I was in the back and the girls said about darts and that they had Elvis in the back. I volunteered myself and the coppers face was a picture. Everyone was laughing including the copper eventually.

Christine also got me some gigs in Sale and Altrincham. The darts team would always be there, it was organised chaos and brilliant for me because all the pubs and clubs wanted was a full house so I would always get re-booked. I was singing over the top of Elvis' voice by now, taking Mick's advice and desperately trying to find backing tracks. It was like finding a needle in a haystack. But I found about three or four and the difference when I sang to these was amazing. So I hoped my dream of having a live band wouldn't be too far away.

We became closer to Christine and the family and when her sister, Linda, said she could sing I decided to try and get her and Donna together for a rehearsal to be my backing singers. I had heard Donna singing along to herself loads of times, she was brilliant but I thought it might work! The only problem was that Linda's voice was completely drowning out Donna's. So with the help of a good mixing desk I got it right and we started doing some gigs. I had to pay Linda of course but I had raised my fees so it worked great.

One of the pubs Christine got me booked into was The Volunteer in Sale. By word of mouth it was always crammed full. On one of those nights there was a kid at the side of the stage. I could tell he was watching everything going on on stage. After the show he came up to me and asked if he could have a word with me. He said he was in a band and I thought he looked too young but anyway he started asking me about being the lead singer and how I dealt with different audiences. He was very polite and intelligent for being young so I explained a few do's and don'ts and how if he had the microphone he was in charge of what was happening on stage. Under no circumstances to give the microphone to anybody especially the audience members.

I could tell he was drinking it all in. I also told him if he couldn't see the audience because of the lights, to pick out three areas in front of him and play to those three areas as if you could see those people. I told him how to handle hecklers. He laughed and thought it was funny. He was very polite and he thanked me profusely for my time. I was just glad to help someone at the start of their career as Jimmy Bond had helped me. A few months later I was watching our local news channel, Granada Reports, and

105

this kid was there singing with his mates, they were good and their name was Take That! The kid I was talking to was Robbie Williams! And I thought good luck to you Robbie, but he didn't need luck of course he is mega talented and I'm proud of how his career worked out for him. Of course I always tell people that I taught him everything?!?!

So it was 1991/92 and I was doing shows in central Manchester and southern Manchester with Donna and Linda my backing singers. We went down really well wherever we appeared. And I added to the show myself talking live between songs. I was a bit nervous at first but after a few shows it was like I had done it all my life.

We finally moved house, this time to a maisonette in Blackley. We made friends with the neighbours pretty quick and soon felt at home. It was another housing estate like Langley so we felt comfortable.

In October 92' Donna told me she was pregnant again. It couldn't have come at a better time.

At first I insisted that she should stop working especially after the last time. But she flatly refused again and carried on working. It wasn't manually hard, she was back working as a secretary in central Manchester.

So Donna carried on working and I kept performing as Elvis. I did however put my foot down on the backing singing. Linda said she would do the driving but didn't want to work my music system and lights so I went to see Jimmy Bond. We had a good long talk and he was more than happy to help with my shows. I also hired Jimmy Bond Jnr. to work the lights, he turned out to be top class, working different lighting effects on the lighting desk. Jimmy Bond Snr. asked if I needed a driver which I did, so he suggested his brother Pete Bond to drive the van. Pete proved to be invaluable in the future. So it was a real family show with the Bonds and Christine's family. I was riding high playing many venues in Sale, Altrincham and all across the North West and The Midlands. The comradrie was great.

Chapter 9

1992-1993......MY BOY

Saturday 4th July 1992 was my twenty eighth birthday and we had been invited to Millie and Joe's fiftieth Wedding Anniversary at a function room in Sale. Christine had insisted we were there as part of the family and not to perform. I thought this was extremely thoughful of her and we danced and enjoyed the night.

Donna was heavily pregnant and due any day. She kept saying she wanted him to be born on my birthday. I've never seen a pregnant woman dance so energetically before and all because she wanted to give me the best birthday present of all.

We went home and i was pretty drunk and we went to bed. About 6am Donna frantically woke me up and saying the baby was coming, I stood up too quick and fell back down again onto the bed, I was still drunk!

Eventually I got dressed and went downstairs to call a taxi. Then I realised Donna was still upstairs and trying to get what she needed for hospital. So I staggered upstairs and tried to help her but I think I was more of a hindrance, she told me to look out for the taxi.

We got to Crumpsall Hospital and the nurses took over which I was thankful for, I felt like I was in a parallel universe, the whole world felt like it was spinning! They took Donna to the delivery room and told me it would be quite a few hours to wait. Someone led me to a room where I could sit down and I fell asleep. An hour or so later I woke up with a banging headache and I located where Donna was. She seemed alright and she told me I looked awful and that I should go to the hospital restaurant for breakfast, so I did.

After breakfast I felt a lot better but Donna was no nearer giving birth so I sat with her till lunchtime then went back to the restaurant for lunch. Then I went back again later for some tea and when I got back she was starting in labour. It carried on till 8.30pm and I was helping giving her the mask with gas and air. Somewhere around 9pm she gave birth to our son Benjamin all seven and a half pounds of him. It was the best feeling ever, ten times better than the best highs of being on stage. The nurse offered Ben to Donna, he was still covered in blood etc. and she said oh no take him away! I took him straight away in my arms. Ive never known an instant love like that, I was overcome with emotion. They say babies cant see anything for a while but I swear he focussed on me and I made him a promise that I would break the cycle of mental abuse my own father had done to me. I told him I would love him unconditionally and I would have his back as long as I lived. My Mums only Grandson and she never got to see him. Maybe she was smiling down on us, It certainly felt like she was. I spent about an hour with him while Donna was checked out and had a bath.

After a while one of the nurses said it was late and mother and baby were being taken up to the maternity ward for the night. Somehow that didn't feel right, I just wanted to be with my wife and new born child. Reluctantly I headed off to get a taxi home. I was on cloud nine and it felt like our little family was complete.

The next morning I was still buzzing and couldn't wait to get to the hospital. When I walked in I was very emotional seeing Donna there with our child next to her. Ive had a few highs in my life but nothing like this. I spent the whole day with her and Benjamin until finally the nurse yet again said I had to leave. This time Linda was picking me up to go see Christine and the family. We went to their local pub The Brigadier to wet the babies head, it just had to be done! I stayed on Christine's sofa that night and we all went to the hospital to see Donna and Ben the next day, even Millie and Joe came, it was a very memorable day. Donna had to stay in for just one more day because it was her first baby, that's what they did back then.

The following day I took a taxi to bring them home it was the proudest day of my life. The nurse told us the do's and don'ts and that the midwife would visit the following day. The mid-wife never turned up! Not that day or any other day, we were left to fend for ourselves which was ok with me I had fended for myself since Mum had died. Donna was a bag of nerves worrying that she might do the wrong things but I reassured her we would be alright, even if I was feeling scared as well! We did alright with him and he slept in a cot next to our bed. I don't think I slept a wink that night, I was listening to him breathe. As the days went by we did alright really, I even felt comfortable giving him a bath. All was perfect with us apart from Donna wanting to go straight back to work. We had a heated discussion and she agreed to have at least three weeks off. In the end she had two weeks off. I should have realized something was wrong at that point but I was flying high in love with our newborn son.

The following week I was back on stage at The Sandringham Hotel Tuesday and Wednesday nights. Donna stayed with Ben and I did the shows without backing singers, Linda drove me. Everybody showered me with cards and good wishes after the show and wanted to know when I was bringing Ben to see them all in Wales.

We got home from Wales in the early hours of the Thursday morning. I paid Linda and thanked her for driving me. She got into her car and went home. I was so tired that I couldn't be bothered lugging the gear inside so I left it in the van, planning on doing it in the morning. You know what's coming next don't you, when I got up I found the van doors open and all the equipment had been stolen. What was worse was the jumpsuits that my mum had made had gone along with my TCB ring that Donna had had made for me that I cherished so much. The police arrived eventually but didn't say or do much. Donna went to look along the river that was opposite our home. She returned with my suits she had retrieved from the river. Obviously they had stolen everything and discarded my suits into the river. We were both devastated! They were totally unusable, I was lucky I had a suit that Donna had almost finished for the next shows. I borrowed equipment off some friends in the business and got by until I could afford new gear.

Donna went back to work and I looked after Ben during the day. There was a two hour gap from me leaving for Wales on Tuesdays and Wednesdays to Donna getting home. Between Christine, Linda and our great neighbours they all took care of him till Donna got home. I would get home from Wales at about 2am and as soon as I had gotten through the front door Ben would start crying. Donna was in bed so after singing songs for two hours I went upstairs, picked him up from his cot and started singing lullaby's. He went to sleep after ten minutes and I would collapse into bed until 7am when Donna left for work, then I got up and took care of Ben again. It was like Ground-hog Day and really tired me out.

At weekends I would carry on doing one nighter's all over the UK. On average I was doing about four to five shows a week including Tuesdays and Wednesdays at The Sandringham. As usual I would give 100% at every show. I would get home at two or three in the morning and that would be Bens cue to wake up and get me to sing songs for him. I was tired but the adrenaline saw me through.

Then one day in late September it hit me right between the eyes – exhaustion. I couldn't get out of bed so Donna got the Doctor out. He told me to have at least three months off or I would end up in hospital! I cancelled all my shows up to mid January. Donna thought it was great, she wouldn't have to pull her weight looking after Ben! The idea was I would be able to have a rest but it didn't work out that way. I got up early with him, then looked after him through the day and then sang songs to him at bedtime. Donna would come home from her secretarial job and go to bed at around 9pm. She literally saw him for five minutes in the morning and two hours at night. So bang went my chance to recharge my batteries.

I decided to go back to work after a month so I tried to re-book the dates I had cancelled. Most of them were happy to do so. I was earning good wages at this time pulling in £150 - £175 per night, clearing about £125 - £150 after paying wages and petrol. At the time one nights pay was equal to a full weeks pay in a normal 9-5 job. I knew if I could stay focused and determined I could earn even more and go up the showbiz ladder. We actually started to save up for our first trip to America. At least I would get to sleep on the plane!

During the summer we had Ben christened at the Blackley Catholic Church. I wasn't a practising Catholic, I had studied different religions since mum had died and had come to my own conclusions. We went to see the priest and I told him I wanted six Godparents. He said absolutely not! So I got up and started to walk out. We were halfway down the corridor when he called us back, he reluctantly agreed. I wanted him christened catholic for my Mums memory and I wanted six Godparents because I wanted to make sure Ben would be thoroughly looked after if anything happened to Donna and myself when we were on the road.

We chose Jimmy and Marian Bond, Christine, Carol and Tommy (mums best friends) and Kevin (a venue owner who became a close friend).
So at the actual christening we had a great time and not one blood relative was there (mine and Donna's choice) just like our wedding. The room was full of the Louis Gates Family. They came from everywhere to celebrate with us. It was the perfect day!

Eventually Linda's daughter, Emily, would babysit Ben on the Tuesdays and Wednesday nights. Then one Tuesday Emily turned up at the back door and as soon as Ben saw her he ran underneath the kitchen table. We all thought he was playing but later it turned out that whatever Emily was doing it had scared Ben to death! I approached Linda about it and said Ben was clearly upset and probably would be best for Emily not to babysit any more and maybe one of her other daughters would instead. Linda hit the roof defending her daughter. Ben was almost two by then and I know he wouldn't have made anything up. I called Christine the following day and explained what had happened. She said that Linda had told her side of the story. Amazingly Christine sided with me and was extremely concerned about

Ben's welfare. Apparently she thought her niece had hidden demons and I was in the right to pull Linda about her. We all fell out which upset me greatly. Of course Millie was heartbroken that she wouldn't see us again. She always said she would look after me because my mum couldn't. She was a good friend to my mum and it was very sad, I never saw her again!

So that was the end of our friendship with Linda. Christine had been told by her father, Joe that she was not to socialize with us any more. The old man was very naive but Christine loved and respected him. However she did keep in touch by telephone and one day she phoned me to say that her Mum Millie had passed away. I was gutted, I thought the family row would have blown over eventually and we would be friends again. Christine said that Millie had insisted to be buried with a picture of me that I had signed for her. I was choking back the tears I couldn't believe it had happened. Christine arranged to meet us in Sale so we could pay our respects to Millie. She took us to Sale Cemetery which I found really tough. It was just so very sad. That was the final time I ever saw Christine it was heartbreaking.

Jimmy Bond Sr, Pete Bond and Jimmy Bond Jr were still working for me though and we had some great nights. Sometimes just Pete and Jimmy Jr would be there. It was on one of these shows we got called to perform at a 21st birthday party. It was at the Irish Centre in Chorlton, Manchester. I had no idea who it was but it turned out to be the lead singer of the band James. It was a brilliant night, they knew how to party.

Another one I did at the Irish Centre was a wedding for one of The Charlatans band. That was sensational, three hundred people bopping away to Elvis. Ive got to say that both of these famous bands were extremely respectful to me and so polite. But they could party that's for sure. I never thought to get photo's at these events I was just living in the moment. With hindsight I should have.

1993 saw us both working hard and saving up for a once in a lifetime trip to America. I had wanted to go ever since my early years and we hadn't had a honeymoon so we went in November.

Avril and Jacqui kindly offered to have Ben for the three weeks we had booked. She thought it would be better for us to have some quality time. I was unsure, I hated the thought of leaving Ben behind but they all talked me around in the end.

We went on Airtours inaugural flight to Orlando. Talk about Mickey Mouse airlines, nobody seemed to know what they were doing. We had to refuel in Bangor, Maine and the airport was a shed with the smallest landing strip you could imagine. We eventually landed at Orlando International Airport and I've no idea why but there was a New Orleans jazz band playing and welcoming us. It was a shock to the system how hot it was. We got our luggage and exited the terminal to go find our rental car. My God it was like opening an oven when we stepped outside. However it was a humid tropical heat and not like European heat. We knew instantly we wanted to live there, there was something in the air that was intoxicating! We got our car and it was huge as you would expect but Donna coped well on our five mile trip to the hotel. The Days Inn Hotel was about three or four miles from International Drive, one of the main roads with it's attractions etc.

We woke up on our first morning, got some breakfast from the IHOP opposite and headed to International Drive to have a look and get our bearings. The first thing we noticed apart from the humidity was how genuinely nice the locals were. My mum had always said Americans were loud and false but I think that stemmed from her wartime memories. We had booked all our theme park tickets at home so everything was paid for and we were due to go to The Magic Kingdom the following day. We acclimatized very quickly and felt totally at home.

I couldn't believe how lucky I was, I had always wanted to meet Mickey, even now as an adult, I guess I'm just a big kid at heart.

I won't bore you with details about each theme park, you probably have been yourselves or heard about it from friends. But we had a fantastic time in the three weeks. The weather never dropped below ninety degrees, it was spectacular and on the way back I couldn't wait to go back again. We landed back in Manchester and we were freezing. Like an idiot I still had my shorts and t-shirt on. So I got the luggage, cleared customs and did a quick change in the toilets.

We had arranged to pick Ben up from Avril in Wales in two days so we could get over the jet lag. Donna had other ideas, she decided she had missed Ben so much we were picking him up straight away. So we picked him up and thanked Avril and Jacqui and headed home. Twenty minutes later and the jet lag hit Donna. As she was the only driver she decided to have half an hour in a lay-by. We got home eventually and she agreed she wouldn't make that mistake again.

We got back to Blackley and our world seemed perfect. However I was about to make a monumental mistake that would affect our lives yet again.

Chapter 10

1993-1996...FOLLOW THAT DREAM

I was performing at many venues across the North West, one of them was The Victoria pub in Middleton Junction. Literally fifty yards from where my mum was born. I was introduced to Marlene and Joanne who offered to be my backing singers so I agreed to audition them. They past with flying colours and I put them on the show the following week.

One night at The Victoria we had the place rocking, Mick and Sue were there and Marlene and Joanne's friends were there, it was bouncing. The atmosphere was fever pitch when in walked my Father and his new wife. It threw me a bit but I carried on. What did he want? We finished the show after several encores and sat with Mick and Sue. Sue kept saying to make friends with my Father, she was really insistent and a bit annoying. Against my instincts and to shut Sue up I went to his table. He had a smarmy grin on his face and said "just as good as you always were". I couldn't believe it, the last time he saw my show I was a mime act and now I was completely live. I didn't know how to take it, was he really that stupid, just being sarcastic or just plain thick?

We got talking and it all became clear later what he was after. He had heard about me having a child and he just wanted to see Ben who was three years old by now. Yet again against my better judgment I agreed to meet him at The Jolly Butcher pub. He said he'd love to meet his only Grandson so I thought about it and I decided maybe he had changed and Ben deserved to have a proper Granddad, Donna's parents had paid no attention to Ben whatsoever. I insisted he came on his own at first which he did. I had heard all about Ann his second wife. She was well know as being the local gold digger in Middleton. But she was my childhood friend Gail's Auntie, so maybe she had changed.

115

The first meeting went alright, he seemed to be just pleased to see Ben. He even seemed to be pleased to see me but I wasn't holding my breath. He came a few more times before I relented and agreed for Ann to visit next time. How wrong I was she was still the same false gold digger as I had heard. I could read her like a book. My Father wasn't a millionaire but with his early pension payout and what he had in the bank after Mums life insurance pay out, he was pretty comfortable financially. She had taken full advantage of him and I just thought its his bed he can lie in it. If he wanted to make a fool of himself then they probably deserved each other. My only concern was Ben but he seemed happy seeing his Granddad so I allowed the visits to continue. This turned out to be one of the monumental mistakes I spoke about earlier but more about this later......

The next monumental mistake I made was that we left Blackley and moved into a council house back on Langley. This might sound alright and I thought it would be, we were on the very outskirts of the estate on Calgarth Drive. But it led to reacquainting with Donna's family who still lived nearby. Donna's sister Leslie came up to me after a show at The Moonraker pub and was very apologetic for what her family had been like, she also buttered me up about how good my show had become. Like an idiot I agreed to a visit which led to more socialising with the rest of the family.

One good thing that happened that year was I met Richard Kelly a local DJ. We soon became good friends. He had his own issues but had a heart of gold. I decided to make the show bigger and employed him as a DJ so it would be like an old fashioned roadshow. I would do two sets with Marlene and Joanne my backing singers and Ricky would do his disco before, in-between and after we had finished. Ricky was as daft as a brush, he'd get dressed up as something crazy and come and stand beside me. He used to crack me up. One night while I was singing " Rock-a-Hula Baby " he came behind me in just a grass hula skirt and his socks! The audience were in stitches. He was such a clown but a great respite for me, taking the limelight off me was always great for me laughing at his antics! He actually made the singing live factor a lot easier.

After he finished his disco we closed the show with all of us onstage singing Tina Turner's Simply The Best. The audiences loved it and when the lights went out at the end we were always greeted with shouts of more, but I totally refused which always led to a rebooking straight away!

I can't remember why but in 1994 i decided to change the spelling of my stage name from Louis Gates to Lewis Gates. Don't know why but it just felt right and it would prove lucky with what would happen from this time onwards.

I got a call from Hilary the owner of The Harbour in Wales. She asked me would I come and perform at her new pub on Queensway in Rochdale. She told me she had sold The Harbour and moved to this new pub. I found out later The Harbour had gone bankrupt, of course all the fans that used to come see me there, all migrated to Maxine's Club, The Sandringham Hotel and Oakfields Club. I had no sympathy for her, I had only asked for a ten pound a night rise which she completely refused. They were taking £1000+ a night behind the bar and couldn't afford a tenner? Anyway I told her my fees had gone up I was now on £175 a night solo no backing singers and to my surprise she agreed straight away. I suppose she had learnt from her past negotiations, if she wanted her new place full it would come at a price.

I did the gig and the pub was fairly full and it was a good night. However it was full of gypsies and they were getting rowdy. I handled them ok but I felt sorry for Hilary, it wasn't the venue for her. I think I was the final roll of the dice for her. She never called me for a rebooking and the last time I passed the pub it had been converted into a Co-op store. And the last I heard of Hilary she was running a B&B in Blackpool. How the mighty had fallen.

We had a show in Warrington and in the interval this guy approached me and was very complimentary about our show. He

117

explained he worked for Scottish & Newcastle Brewery and would I be interested in doing a North West / North East tour of their pubs. There would be around thirty gigs and it would be promoting Strongbow cider. And the best part was it would be mid-week gigs which meant I didn't have to change my weekend shows. The only stipulation was I had to be totally live. Up to this point I was still singing over the top of Elvis but talking live in-between each song. I told him I would do it even though I was panicking inside. I had just a few backing tracks, there wasn't many around back then. I told Pete and Ricky and they said it was a brilliant opportunity to progress in the business.

Pete said he knew a way of taking Elvis voice off the original recording then I could sing freely. Wow it was really going to happen!

We actually ended up doing twenty eight pubs from Penrith to Hull and everywhere in-between. There was all sorts of merchandise given out at every show and we all ended up with T-shirts etc. The brewery had contracted their own DJ for the tour but I kept Ricky on as a roadie which was cool because of his personality we never stopped laughing. Of course Pete Bond did all the driving and sound mixing desk. The tour was a huge success but they refused to do another tour the following year? That s showbiz I guess! I was learning not to take things so personal with the powers that be.

We were not at Calgarth Drive long when Donna told me her old family house was up for sale and we should go for it. I was unsure at first, it was closer to her family. However I relented and we went for a mortgage. The price was only £15,000 but it needed a lot of work doing to it. We finally got a mortgage with Nationwide and instantly got an improvement loan of £6,000. We used all of this because the house was a mess. In the kitchen there was just two water pipes where the sink should have been. Upstairs the bathroom consisted of just a hole in the floorboards where the toilet should have been. All the windows were boarded up but when we opened them up it was clear we needed new windows all round. We went back to Nationwide to get a top up loan of another £6,000 and along with the other £6,000 we used

118

almost all of it on windows, doors, bathroom, kitchen and carpets. It took us about six months to sort it out. It wasn't perfect but we felt a great achievement and it belonged to us. The first home we had ever owned!

Donna got a well paid job as a secretary at a huge cable factory that supplied to Sky and BT. She was only on twenty odd hours a week but she was pulling in almost £1000 a month after tax. Along with my income we we doing really well financially. So we decided to go on holiday to America again. This time Ben would be with us. It didn't sit well with me the first time leaving him at Avril's he was only one year old then. This time he would be about three and he adored anything Disney.......

We decided to do a bit of a road trip and visited Nashville first, Donna loved country music. We saw Studio B where Elvis had recorded loads of his hits, I couldn't believe how small it was but it was great. Then we went to Graceland in Memphis, the holy grail for Elvis fans.

When we got to the outskirts of Memphis we got a bit lost so I told Donna to pull over at the seven eleven drug store and I got out to ask a group of black teenagers the direction. That was Donna's cue to lock the car doors. The kids were brilliant with directions and when I got back to the car I asked her why she had locked the doors. She said she thought the gang could possibly beat me up so she locked the doors. I thought great thanks Donna don't worry about me. But i just knew the locals would be ok, I just had a feeling and I was right.

We finally got to our hotel, the Days Inn Graceland just a hundred yards from Graceland mansion. The hotel was resplendent with its own guitar shaped swimming pool.

The following day we visited Graceland. Ben was just three years old and he couldn't understand why I would want to and go see one of my old houses? Let me explain, whenever we would have an Elvis movie on at home Ben used to shout Daddy when he saw Elvis on screen and at that age it was easier to just go along with it. And anyway we could explain when he got a bit

119

older when he could understand. He was incredibly inquisitive and it was very hard work I can tell you.

We walked through the front door and I could feel Elvis' presence it was so strong. I looked at Donna and she had tears in her eyes, it was so emotional. She wasn't really an emotional person but she felt it that day. The mansion itself was smaller than I had expected but it had a homely feel to it, you could envisage Elvis living there and being so happy.

So we were looking at all the rooms and Ben decided he needed the toilet. Great, you know what's coming next. I told him he would have to wait. But he was determined and kept saying " you said it used to be your house you know where the toilet is"

That came back to bite me didn't it. Donna took him outside and asked security for the men's room, catastrophe avoided.

When we came outside from the famous Jungle Room we walked straight ahead towards Vernon's office. This was where Elvis did his famous interview to the world when he got out of the army. To the side of the separate office building were Lisa Maries Presley's swing and slide from when she was young.......Ben headed right for them, climbed the fence and was almost on the slide when I dragged him back. He just couldn't understand why he couldn't play on them especially as it used to be "my house". He was just so very funny.

We finally arrived at the Hall of Gold, all of his gold and silver records. My jaw dropped, that's when it hit me just how successful Elvis had been. It was about fifty yards long and they were on show from floor to ceiling with the silver and gold records. It was truly awe inspiring, the largest collection of gold records in the world! We exited the Hall of Gold and made our way outside towards his racquet ball building. The first thing that hits you when you enter is the small lounge area with leather seats etc. and the last piano he ever played on August 16th 1977. He sang Unchained melody and Blue Eyes Crying In The Rain for his girlfriend Ginger Alden. That moment was very poignant.

We then headed into the actual racquet ball court and I was overawed yet again with more gold and silver records, official awards and presentations from all over the world. They lined the walls from top to bottom, I was totally in awe. I'm not often stuck for words but my God how impressive was this collection. Also on show were some of his jumpsuits. Specifically his Sundial suit. The last one he wore on the last tour. My mum had promised to make me one but fell ill and never got around to making it. So I stood staring at the suit for a while with a tear in my eye.

As we came out of the racqetball court we walked across to the meditation garden. Elvis, his mum, dad and grandmother were buried here. It was very solemn but it felt like something wasn't quite right. We walked back to the fourteen acres of pastures at the back of the mansion and it was then I could tell the story was true. It was heavily rumoured years ago that because of the threat of someone stealing his body for ransom. They buried him in the pasture so no one would know. When they brought his and his mums bodies back to Graceland from the Forest Lawn Cemetery in October 1977 a reliable witnesses said the coffins didn't look real. Especially his mums coffin that looked brand new after being in the ground for nineteen years?

The following day it was teeming down with rain, I've never seen rain like that before. Anyway Donna suggested I go back and visit Graceland again because the day after we were set to leave Memphis. So I went back and spent a long time taking it all in. I got the same feeling at the graveside, in my mind he wasn't buried there at all. Years later I discovered proof but more of that later.

The following day we set off from Memphis heading for Daytona Beach in Florida. As we left it was snowing heavily. So in five days in Memphis it had sunshined, rained, gusty winds and snowed.

As you can imagine it was a long drive. We passed New Orleans where I had wanted to visit but Donna was adamant she didn't. After six hours of driving we stopped in Pensacola at one of the many motels along the Mississippi/Florida gulf coast. It was cheap and cheerful but it was alright. Next day we set off for Daytona Beach, we arrived mid afternoon and checked into the Marriott Hotel situated right on the beach. I couldn't believe the view. It was right on the ocean and had spectacular views. I took

Ben onto the beach and tried to get Donna to teach Ben how to swim in the hotel pool. She flatly refused which upset Ben.

We stayed there for two days and then headed off to Orlando. As we pulled into The Hotel on International Drive it felt like Pontin's back in the UK. Loads of English family's but I thought it shouldn't be a problem. I had taken a lot of horrible mickey taking back home with regards to my Elvis haircut and large sideburns but I hoped these Brits would be ok. And they were to a large degree, only getting one mickey take in the whole week.

Ben loved Orlando, especially The Magic Kingdom where we all met Mickey Mouse and all the other Disney characters. It was Thanks Giving while we were there and all the hotels dressed up their front lawns with Christian themes and celebrating when Jesus was born in their Nativity scenes. Ben loved walking around the hotel grounds looking at all the Nativity scenes, there must have been about thirty and we had to take him around all of them at night time when it was all lit up. It was truly magical.

We had fallen in love with America, not just the tourist places but Main Street USA the normal America. We both agreed to look into emigrating to the land of opportunity! Not just for us but mainly for Bens future. We were filled with optimism.

On the plane on the way back I was thinking of ways to improve my show. I decided to ask Jimmy Bond to come back again and do as many shows as he could. He ended up doing the "Charlie Hodge" job of looking after mc on stage, giving me scarves, handing me water and standing with me afterwards handing me each photo that I would sign for the Elvis fans. So now I had Pete Bond as my driver, Jimmy Bond Sr as road manager and Jimmy Bond Jr. working the lights. Along with Ricky and the backing singers it was quite a large show. We always got rebooked at every venue and we were doing about three to four shows a week throughout the north west of England.

It was great for about six months then I got a phone call off Marion Bond saying she didn't think Jimmy could make it to that nights show he had collapsed and was in bed. He had been doing his day job then and working with me at the night time. He had exhaustion. I was gutted and hoped he would be alright. I went to see him a couple of days later and he was so sorry for letting me down. I stopped him dead in his tracks and told him his health was priority and he could never let me down he was my friend, the show would always be ok. I just wanted him to be healthy, he was my mentor and best friend. He looked relieved that I understood and we concluded that he could always come and watch the show anytime he wanted, I would send a car for him and Marian.

I had started working for some new agents notably Nigel Round Agency. Nigel got me lots of bookings further afield and much nicer venues. I remember he had me resident in a small pub in Preston every Monday night. It was a bit surreal, there was never many people in and we had to perform at five thirty to seven o'clock. I think it was just the Landlord that liked Elvis which was fine by me, I got to sing some of the lesser known Elvis songs. Monday night bookings were unheard of so it was great.

Nigel got me a gig in Walsden near Todmorden in Lancashire. It was a charity event and Bobby Ball was the celebrity to appear and draw the raffle etc. I was on stage when he walked in and instantly his eyes lit up. He sat right at the front and half way through the first set off mic I asked him if he wanted to sing a song, he was clearly enjoying our show. He declined saying he had the utmost respect for me and it wouldn't be the right thing to do. I started the second set in my white suit and I could see he was itching to get up. I think he wanted me to give him another nudge. So I did and he got up and sang "Lets Have A Party"! I asked if he wanted to do another and he replied he didn't know all the words but could he stay up and do backing vocals with Marlene and Joanne. It was a brilliant event although a bit surreal. However I can always say I had Bobby Ball as my backing singer! God Bless you Bobby and Rest In Peace......Legend!

It was around this time that Donna surprised me with tickets for us to see Elvis original backing band and singers. Guitarist

Scotty Moore and drummer DJ Fontana were awesome. While The Jordanaires were outstanding. You could see why Elvis had them play with him. After the show we got to meet all of them and they were all so nice, polite and full of humility.

What a great surprise, it was brilliant!

One venue sticks in my mind was The Sale Hotel on my birthday 4th July. Everybody wanted Elvis on American Independence Day. Anyway the show was going well it was just me, Pete Bond working the sound and Ricky being the DJ. So Ricky decided to play a trick on me by substituting my glass of water with a full glass of vodka, about six vodka shots. I was singing American Trilogy, took a swig and spluttered it out. He got me, so he thought. In the quiet bit when I sang "all my trials Lord will soon be over" I walked over to him and poured the full vodka over his head! He just stood there stunned, everyone else was in stitches laughing. He never tried that again, he said the joke cost him too much!

I can't remember exactly when but Donna had become distant. I had helped her lose some weight by enrolling her with Lipotrim at the hospital. It involved drinking three of their shakes a day for three months but no other food at all. She did really well and lost about three to four stone. But she started ducking out of more and more shows. I still called on Marlene and Joanne to do the backing vocals and Marlene would drive the van so I wasn't too perturbed about Donna's absence. I thought she was just tired, little did I know..........

In 1996 my dream of having my own live band became a reality. I decided to advertise for auditions. I held them at our local pub, The Falcon in the back room. However there was only a small response. A bass player who was very inexperienced but I took him on out of desperation. Two teenager friends from Salford University turned up. Guy Shalom on drums and Neil Bowden on keyboards. My God they both blew me away especially Guy, it was like listening to Ronnie Tutt (Elvis 70s Drummer). Neil's piano, brass and strings were also of the highest calibre. I couldn't believe my luck. I learned after the

124

audition that they had both taken Elvis' music as the course music at University and it paid off for them both. The future was beginning to look bright.

However we still needed a lead guitarist. We auditioned a few but then the right one came along in the shape of Alan Faulkner. Wow! Could he play like Elvis' guitarist James Burton. He sent shivers down my spine, it was quickly taking shape. Ive recently found out that Alan was in the sixties band "Money" who had a couple of hits back in the day and were popular on radio one. No wonder he was extremely good. Apart from that I liked his humble character.

We rehearsed twice a week in my large kitchen for about six months. I got us a local gig at a pub called The Moonraker. We just about had enough songs perfected to do a gig. Marlene and Joanne were on backing vocals and it was a great night. Neil came up to me afterwards and said we might need another bass player as the inexperienced one we had had been asking him what key each song was in. Not a good sign. So at the next rehearsal I let him go and advertised in the Stage Newspaper for a bass player.

Garry Marriott was another agent that got me solo work. He put me in The New York Club in Southport and I thought it sounded really cool I must be getting up the ladder a bit. When I got there I nearly died, it was up four flights of stairs. I had just bought new speakers designed specifically for the new band and they were big, really big and heavy. Anyway we got to the top and walked in to face the stage full of equipment. Absolutely nowhere whatsoever to put my gear. I was the support act to "The Amazing Blues Brothers Show". I was now buzzing, I had never worked with a pro band before. I found a tiny space onstage for my mixing desk if the bass player would just nudge up a bit. I asked him and he replied "No F**k Off"! I was shocked but didn't let it bother me too much. I was down to perform one sixty minute set in-between the Blues Brothers sets. I must have done something right because when I came off The Blues Brothers wouldn't go on until the crowd had stopped chanting "we want Elvis". Jeff the lead singer of The Blues Brothers wasn't best pleased but I had only done my show my way. I was told later by the agent that they didn't want me as support ever again it was too much competition. My God I was a solo singer and they were a nine piece band, some people are so fickle, just do your job man!

So we were holding auditions for a bass player, we had our first official show at a hotel in Frodsham, Cheshire in seven days and we were pretty desperate. I got a call off this bass player called John from Bury. He sounded as though he really knew what he was talking about and i asked him if he could learn three songs and audition in two days time. It was only then I realised who he was, he was that grumpy bass player from The Blues Brothers band that had swore at me! I had no time to worry about that and hoped he would be nicer this time. He turned up on the Tuesday and was totally opposite to grumpy. He played the three songs top class so I took him on straight away and asked if he could learn the whole two sets by Saturday, he said no problem. And it wasn't, he was a true professional. The show at the wedding went down extremely well and he turned out to be a life long friend and my right hand man with the band for over twenty years. In fact John painted the artwork for this books front cover.

Chapter 11

1996-1998...THIS TIME YOU GAVE ME A MOUNTAIN

1996 and all my dreams were coming true. We had been to America twice, visited Graceland and Nashville and was looking into emigrating. My show was going from strength to strength and I finally had my own band. But much more than that, I felt alive on stage. Similar to when I first started my career but multiplied by ten. It was unbelievable!

After the adrenalin rush of the first show, all the hard work had to begin. We rehearsed twice a week for about six months. We did some low key gigs along the way. I stopped taking bookings for solo gigs because they would clash with the band project. I wanted the band to be really tight and after a couple of months they were. I really worked them hard during rehearsals. I had given all of them audio tapes of the exact song versions from Elvis; concerts that I wanted and it paid off extremely well. They played to an unreal standard and John on bass gave it a real live Elvis feel, slightly different each night and the feel was just like Jerry Scheff had done for the King. I didn't just want an average backing band I wanted it to be the very best. I wanted to take the show into theatres and corporate events. Although we had to work up to that I was buzzing with excitement of the prospect of it!

However i called a Florida lawyer who specialized in emigration who told me initially that we passed the criteria with Donna's job. However I had to apply for the paperwork from the American Embassy in London. I phoned them and they agreed with what the lawyer had said and they sent me the paperwork. We had to fill it in send it back and wait for an appointment to be interviewed at the Embassy in London.

We were overjoyed with excitement.

In the meantime we went on holiday again to Florida. I suggested we take Donna's dad Tony with us. He had been babysitting Ben when we were out gigging. Mind you we had to pay him a fiver, he insisted? Anyway we took him with us and stayed in a villa for the first time. It was great in the villa not having to be next to the Brit holidaymakers, they were a nightmare. As was Tony! Absolutely nothing was right with him from the heat to the food and the vastness of America. I think he was overawed. He was moaning that much one day that Donna threatened to take him to the airport and put him on a plane back to Manchester. He thought she was joking but she wasn't, she started packing his suitcase. So Tony relented and stopped moaning for the rest of the holiday. He was very tight with his money, he used his babysitting money from the previous year for spending. He promised to buy us a meal before we went home but he never did. We had paid for everything for him and the only thing he got us was a small $5 cuddly toy for Ben, he was unbelievable! He was the only person I know that actually went home after visiting Florida with money left over!

When we got back I got a call from Granada TV to be interviewed on Granada Reports. It was for the twentieth anniversary of Elvis passing. They told me that Colin Paul would be there dressed as the young Elvis and they wanted me as the Vegas Elvis. They asked me to bring more than one costume in as I would be singing live as well.

We got to Granada and met up with Colin, I nice lady escorted us to our dressing room. And as we walked past all the dressing rooms I couldn't help but imagine the cast of Coronation Street using the same rooms. Donna had flatly refused to go with me which I was pretty upset about but her dad Tony offered to take me, I think he thought he'd look good as security.

Anyway Lucy Meacock, the TV presenter, introduced herself to us and we followed her to the set. They said we would be interviewed live but we would have a rehearsal beforehand. We did the rehearsal and I was quite happy with it so I asked which song they wanted me to sing, I wanted to hear the sound levels etc. Then the director said he didn't know anything about a live song, I was furious, the whole idea of me consenting to the show was for me to sing. I felt duped. Colin said not to worry at least we'd be on TV.

Come time for our bit Colin and I were dressed in our outfits and sat on the TV sofa with two of my other jumpsuits on mannequins behind us. Then this supercilious man approached with two cushions to put behind me to give the impression I was the overweight Elvis. I couldn't believe it, we were twenty seconds before going live. I just went with it there was nothing much I could do. I looked like Bernard Manning with a white Elvis suit on! Then the best part happened, they asked completely different questions to the rehearsal! Colin and I must have looked a bit stupid with our mouths wide open! We got through it somehow and Lucy insisted we sang a verse of a song each. Colin sang Love Me Tender and I did I Just Cant Help Believing, then cut!! Lucy was great and apologised to us both, we must have looked bemused.

I made a mental note never to appear on TV again after this experience.

I started sending publicity for the band out to venues and agents. But it was a slow start and we didn't get many gigs at all. This played into Donna's hands, she constantly argued with me that the band was a bad idea.

Then I got a gig at The Park Hotel in Prestwich, Manchester. I think we got paid £250 between all of us which left no profit for me. However I had called an agent called Phil Hughes who ran Ambassador Promotions in Manchester. I just hoped he would turn up, I knew if he did he would get us some bookings. There wasn't many in when we started but it filled up a bit during the night. It ended being a great atmosphere and the band and backing singers were superb. After I got dressed out of my jumpsuit I headed to the bar to get a round in for the band. This tall balding man approached and introduced himself as Phil Hughes. He had a look of a young Colonel Parker. He said he enjoyed the show and it was really good. I plucked up the courage to ask if he could get any work for the show. His reply stunned me, he said he wanted to personally manage me and the band! I was in shock I couldn't believe my ears. He gave me a card and asked me to call him on Monday morning.

I told the band and the girls what had happened and they were all really excited. Apart from Donna!

I called Phil on the Monday and he again repeated his desire to have sole management of my show. I agreed and we set up a meeting for the Wednesday. I had no idea at all what sole management entailed. Don't forget computers were only just coming out so I couldn't google it. I called John the bass player. He was very helpful and explained the benefits and pitfalls of sole management. It turned out that if Phil wanted to sole manage me he had to supply a certain amount of work per year that was mutually agreed.

I spoke with Donna and explained what would be happening but she just wasn't interested, something was clearly wrong. But my head was in a spin with the prospect of my career advancing, and with it a higher income.

The following week Gary Marriott from Omega Promotions called me and booked us into Johnny Balls New York Club in Southport with my band for £450, things were looking up. We were booked there several times and soon we were the headline act there. We had some fine solo tribute acts as support notably Liam Bray as Phil Collins and the legendary TJ Slater as Tom Jones. When TJ was on with us he always ended up singing backing vocals with the girls. He was a real character and we became friends, he was a true professional.

Johnny Ball had another venue in Formby called Shorrocks Hill Country Club
and he had us on there too. One night we had support from the guy that won Stars In Their Eyes John Finch as Marty Pellow. In the dressing room all he could talk about was himself, talk about huge ego! One by one the band left until it was just me and Ricky. So we left and on the way out I saw him preening himself and still talking, but by then he was on his own, Ricky and I went in search of the band and when we found them they were in hysterics that I had been left there on my own. Marti Pellow

130

didn't go down well they were all chanting "we want Elvis" again! So we came on and blew the place apart. In fact security had to stop the show for five minutes the audience was getting too rowdy!

We did a show in Stoke-on-Trent at a rock n Roll Club. It was a door take so our fee would be whatever we took on the ticket sales. Our good friend May Whitby from Stoke offered to help on the door and take the tickets or cash. It was a huge flop there was only about twenty people attended in a room that held five hundred. All the Rock n Roll bands used to fill the venue, but not us. We did a great show and used it as a rehearsal, the band were really hot. When we finished I noticed Neil's fingers were bleeding after playing the piano so hard. With a big grin he said " what a great gig "! Donna came backstage afterwards and said to the band "well that was a rubbish performance". I was so embarrassed and apologised to them. I think they were embarrassed for me. Something was very wrong!

In the meeting with Phil we agreed that we would work on a handshake, that way either of us could walk away and not incur any payments. I was a bit deflated because this meant of course that he didn't have to supply a certain amount of shows each month. But when I thought about it I had nothing to lose. Phil agreed for me to get any gigs of my own and just charge me ten per cent. He would charge me fifteen percent on any bookings going through Ambassador Promotions office. I was agreeable to this because usually sole management charge at least twenty per cent. I could see a bright future.

But then completely out of nowhere, Donna started to be distant. She said she didn't think the band was a good idea and that it would mean losing income for a while. I said it would be alright as we had her income which covered all the bills and food etc. She wasn't having it though. We did a couple of gigs in Stoke and Manchester with the band and she was very rude towards them! What had they done? I was absolutely embarrassed and apologised to them again. I couldn't get any sense out of her. My idea for the band was to get the show into theatres and earn more money for us as a family. She said it was my ego. I wont lie, creatively it burned inside of me, a little boy from Langley making it into theatres was the stuff of dreams. But the financial side of things looked so positive for our family.

There was a party for Donna's work and she wanted to go even though I had a gig that was contracted. Marlene offered to drive and also offered for Ben to stay with her husband Neil. I was so relieved I didn't have to cancel. Though Donna didn't seem to be bothered. She went to her party in Manchester and because she would have got home long before me, we arranged that she would pick up Ben. I got home and she was just about ready for bed. I asked her if Ben was alright and she replies she didn't know? She said she had forgotten to pick him up! How do you forget your own son? I hit the roof but she didn't seem bothered. It felt like she was distancing herself from her own son! I was so angry with her attitude, I couldn't comprehend it. She said I could get a taxi to pick him up, a taxi!! When we had a perfectly good car outside. I made her go pick him up. I should have noticed the signs then, maybe I did but didn't want to admit it.

Easter Sunday, Donna, Ben and I went to Southport for the day. There was lots of rides on the fairground for Ben and he had a ball. On the way back Donna said she had something to tell me. At first she said when we get back home but I insisted she tell me there and then. So she came out with it, she felt she had to leave me and Ben. I was stunned but I should have seen it coming, my whole world was falling around me. I said nothing all the way home. When we arrived I set Ben up with some toys to play with in the living room and we went upstairs to talk. She insisted there was no one else she just needed to be on her own for a bit. I tried reasoning with her but she was adamant. I sat on our bed and started to cry uncontrollably, I couldn't stop. She sat next to me and tried to comfort me which just made it worse. Then we started to talk and she felt she had missed her teenage years because she was with me. I couldn't understand that because I never stopped her going out with her friends, it was always her choice to be with me. She then came out with it, she had met someone else. I was livid, she said I didn't know him and that he worked in a bank in Manchester. That was a lie has I found out later he actually worked where she did. Donna knew I would go to her work and knock him out hence the lie about the bank.

That night was the last night she stayed with me. I put my arm over her as we lay in bed, I didn't want the night to end and I didn't sleep a wink.

She said she wouldn't take Ben away from me and she would come home after work and have tea with us for a few days until I had told Ben his mum was leaving! Hold on I said if she was leaving us she had to tell Ben herself. She did this under duress when she got home from work that day, it was very emotional. He was only five years old and didn't understand. For the first time for many years I had to pick up the pieces. When she left that night Ben and i stood at the front door but she didn't even look back, we were both gutted and Ben cried for a very long time, eventually crying himself to sleep. Looking back she didn't want to take Ben because she didn't want to be strapped with a child it would have stopped her going out with her new boyfriend.

I could actually feel the pain in my heart. Perhaps it was payback for all those times I played the field and breaking other hearts.

Ben finally fell asleep and I put him to bed but I couldn't face our bed, not without Donna there. I found a cardigan she used to wear and eventually fell asleep on the sofa.

Easter Sunday was exactly thirteen years to the day that we got together, that was freaky. The following Thursday we had a booking at The Rhythm Station in Lancashire. It was our first real music venue and despite the band advising me not to do it because I was too upset. I insisted we did. I probably shouldn't have because it was really hard to take to the stage with Donna gone. There's a really grainy video of the show and its clear I was almost breaking up especially on "Hurt" and "Always On My Mind". But I could feel the band and and the road crew rooting for me. They will never know how much that meant to me.

133

Then two weeks after Donna had left us, the paperwork and an interview date arrived from the American Embassy. I can never explain how I felt it was like a knife through my heart, I felt gutted for Bens future he would have had lots more opportunities in the states.

We had always wanted to go and live in America but now that chance had gone! They wouldn't accept me with my job. They had all the Elvis's they needed and another one wouldn't be a positive for their country. I did call to enquire but they just told me what I already knew, The dream was over!

Meanwhile Phil Hughes was hard at work getting bookings for solo gigs and band gigs. He did really well, quite a few venues were booked in advance from July onwards. That's the norm with Tribute Acts, three to six months in advance. Almost immediately he had me booked into hotels and restaurants as a solo Elvis show. He said he didn't know if he could get the band bookings but he would try.

As the contracts came rolling in I couldn't believe how much the fees had increased. I was making £150 - £200 per night before but these contracts were double that. So as if by magic I was performing for £400 - £500, at last I was going to make really good money and play in excellent venues rather than just pubs and working men's clubs. In pubs the act was an added attraction and in working mens clubs bingo was top of the bill. This step up the ladder meant that people had actually come to see my show. I'd been working a long time for this.

However this was all happening from July onwards and I had literally no money until then. I phoned Donna and explained but she said it was my fault for cancelling those solo shows to concentrate on the band. She did say she would bring some food the following day. The next day came and she arrived with a bag full of Bens favourite food. She said "this is for Ben, you can starve". I was gobsmacked, what had I done for her to treat me like this, after all she was the one that had left me. I never found out the reason for that and I didn't know it then but it was the start of Donna being downright nasty and eventually leading to me and Ben left homeless!

Ben said never mind Dad we can share the chicken nuggets! What a position he found himself in at five years old. I was so proud of him and told him not to worry about food, we would get by.

I had no choice but to seek help from the DHSS. I needed money to live. Don't forget I had no solo gigs and the odd band gig was very poorly paid and more often than not I ended up with nothing.

I explained everything to the DHSS and they told me to fill the form in which I did. They told me a decision would be made and I would be notified. A couple of days later I received a letter off them explaining that the previous year I had earned quite a bit, which I had. I was not entitled to a penny. We had spent it on our USA holiday and I had no savings. I called them back and said my new to be ex-wife had left me to bring my son up on my own. She called me back an hour later and said I was still not entitled to anything. I was furious, I knew it was my fault not having any savings but it was not my fault the way Donna was acting. I took Ben with me and marched in to one of their offices, I was so angry! I spoke to a woman who looked at my file and said there was nothing she could do. So I said "fine can you feed and shelter my son then" and got up to leave without Ben. She called me back in. I sat down as she explained they could sanction some money but I would have to pay it back and by law I would have to apply for CSA Government enforced Child Benefit. I calmed down and said I would quite willingly pay it back. She went out and came back and said they could lend me £32 a week.

I was stunned, how could we live on that. But it was better than nothing I just needed Donna to keep paying the mortgage and the bills. She flatly refused! I told her if she could just do it for a few weeks then I would pay her back. Again she refused, she wasn't interested in Ben or me, it was all about her new life. I told her I had to apply for CSA by law and she hit the roof shouting I wouldn't get a penny. I said its not for me its for Ben, she was completely psychotic, she wasn't bothered and said her solicitor would be in touch.

Phil Hughes had got my diary almost full with at least two shows a week pulling in £450 - £500 per gig from July to December, more than double what I was earning before and only having to perform for an hour rather than the obligatory two forty five minutes. He got me work through other agents as well like John Henderson Management, Omega Promotions and The Peller Agency. This got me onto the same tribute circuit as most of the Granada TVs "Stars In Their Eyes" artistes which was great, I was really moving up the ladder.

What I didn't know was that Phil was just starting off his agency Ambassador Promotions. He had been the General Manager of Heywood Civic Centre in Rochdale. He used his artiste contacts to boost his agency and at the same time move me up the ladder.

Donna's sister Lesley had sent word via Pete Bond if I wanted to Ben and I was welcome for Sunday dinner at her house. She had got together with Pete six months previously. For Bens sake I agreed plus I was hoping to see if she could ask her sister to see sense and play ball. I had lots of money coming in that summer it was surreal. I walked into Lesley's dining room and I was faced with Steve Grayson and his wife Pauline (Pauline was Donna and Lesley's auntie). Straight away Steve apologised for what had happened years ago and shook my hand. I didn't really have a choice but to accept his apologies and besides Ive always said if somebody has the strength to apologise then you should always accept it.

Later I spoke with Lesley about Donna and she was very sympathetic and said she would see what she could do. I felt a big sigh of relief!

Phil got me some midweek bookings in smaller etc. for slightly less than the bigger bookings. It was mainly to put some money in my pocket straight away. It was a huge relief, I had worked for years in pubs for £150+ but it was always on the weekend. Plus he said he didn't want any commission if the booking was below £250 which was really good of him. So I did some Tuesdays and Wednesdays and it was great. I kept Ricky on as a roadie and it paid off because he did most of the loading and unloading. I didn't tell Donna , she would have hit the roof, which she did later on when she found out.

Then Phil got me a gig in Stretford, Manchester on a Monday night. He said it was a slightly different gig and that I was to be the compère of a Ladies Night, male strippers, the lot. He told me don't forget just say good evening ladies, no gentlemen. If he told me once he must have told me ten times. So as you can guess I walked out on stage and said "Good evening Ladies and Gentlemen" oh my God I wanted the stage to swallow me up. It turned out ok in the end, I sang two or three songs in the interval. I got £150 and told Phil never to book me as a compère again. My first and last gig as a compère at a Ladies Night.

My dole money came in, all £32 of it and Pete took me to Morrisons where me and Donna used to shop. She got wind of it and hit the roof in a telephone conversation. There was no appeasing her, I just didn't know what was happening, my head was in a constant spin and my heart physically hurt. I carried on as best I could but at each new day it seemed Donna was being even more horrible. And to think it was her that left not me. I just couldn't figure it out she was my soul mate, or so I thought.

The paper work arrived for the CSA Child Maintenance. I called Donna and told her it was out of my hands. She went ballistic again telling me I shouldn't have told them anything and she would treat me right for money. Yeah right she'd been so nice up to now! It turned out that she had to pay a percentage of her wages, £220 into the CSA's bank account every month or they would take it directly from her bank. When she found out she had to pay this amount until Ben was eighteen she went off her head again! I didn't think things could get worse but they did. With the midweek wages I had I had invested in a professional radio microphone. Phil had suggested it would be better for when I started playing the bigger gigs. Donna turned up at the house on the pretence of seeing Ben. In actual fact she had got word of my new microphone and slyly slipped it into her handbag when I wasn't looking.

After she had left I realised what she had done so I phoned her and asked for it back. I couldn't believe my ears when she tried to blackmail me. She said i could have my microphone back if I stopped the CSA money. She just didn't get it, it was irrelevant what I said to them, it was law that they start those proceedings. After about a week I found out it was at Tony's, her dads where she was staying. I went to his flat and rather conveniently she wasn't there. Tony gave me the microphone and I had a go at him about it. He said he didn't know what she had done. From a family of liars I found that hard to believe. Donna still had her house keys so the following day I changed the locks on the doors. I never thought she would do something like that after everything we had been through throughout the years.

So I started life as a one parent family. Pete Bond invited me to call at his and Lesley's house for a brew after I had taken Ben to school. It became a daily thing which I was grateful for, going back to an empty house was so hard. But I had to face the emptiness so I tried to keep busy by throwing myself completely into the business. I used the phone book and yellow pages to get phone numbers of venues and agents (computers had only just come out, I would get one eventually but for now it was the old fashioned way).I did alright and got some midweek bookings at my new prices. Phil asked me if I wanted to go to his office and try to generate bookings. I got Pete to take me to Phil's office in Radcliffe most mornings, then Phil would drop me off at 3pm at Bens school for home time.

I got pretty good at cold calling hotels and restaurants. I used the approach of saying " hi this is Peter from Ambassador Promotions ". Therefore they didn't know I was Lewis Gates so I could tell them all about this Elvis show, unbiased of course! Slowly my diary started filling up with weekend gigs as well as midweek gigs varying from £350-£600 it was exhilarating, it was the break I had been waiting for for years.

Phil put me and the band in at The Midway Park Hotel in Rochdale. It was a small hotel with a decent stage and Phil's best mates place. We were made very welcome by Patrick the Manager. We went down that well that Patrick was asking for a re-booking almost immediately after we finished! I told him Phil would sort it out. So Phil did but the only trouble was that he booked us at the Blackpool Music Festival in the afternoon then back to The Midway for the evening show. It would have been alright if I had been solo but the amount of equipment and the time it takes for a band to set up and pull down was a huge undertaking. However we had a blast at the festival there was around 20,000 people there and Jane McDonald was on after us. You should have heard her moaning at the promoter and stage manager, I'm sure she thought she was a bigger star than she was. I felt sorry for the organisers running around after her. She had a huge ego and not a very nice lady! We saw all this as we were waiting in the wings it was so funny, then we walked on stage and rocked Blackpool.

We got back to The Midway Park at around 5.30pm set up the gear, went on stage at 9.30pm and rocked Rochdale as well. I had arranged and paid for my dad and his new wife Ann and my auntie Joan to prime seats. I think they enjoyed it but when I came out after the show they more or less made their excuses and left. I stood there in disbelief thinking about what we had achieved that day and my dad just didn't seem interested. This would happen more in the future, I should have known better but we all want our parents to be proud of us and I was no different.

Phil got me and the band on a showcase in Sheffield for Johnny Peller Agency with view to bookings in Europe and nightclubs in the UK. My usual lead guitarist Alan couldn't do it as it was during the day and he couldn't get time off work. So he sent his brother Dave. It was a good job I trusted Alan because Dave did a fine job. While we were there we watched a good Duran Duran tribute band, well they were good until the CD went funny and they sounded like Mickey Mouse. They stopped the disc and of course there was no live music, they were miming, a full band miming! Johnny Peller hit the roof and showed them

139

the door. Johnny was a classically trained singer which was great by me, I would learn a few things from him in the future. We ended up getting some bookings off Johnny and my relationship with him and his staff lasted right up to me retiring.

Johnny Peller owned a snooker club in Sheffield and at the back they converted it into a cabaret club. Of course all the main Tribute Acts appeared there. When I was sound checking I went to the back of the room to check it sounded alright. Johnny was stood there and said to me "Lewis what you have just sung was superb you have the best Elvis voice I've ever heard" I graciously thanked him and then thought that it was such a nice compliment as Johnny Peller was a classically trained operatic vocalist in his day. It gave me a huge boost. I suppose that's how the old school agents worked to get the best out of their artiste.

Phil got us a stream of band gigs at Brannigans nightclubs throughout the UK. We had auditioned for Henderson Management about a year ago and it had taken this long to come in. Anyway we got about fifteen gigs in one phone call, contracts from Manchester to Essex and further afield.

At this point Alan told me he was too old to do all the travelling but he would stay until we found somebody else. I was devastated, his guitar playing was exactly like James Burton's. So we started auditioning at The Midway Park Hotel for a new lead guitarist Out of the six that applied there was only one that was suitable. Chris Williams had played with Stax Of Soul and several rock n roll bands. However his playing didn't sound like James Burton but it did sound uncannily like Scotty Moore, Elvis' guitarist in the 50s and 60s. So I thought about it and John and I decided he would be alright. We could give him a few tips of what we wanted along the way.

At Brannigans near Gatwick Airport it was empty at 8pm but the manager said it would be heaving by 9pm because it was airplane stewardesses end of shift and turn around. He was right it was bouncing by 9pm. My guitarist Chris Williams had a wireless guitar and as I introduced him he would go straight into Johnny B. Goode. This time he dived right into the crowd and on to his knees. All the stewardesses piled on top of him. Talk about baptism of fire. It was hilarious, he got back on stage and said "these southern women can kiss you know!".

He did the same thing at Derby University. It was their summer ball. Chris turned up just in time for the sound check. This venue was huge there was approximately two to three thousand there. It was a full nights entertainment with tributes to The Beatles, Abba, Robbie Williams and of course Elvis. The stage was very high probably ten to twelve feet high. When it was our turn, I knew what Chris was going to do so I warned him of the high stage but he just shrugged it off. With him arriving late he hadn't seen just how high it really was. When it got to the part when I introduced him to the audience I said to him, off microphone, the stage is high so don't dive off. He just smiled, I introduced him and he played the iconic riff of Johnny B. Goode and proceeded to dive off the stage. It was hilarious, all we heard was this big scream and when he landed his guitar screeched and grinded. He ended up going backstage changing his guitar and got back on stage just before the end of the song with a rather sheepish look on his face. We were all in stitches laughing as were the audience! He never dived into an audience ever again but he could really play that guitar. He passed away in 2017 R.I.P Chris we miss you......

My days were filled with the same regime of school, Pete and Lesley's then home to try get some gigs. Or it was school, Pete and Lesley's, Phil's office then back to pick Ben up from School. I never ever let Ben down for school or anything else, I felt I had to keep busy because every time I stopped I was thinking about Donna.

When I saw Steve Grayson at Lesley's for Sunday dinner he asked me if I wanted to join him for a pint or three at The Woodman pub that night. Lesley said that Ben could stay there and play with his cousins. I felt terrible leaving him but like everyone said I needed some me time for my sanity, Donna never offered to have him on the weekend. So we went and it was pretty early, about 7pm. When we got there Steve ordered his lager and I had one to. But my God he almost downed it in one, I couldn't

141

keep up with him so I changed to Boddington's Bitter, less gassy. I could keep up with him now. I think we had about twelve or thirteen pints each come last orders at 11pm. We were both swaying out the front door to the taxi. I picked Ben up and we went home in a taxi. Ben seemed happy enough he seemed pleased that his dad was smiling for the first time in ages.

The only problem with Sundays with Steve was that it was power drinking which can be a bit dangerous but I was ok for the time being. Steve suggested I should look for a girlfriend so like fool I went to see Cath!

She was her same old self, very kind and sympathetic to what had happened to me. Her girls Rachel and Stacey were both teenagers now but they remembered me and were only to pleased to have me back in their lives. So we started seeing each other and it was great, neither of us were looking back on previous times. We both agreed it was a new relationship with a clean sheet.

Cath was very eager to see me with the band so I took to a show I was doing with Colin Paul and The Persuaders. Colin impersonated Billy Fury and I knew him when he was the compère at the PCM club in Sale, he was a nice person.

Colin insisted that the band and I went on first. So I thought ok no problem. The whole room erupted when we started and we went down extremely well. Colin was miffed but I was only doing my job I seriously wasn't playing one-upmanship or anything. He refused to go on for twenty minutes to let the audience cool off and he seemed very miffed. It wasn't my fault I was just doing as I was told. I never worked with Colin again which was a shame.

Cath loved it and wanted to go again. Life seemed good again.

I was working at Phil's office when I convinced The Cairndale Hotel in Dumfries to put a programme together of tribute shows. Phil was pleased and he put me on first. He said he wanted a guaranteed first night success. This happened at a lot of venues. I felt quite important until I realised all the other tribute acts were getting £500 and I was only getting £400. Phil said he would try and push the money up the more I played there which he did eventually to £450. He explained it was a strategy to gain more contracts for everyone and he pointed out my private life needed the constant work. He was right I suppose but this just lay the foundations for him to syphon off my wages. All the fees were paid direct to him so there was no way for knowing what he was charging the venue for me.

As it got nearer to Christmas my diary was pretty full with hotels, restaurants and some private parties. I asked Donna if she could help out with looking after Ben when I was working. I got an absolute NO! So I asked her when she wanted to see Ben at Christmas, I was quite happy if she came to the house, my main concern was Ben having a nice Christmas. She replied with she would see him on Boxing Day. I couldn't believe she didn't want to see her son on Christmas day and was spending it with her new boyfriend. I wasn't having that, Ben deserved better, he had done nothing wrong. So I took her to court to make her see Ben on Christmas day. Unbelievably the judge said he was happy with her to see Ben on Boxing Day. I couldn't do that as I was taking him to Wales to see Avril and the family. So the judge ordered her to see Ben on Christmas Day. And also made an order for us to mediation, he thought it would help. I was happy to do that but she kicked off in court and outside and showed herself up.

I went to mediation and the lady was very nice. Donna, on the other hand just started shouting that she wanted the microwave, the TV, the video player and other things. I stayed calm and said obviously they were all things that I needed for Ben. She got up and stormed out shouting at the mediator "who's side are you on"! The mediator tried to diffuse the situation but she stormed out the door. The mediator just said she was sorry for me and mediation wouldn't work. She said she had never seen a situation like that before and she felt Donna had some serious mental health problems. She genuinely felt sorry for me.

She came to see him on Christmas Day, stayed in the kitchen with him for about thirty minutes and she was gone! Ben was extremely upset, she could have stayed longer and as usual I was left to pick up the pieces......

Now that I was seeing Cath, Donna started being even more difficult with Ben but Cath was very good with him and we had a relatively new family. I never thought I would have the chance to be a stepdad figure to two lovely teenage girls. For once life seemed rosy.

After Christmas I spoke with Phil about trying to get a summer season in Rhyl/Towyn. I told him how popular I had been at The Harbour Hotel, Maxine's Nightclub and The Sandringham Hotel. So we put our heads together and we approached Rhyl's Coliseum Theatre. The outcome was me and the band were to perform every Monday night for eight weeks during the summer. The theatre's capacity was six hundred and we would take seventy percent of the box office, the theatre taking the remainder thirty percent.

I decided if all my friends and fans in North Wales were to see me with the band I wanted it to be the best I could do!

I started rehearsing with the band on a new stage show. It consisted of three costume changes and narration when I was changing outfits. It started with Elvis in the 1950s with lots of early Elvis hits. Then I would change into a GI uniform to do Elvis in the army and the 1960s. Then the interval which was followed by a full Las Vegas show. I did songs that others were not doing at the time like "Kentucky Rain" "Bridge Over Troubled Water" "Just Pretend" and "Hurt". It was a big undertaking but I thought it would be good grounding for future theatre shows.

Cath agreed to help me with the costume changes which was great. However one night she had put me in my GI uniform, I walked on stage and after the the the song "GI Blues" my niece Jamie Lee who was only four shouted " Big hunk your flies are undone"! Everything went silent as I looked down she was right. Talk about embarrassing. She called me Big Hunk because she liked the song Big Hunk Of Love and obviously I was her uncle. It was hilarious though, Cath was laughing her socks off in the wings, Phil was stood at the back in disbelief and I just carried on. Every time I looked at the band they just cracked up.

Alas the summer season at The Coliseum was a financial disaster. The most we had in was sixty four people in a six hundred seater theatre it was a bit embarrassing. I honestly thought all my fans who had flocked to see my solo show at the hotels would come see me with a totally live show. I was wrong!

Everything was going well with Cath, I would stay over at her house sometimes and she came to see the show sometimes. But later in the year it all came crashing down on me. Cath loved cats! And I was allergic to them! Anyway we worked around it after all I wasn't living there permanently. One afternoon I went to her house to have some tea with her. When I got there Cath was really upset, her cat had passed away. I tried consoling her but she was inconsolable, she really was. I didn't know what to do but be there for her. After a few hours she finally started to calm down. Then she hit me with it. She said "I cant be in a relationship with you because she thought more about the cat and she wanted to grieve"? I was stunned! I mean I understand about pets being part of the family etc. I tried to talk her around but she was absolutely certain what she wanted. I would miss out on seeing her girls grow up, I was gutted. To end our relationship in that way was cruel and just too much for me. I went back to Pete and Lesley's and told them that Cath and i were through because the cat died! They both burst out laughing at first they thought I was joking. Then they realised I wasn't and said they couldn't understand it at all. If Disney had wrote my life story nobody would believe it!

I was back to square one, just Ben and I against the world......

LOUIS Gates, pictured above, presents his *Spirit Of Elvis* show at Maxines of Rhyl on October 6 and 7 and every other weekend from 9.00am to 11.00am

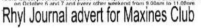

Rhyl Journal advert for Maxines Club

at Maxines Club 1990

With my mate Rob Banks at
The Sandringham Hotel 1990

With Mick at Maxines Club
as always daft as a brush

Sandringham Hotel 1991   Maxines Nightclub 1991

Mine & Donna's Wedding 1991   With Millie & Donna 1991

Manchester Pub & Club News
with Interview 1994

Ricky my friend & Road Manager

18 day Scottish & Newcastle Brewery Tour

148

The Sale Darts Team......My Little Sister & Christine holding Godson Ben

Millie with Ben at 1 day old

Bens Christening with Godmother Christine
& children Lisa, Ellen & Mathew

1956
Pink &
Black

GI Blues
& Movie
Years

LAS VEGAS
1970

Ben's 2nd birthday

Zonked

L - R   Jimmy Bond, Donna Gow, Me, Pete Bond, Hilary Brereton,
Linda Goonan, Jimmy Bond Jnr, Christine Roberts

White Fringe Suit

First time in Orlando we met Cannon & Ball
Four weeks prior Bobby Ball sang backing
vocals for me

Graceland and Ben wanted to have
a go on Lisa Marie Presley's swing

Old Town, Kissimmee, Orlando 1997

1997 First Band L-R...Guy, Marlene, Big John,
Me, Alan, Joanne, Neil, Donna

Joking with Marlene

Blackpool 1997

Nightclub, Edinburgh

Heywood Civic Center

153

Buxton Country Music Festival   Northwich Memorial Hall

Corporate Event, Marriott Hotel, Stoke-on-Trent

Me and my Beautiful Jacqui 2000

First suit Jacqui made me
it had over 2500 stones

Second suit Jacqui made me
The Cisco Kid suit

Jacqui with sisters Michelle & Pamela
The first of my Little Sisters

Chapter 12

1998-2000....RIDING THE RAINBOW

If 1998 was a breakthrough year for me then 1999 was a roller coaster going straight through the stratosphere! It started on 8th January when Phil had booked me and the band onto The Stage Newspapers Showcase in a five star cabaret room at Blackpool Pleasure Beach. I was a bit put out to find we were on first in the afternoon slot, not the best slot. Anyway we played our hearts out for the twenty minutes on stage and blew the audience away. Phil was in shock he had never seen me perform to that standard before. I was annoyed that we hadn't been given a later slot, other artistes that Phil booked were on at the nighttime, Phil said it was because we were a last minute addition. Nevertheless he made himself busy mingling with all the other agents trying to get me and the band bookings. In the end we didn't get one booking which I found extremely strange. Phil said there was a lot of interest in booking me solo. He said it would be good money £500-600 so I calmed down, but it was a sign of what was to come, I just couldn't see it....

On a positive note it was at this showcase when I met Stuart Keen the lead singer with The Ambassadors tribute show. We went for a drive around Blackpool, I think he could see I was a but ruffled about the showcase. He told me to stand up more against Phil if I wasn't happy. He reminded me that Phil worked for me not the other way around. We became friends and in the future I would stand in for his brother Steve who did the Elvis section of their show. I really enjoyed it. At The Cairndale Hotel one night I came on stage and after my first song Stuart had given the audience in the front row big cards with numbers on so they lifted them up with numbers like 1 / 2 / -1 / 0 etc. it was really comical!

In my private life Donna was making a show of herself. She would turn up at Lesley and Pete's house knowing I would be there. She would have several different boyfriends in tow and dressed in leather trousers. She had piled on the pounds again and so she just looked like a leather chesterfield suite! It was embarrassing! My one time soul mate had turned into a caricature of herself. I cant tell you how bad I felt I still loved her but my wife had gone and it seemed she was twisting the knife each time and enjoying it, it hurt.

The court decided that we had to agree on custody of Ben seeing as mediation hadn't worked. So in court she said she wanted to see Ben once a month on a Friday and Saturday. I argued that Ben would need to see her more than that, I suggested Friday and Saturday each fortnight. No word of a lie she jumped up and said I was just looking for a baby sitter to allow me to do my gigs. Unbelievably the judge looked at me and asked for a reply. I told him I had baby sitters all week if I needed and that Ben needed to see his mum. It would have been a lot easier if I had accepted once a month but as always I was thinking of Ben who was just seven years old. The Judge decided that Friday and Saturday each fortnight was his decision and that was that. Donna stormed out of court, she called me later to say I wasn't gonna get my way. I tried to reason with her that I was only thinking of Bens best interest but she just flew off the handle and hung up on me.

That spring i did a prestigious Sunday gig at Cleckheaton Castle in Cheshire. It was a wedding and they wanted me to sing at the reception as well as during the ceremony in th castles chapel. I found myself singing " Can't Help Falling In Love " while they walked down the isle. Then "I Just Cant Help Believing " while they signed the register and finally " The Wonder Of You " while they skipped down the isle afterwards and all the congregation joined in with me. It was like one of those Hollywood romcoms.

Pete and Lesley couldn't do this gig so Steve Grayson offered to drive me with the condition we were back for 7pm so he could go in The Woodman. Ricky was with me he couldn't drive but he worked the sound system. They had the reception early at 4pm. I made an excuse that I had another booking in Leeds that I had to get to before 7pm. The Bride and Groom were made up with what I had done for them and we got back to Middleton at 6.45pm so Steve could get to his precious Sunday night in The Woodman. The things I had to juggle just to get the shows on and money coming in!

Then one day while I was on tour in Essex I lost my voice. I had strained it on stage with the band at Jumpin' Jacks in Basildon. At hospital I had the camera down my throat and the Doctor said it was just a strain and not damaged nodules which would have needed an operation. So he gave me a list of do's and dont's and a vocal exercise regime. I had to take three weeks off. When I got out of the hospital my phone went and it was Donna screaming at me for something! I had no idea nor could I understand what she was saying so I hung up. She kept trying to call me but I refused her calls every time. I hardly had a voice let alone to argue back. The worst thing was she knew I was having my voice looked at that day so I suppose she was just being cruel.
My voice got stronger on a daily basis and I got back to entertaining.

Phil suggested I record an album with the band for promotion purposes and to sell after the shows. He found Testa Rosa Studio in Manchester, John Bass Player said it would only take about three days as we were very tight as a band already. So I booked three days in the studio. The recording engineer was only young but he seemed to know what he was doing. However the first thing I noticed was it felt slightly damp which wasn't good for my asthma. The first day the band laid down the tracks using my vocals as a guide. The second day I put my vocals on properly but by now I sounded a bit hoarse because of the damp. Phil turned up with Patrick, neither of them had been in a recording studio before and there's me trying to belt out these Elvis songs suffering with my asthma.

After doing the vocals for Suspicious Minds the engineer called me into the mixing room and showed the band and I something strange. He played our Suspicious Minds along side Elvis' Suspicious Minds on the led monitor and another device.

It showed my vocals were exactly the same as Elvis'. Then he played two or three more and it was the same again. He told me " you have the exact same vocal range as Elvis had ". I was shocked as were the band. We all knew how close I was to Elvis but I never envisaged anything like this. Apparently all those years ago when I was miming I was actually singing into a dummy microphone and therefore training my voice without knowing it. I had Elvis as my vocal coach!

Donna brought Ben to see me halfway through the sessions, I think she was just being nosey and a bit miffed because her ex-husband just might be going places.

I brought Graham McGrotty in on lead guitar because Alan couldn't do the sessions for some reason. He did a really good job and I used him for live gigs whenever Alan wasn't available, what an unbelievable talent he was. He used to play Johnny B Goode using the neck of a Budwieser bottle, he was something else. He's currently working as a session musician in Nashville and I wish him all the very best.

So we now had a full album of songs we were doing on stage and I was on cloud nine!

Phil got a call from Erica at Henderson Management wanting to know if I was available on this particular Wednesday. The venue was Planet Hollywood in the west end of London. Phil relayed the enquiry and I was in disbelief. This was in the theatre district and yet another rung up the ladder. I was to work for Bob Carruthers the movie producer and music producer. Apparently he had heard about me from somewhere and he wanted a good soundalike Elvis. The event was for Uriah Heeps Platinum DVD Award and they were adamant they wanted a proper Elvis that could sing for their awards party. Bob had also booked Ged Bolton (Rod Stewart tribute act) to be my support. Ged called me up and we arranged to travel down to London together to save on petrol. I took Pete Bond to work my sound and Ricky came with us as well. After we had set up the equipment Bob arrived, he greeted us with a big smile and gave me and Ged £50 each to go and get some food. I was a bit star struck because Bob had produced movies such as Romeo and Juliet and Saving Private Ryan. His company was called Cromwell Productions and he produced many historical films that we all loved. He had also produced Uriah Heep's music video and many more such as Pink Floyd and The Who. He owned Classic Rock Magazine.

We went outside into the west end and it was really busy. Ged and I were walking and talking when a black stretch limousine pulled up with a load of young ladies who were obviously half drunk on their hen night. They shouted for Rod Stewart to jump in for a ride. I was gobsmacked, he got in and found us later on with a big smile on his face. He did look like Rod, if only I looked like more like Elvis.

He went onto the stage to start the show and he went down a storm, I was thinking to myself just do what your good at, be yourself. I had Jimmy Bond's voice in my head. Anyway when I came on later the place erupted and I thought yes I could get used to this. Part of my show consisted of walking around the audience singing Love Me Tender. I had to do a double take, it was only Brian May from Queen stood at the bar. He was loving it, big smile on his face and nodding in approval.

It was a huge success and after I had changed and came out I was hoping to get Brian Mays autograph, unfortunately he had left. However we got to party for the rest of the night. Lots of people asking me questions about my voice and how long had I been performing. When I look back this night was the making of me, I felt like I had arrived. It had taken me fifteen years to be an overnight success!

We loaded the van at the end of the night and was all ready for our journey up north when a policeman waved us down. The van was still on the pavement outside the Planet Hollywood. Ricky was sat up front and me, Ged and Pete were stretched out in the back completely drunk. Some girls passed and shouted " hey its Keith Richards " to Ricky, he did have a resemblance. The copper looked to see if it was true. Ricky said " your not gonna believe who's in the back, Rod Stewart and Elvis! " The copper was getting agitated so he slid open the side door and there we were! He just shook is head and told us we could go. Ricky dined out on that one for years.

160

The following Monday Phil called me and said would I be willing to go to Malaga in Spain and perform three shows in one week. Although it only paid £150 per show it would be like a paid holiday. The flights were paid and I would stay in the promoters villa. I said yes of course I would when will it be? He said tomorrow the flight is 9am. It was short notice but it was midweek so I did it. I got Lesley and Pete to look after Ben, it very was hard leaving him. I got to Malaga airport and the promoter, Tony Reddin, picked me up in his minibus. What a character he was, he said we had to stop off at that nights venue to set up the sound system. So I ended up lugging these huge speakers into the hotels marquee. By the time we got to his villa I was already tired especially in the heat. Tony was living with an Indian lady who was lovely but he treated her like dirt, I don't know why she stayed with him. Tony was a typical cockney wide boy but he was ok with me.

I did the first show in Malaga in the marquee and it went extremely well until I got towards the end. I had shown Tony how my show worked and he was working the minidisc and sound system and he just kept putting more and more backing tracks on without telling me what was next, geeing up the audience at the same time on his microphone. I ended up doing two and a half hours instead of ninety minutes. I felt like a human jukebox. I was furious with him and I told him if he ever did that again I would walk off and go straight to the airport. He could tell I was serious so he apologised.

The next show was at a restaurant owned by a Hungarian couple from Oldham who were really nice. The show went well and Tony behaved himself that time. After the show he told me the third show had been cancelled and there would be no cancellation fee. I wasn't best pleased but what could I do but try and enjoy the rest of the week in the sun. Tony said he definitely wanted me back again. So I asked if I could bring my seven year old son with me and he agreed.

It was only a month after I had been to Spain when Phil called and said Tony wants you back in Fuengirola, Spain again. So I

161

took Ben with me he was about seven and he had a great time. Tony had friends staying with him so he rented a villa for Ben and I. Ben was in his element because the shared pool was about ten yard's from the villa. All three shows went well and Tony was happy. He wanted me back again sometime that year but I had a full diary of midweek and weekend bookings so he said to book it for the following year.

Life was good and I couldn't believe after fifteen years chasing the dream with Donna it was starting to happen, but it was just me and Ben now and I was full of optimism for the future.

Pete Bond and Lesley used to alternate driving me and doing the sound and lights etc. On this particular gig it was Lesley and we were booked to do a nightclub in Carlisle, Cumbria. Phil gave me the details so as usual I pin pointed the address from the post code, there were no satnav's back then so we used the old fashioned maps. We got to the venue in Carlisle and it was a large pub the same name as on the contract. I showed the doormen my contract and they said I'd got the wrong place it was about thirty miles away in the Lake District. I couldn't believe it, I called Phil and he said they were the details the other agent had sent him. So we headed off into the wilds of the lake district in the dark trying to find the venue. After forty five minutes we finally arrived to be faced with three flights of stairs! We had about fifteen minutes to get the gear upstairs and set up before starting the show. Lesley earned her money that night, when the gear was upstairs she virtually set everything up on her own while I got ready backstage where I could hear the "why are we waiting" chants. I finally got on stage and blew the audience away. The manager wanted me back but I refused, talk about stressed, it was one show I wanted to forget.

Me, Pete and Ricky did a 21st birthday party at The Irish Centre in Chorlton, Manchester. We got there and set up in the large function suite. I went on stage to rapturous applause and went down really well for the first set. In the interval this guy came up to me and asked for a request, then he told me the guy who's 21st it was was in the band The Charlatans. In fact all the

162

band were there and they were loving it. They came up to me afterwards and introduced themselves, they were so friendly, respectful and unassuming.

We did another one for the band James and they were just the same Its amazing how many pop and rock stars still love Elvis, even today!

I was at Pete and Lesley's one morning when Donna walked in all cocky saying how happy she was, she had received her decree nisi papers. I had dropped Ben off at school and had not yet been home for the mail. She was acting as if she had just won the lottery, I couldn't comprehend it and Pete and Lesley looked embarrassed. I did get the papers when I went home and i had a cry for me and Ben, it was official it was over!

Bob Carruthers had me back at Planet Hollywood in London again. And again it was Uriah Heep that had specifically asked for me. I couldn't for the life of me understand why a rock band would want Elvis entertaining them. I was saying this to Ricky just before I was due on stage and a voice from behind me said " cos your the F***ing best Lewis ", it was Mick Box the guitarist from Uriah Heep. It gave me a huge boost and I pulled out all the stops and rocked the place again. All of Uriah Heep and the audience were bowing to me begging for more. I think I must have done ten encores. It was great this roller-coaster I was on and I was riding it at max-speed!

Erica from Henderson Management called Phil and asked if I could fill in for Steve Preston's Elvis Show the following Thursday at The Village Hotel in Nottingham. When we arrived the manager came running across to the stage and was almost pleading with me not to mention my name and to make out I was Steve Preston. The cheek of it, I know the billboards had Steve Preston's name on them but that wasn't my fault. After all I was helping them out. This manager was quite adamant so I said to him look I won't say anything on stage but if someone asks me my name I have to tell them. It looked like he was going to blow a gasket! So I told him that I can always just go home. At that point he stormed off muttering to himself. I wasn't being awkward I was just trying to build up my name and reputation. I wasn't likely to say I was someone else. The show went really well and a few people wanted autographs and photo's and when they called me Steve I told them what had happened and that I was just helping out. They were all so gracious and thanked me for entertaining them. I signed as Lewis Gates.

Erica, who by now had started her own agency called Big Foot Events, called and said would I like to do a tour of Brannigans nightclubs with my band. Again the money wasn't great and I had to pay the band most of it. Anyway we went everywhere from Ipswich to Basildon to Manchester. In Ipswich our guitarist Chris was mobbed and he had to sign signatures, one of them on a woman's breast, it was unbelievable, Chris was embarrassed but I think he liked it.

It was my birthday in Brannagans Manchester and every man and his dog turned up to party with me. God knows I had been to hell and back by then. It was like a coming home show. Even the management left a bucket and ice with bottles of champagne in it in the downstairs dressing room. Mick and Sue and their daughter Tracy who used to do backing singing years ago came. As did my dear friend and little sister Christine with Lisa and Christine's friend Brenda. I had done the first set and was downstairs with my feet up when Christine walked in. I was an idiot! I was on different medication at the time some prescribed and some not. I'm totally ashamed to say I didn't even get up to greet Christine, I thought I was a rock star, it still haunts me today it was the last time I would see her.

On the way home we gave a lift to Mick, Sue and Tracy and my sister in law Tracy who had always held a torch for me. Needless to say I ended up in the back seat of the van with both Tracy's, very rock'n'roll indeed!

Then Phil got me a show in the Isle Of Man at the Villa Marina Theatre. It was the Country Music Festival but they wanted me to do my normal show with just a few of Elvis' country songs. I took Lesley with me and it was going down really well until I did American Trilogy. On the slow part in the middle when the flute plays I always turned my back to the audience and raised my cape at the crescendo just as Elvis had done in the seventies, it always got a great reaction. It did this time but when it reached the crescendo and my cape was outstretched there was three gun shots! It scared me to death, Lesley had this look of panic on her face I thought I'd been shot! I turned round quickly only to see all the audience that were dressed in cowboy outfits shooting blank bullets in the air. What a relief, they told me they always did it during that song. I just wish they would have told me beforehand.

Another gig Phil got me was at Bury FC. This was when I met the legendary TJ Slater (Tom Jones) for the first time. We were to perform in the interval of the match. It was really cool they had set up a stage on top of the Chairman's hospitality box. I watched as TJ did his part then he introduced me and the whole crowd just erupted, it was brilliant. TJ became my mentor and life long friend after that. He taught me everything I needed to know about being a tribute act. We did many Las Vegas shows together over the years. I owe him a great deal God rest his soul.

Saints & Scholars restaurant in leafy Style in Cheshire was the first time I met Big David Elliott. Phil was supplying Dave's restaurant with tribute acts and he booked me in there. It was tiny, about forty seats. Anyway I got changed across the road in an office that Dave owned. The restaurant had large glass windows so I tried not to be seen before I entered, trying to keep the mystique as I always did copying Elvis. So I heard the intro music and then my cue the drums for CC Rider. The only trouble was the road was busy and all the audience turned around looking for me and I'm stood there like a prize idiot waiting for the traffic to pass. I made it just in time, much to the amusement of the audience and Pete who couldn't stop smiling!

I went down really well and exited the restaurant to face the traffic again. Luckily I was alright that time. I walked into the office and took off my jumpsuit wondering what this Dave was like, he'd been cooking all night so I didn't know what he looked like. When all of a sudden the shower curtain swung open and this huge 6'6 Yeti walked out " Hiya Elvis I'm Dave ". So I'm stood there in my pants and he's stood there butt naked! He

165

treated me with the utmost respect as we talked for a while. He told me I was better than Stuarts Ambassadors, he had refused to pay them he said they were rubbish, I didn't comment.. Good job I went down well! It was the beginning of a friendship where we both referred to each other as ' Brother '.

I performed at all his venues in the future. In fact my final show was at his legendary Elvis Kitchen Restaurant in Hazel Grove in 2018.

Another strange gig I did was at Sunderland's huge shopping mall. It was for a store that sold all music memorabilia and odd musical things. It was the stores launch and they had me in the middle of the mall singing for fifteen minutes then promoting the new store for fifteen minutes and so on for three hours, starting at noon. We were travelling to Dumfries for a show at The Cairndale Hotel that night. I thought it would be a breeze just singing for fifteen minutes etc. but it was pretty tiring. At the end the manager told me I could have some of those Elvis bobble heads, he was really pleased. So we ended up with three boxes of these Elvis bobble heads and sold them after the shows for the next three months!

At Brannigan's in Blackpool one night with the band. The place was rocking and when I finished the second song Burning Love I took the guitar off and threw in the air behind me for Ricky to catch it and the band would finish the song in sinc with the catch. The only problem was I had forgotten it was a low ceiling on stage so the guitar never reached Ricky it bounced off the ceiling and completely broke the guitar in two. Ricky didn't know if I was going to shout at him but I burst out laughing as did the band. The audience thought it was part of the show and I needed a new guitar!

We did a show at Bradford City Football Club's Social Club. I was ill. I couldn't stop vomiting. Lesley said we shouldn't do it, but I insisted we did. I was contracted to one sixty minute set and I always performed for longer usually seventy five to ninety minutes. On this particular night I was being sick in the dressing room even as my entrance music was playing. I made it on stage,

Lesley had a worried look on her face but I continued with the show. I did sixty minutes, sang the last song and walked off stage and proceed to vomit again. All the audience were on their feet cheering so like the pro I am I went back on to do an encore, Lesley pleaded with me to finish but I did two more songs. When I finished and walked off the audience were all cheering again while I was throwing up backstage. I said to Lesley one more then that's it. So I did the one song and finally finished. Again I was throwing up backstage when I asked Lesley to go pick up the fee. She came back and said the Chairman was refusing to pay unless I did one more encore. I saw red, I got dressed and stormed over to where he was sitting. He said again I couldn't have my wages unless I do a couple more songs. I just replied "fair enough I'm going home now but first thing in the morning I'm gonna contact The Musicians Union who will get my fee off you plus any other costs, its your choice". And we proceeded to strip the gear down. Some of the audience came up asking what was wrong so I told them and they were shocked. They said I was the best tribute show they had ever seen and couldn't believe I wasn't getting paid. We loaded the van and I went to see if the chairman had left my fee but he had gone home. There was an envelope left with my fee minus £100. Apparently he left a message saying I hadn't done my full show. The barmaid looked at it in disgust, went into the till and paid me the £100.

On the Monday Phil got a call asking for a rebooking. He just declined stating that I wasn't being treated like that. It was a great shame because the audience were terrific.

Another strange one was in Altrincham, Cheshire one Thursday night. It was a tiny pub about the size of The Rovers Return in Coronation Street. When I walked in and introduced myself to the landlord he pointed to where I would be singing, the fireplace. So I thought well I was on £450 so it was great with me.

Come time for showtime there was about ten people in. The landlord said to start and hopefully more people would come in. They didn't!

I was getting towards the end of the show and a barman walked up to me with a brush and proceeded to sweep around me. Ive no idea why he would insult me like that, I'd been super professional since I had walked through the front door. I just ignored him and when he realised he wasn't getting a reaction from me he walked off and as he did I told him on the microphone he had missed a bit. It went straight over his head.

Firstly I don't know how a tiny venue like that could afford the fee unless it was a front for a drugs gang (which I experienced quite a few times later on). And secondly I couldn't figure out why someone would sweep around me while I was performing. Some things you never understand. I got my wages and left quickly.

While we had been doing all these shows Pete, Lesley and myself had been saving up to go to Orlando. It was the only way Ben and i would get to go again! I needed someone to drive while we were there. In the end Pete chickened out of going so it was just me and Ben, Lesley and her four kids and Lesley's mum Ann. We went in November to miss hurricane season. It was great for me and Ben but Lesley's kids were always showing us up. Culminating in Lesley head butting Laura while we were at The Magic Kingdom waiting for the fireworks display. I couldn't believe what I saw but I suppose I shouldn't have been surprised Lesley was always screaming at her kids at home. Anyway Ben and I went to America again when I never thought I would have got there on our own.

Avril and Jacqui turned up at a band gig at a Catholic Club in Blackley. It was a great night we went down a storm. Avril and Jacqui had never seen me with my band and I think they were quietly impressed. Afterwards I sat at their table and had a catch up. When they were about to leave Jacqui said something (that I cant repeat or I would get lynched) that made me blush and she promised to call me to arrange to come up to see me when Phil had his showcase on in Yorkshire in a few weeks time.

Jacqui duly turned up on the train with a big smile on her face and long flowing auburn hair. Wow! She couldn't be interested in me could she? I was her adopted big brother. Pete brought us both home from Manchester and that afternoon we got ready to go to

Phil's showcase. I still had jet-lag when we arrived I had only been back in the country for about six hours from Orlando!

Phil approached me and said where we could set up the band. Basically he had given all the other bands the best positions and my band would be scattered about the stage, it was like a Carry On movie. I hit the roof, I told him he should have given us priority as he was my manager. Jacqui looked at me and was surprised, she hadn't seen me raise my voice in anger before.

Anyway instruments and amps were moved so we could do our show properly. Jacqui stuck to me like glue all night and I felt good for the first time in ages. She stayed at my house overnight sleeping in Bens room and left the following day leaving me to catch up with the jet-lag I still had.

I wondered what would happen next. She called me and I invited her to our Christmas Lookalike Ball in a few weeks time in late January. In the meantime we phoned each other quite a lot and I soon realised she wanted a relationship. I could have cried with happiness I had always fancied Jacqui but she had always been out of bounds being married. She said her marriage to Steve had come to an end and she was going for a divorce. So I felt more at ease learning of this.

She came to the Lookalike Ball but more of that later......

The month before Phil said that Bob Carruthers office had been on the phone and wondered if I wanted to got to Cannes in France. Bob had a film showing at the festival and he wanted me to entertain his guests at the after screening party at Planet Hollywood. Are you kidding me of course I would do it, I'd do it for free if necessary. Anyway Bob was flying me and Lesley to Nice and putting us in two rooms at a five star hotel for three days. On the middle day we were to get a taxi to Cannes which he had already paid for.

All I can say is WOW! Nice was beautiful we went for a stroll down the promenade de englaise, it was a really humid night and when we headed back to the hotel and I looked up into the sky a grapefruit hit me in my right eye. I kid you not, it hurt like hell,

Lesley couldn't stop laughing. I suppose it was funny but later on it would cause me mega problems. But more about that later on....

We arrived in Cannes the following day exited our taxi and we were both just in awe of the place. I had seen Cannes on television like everyone else but in reality it was even more beautiful. Its only small though and we pretty much saw most of it before we went to soundcheck at Planet Hollywood. Bob had hired a local radio station to provide the sound system. We got on great with them and got a good sound then sat and waited for Bobs arrival. When he got there he asked if everything was ok and not to worry about the audience that night they probably wouldn't get up and dance like in London. They were all movie producers and directors, he called them stuffed shirts, I knew exactly what he meant and I was confident that my voice would win them over whatever show I did!

Bobs guests started to arrive so Lesley and I went to the dressing room to keep out of the way until showtime. About ten minutes later Bob put his head round the door and said "about five minutes Lewis" I replied he'd have to wait fifteen so I could blow dry my hair then I would be ready.

When I was dressed and ready I sent Lesley out to start the intro but Bob wanted to announce me and said I was from of all places Macclesfield! Anyway I walk out to tremendous applause and I knew there and then I had won them before a note had been sung. I told Lesley which songs to put on to keep it up tempo. One thing I'd learnt from TJ Slater was once you've won an audience don't let up keep the tempo high. Second song was Suspicious Minds and they were all up dancing on the tables and the floor in their long evening gowns and tuxedo's. I looked over at Bob and he smiled and nodded, I gave him a look of "its just what I do". Next thing he was on the dance-floor and singing along. I had them all waving their arms etc. it was amazing!

Towards the end of my set I noticed a white haired man stood near the front with his eyes closed. I racked my brains wondering what he was doing. Afterwards he introduced himself to me as Dennis Hedlund from New York Films Inc. and asked did I know why he had his eyes closed, I shook my head. "Well" he said, "him and his family were personal friends with Colonel Tom Parker and Elvis", He had seen Elvis fifty or sixty times in Las Vegas. He said "that my performance was the nearest vocally to the king he had ever heard". He was concentrating to see if I made any mistakes on stage, he said he didn't and it was flawless. I couldn't believe what was happening to me. I had to pinch myself. We swapped business cards apparently his family more or less owned a small town in Texas called Fort Worth! Oh my God he must be a millionaire! He said to call him anytime I was in the states. Was this really happening to a kid from Langley!

Bob had arranged a meal for Lesley and I on the outside terrace while he took his party to a smaller restaurant to party, we were to follow after we had eaten. He left his Pa to make sure we didn't get lost. When we arrived at this small place the whole of his party cheered. I sat next Bob and Lesley sat opposite. They were all eating posh French food, we were offered but we had only just finished our meal. On the table was five buckets of champagne and Bob poured me and Lesley some drinks. He kept asking if we were alright I think he was still on a high, the event at Planet Hollywood went down better than he thought it would. There was an entertainer singing songs on his piano and accordion. I knew what was coming and it wasn't long before Bob asked me if I would sing a few songs. So I got up to a big cheer and spoke with the entertainer about songs, he asked what keys and I replied in Elvis key he looked surprised but we did Cant Help Falling in Love, Always On My Mind and Suspicious Minds. The place was rocking but it wasn't my show and I left the entertainer to carry on his show.

Bob had finished his meal when he asked if we wanted to stay for the full week. He was filming a movie about an hours drive away and we could see how everything works. I was gobsmacked, me being catered to by a millionaire. I looked at Lesley and she said I've got Ben to think about and of course she couldn't stay because of her kids. And anyway by this time I had no money left. I explained to Bob and he said he would cover all expenses etc. which was very generous. Still I had to decline,

171

Ben's head was not in a good place due to Donna messing it up and I felt I needed to be there for him. Bob was ok with that he understood about family, he now considered me as family.

Lesley looked so out of her comfort zone but I just wanted the night to carry on forever, I might not get to this level again. But too soon the night ended and we headed off to our hotel in a taxi. The following morning we caught the flight home and I wondered what Bob had in store for us next.

I was still on a high the next day but i had to perform in a pub in Rotherham for £500, my head was spinning. Talk about bringing me down to earth. I felt like I was living in a parallel universe!

One huge gig the band and I did was at The Americana Festival at The Newark Showground in Lincolnshire. The main stage had well known American country singers and bands while we played on the tribute stage which was just as big but at the opposite end of the showground. The band and I were on second to last just before the headline act which was Jerry Lee Lewis's sister Linda Gail Lewis. I thought it was really cool and couldn't wait to meet her.

There were other tribute bands on before us, Eddie Cochran, Bill Haley & The Comets and Buddy Holly.

We watched them all and they were excellent. Then it was time for us to go on. The green room was a huge Portakabin backstage and we thought it was cool. When I got on stage I couldn't believe how many people were in the audience, probably about 3000 or so. I was in my element I got the place jumping and the crowd were bouncing. I finished with An American Trilogy and in the middle bit when the flute plays, somebody shouted really loud " We love you Elvis " . It sent a tingle down my spine. As I took my bows and walked off stage the audience was bouncing. And then it started with the chants " We Want Elvis " over and over for about ten minutes. The organisers said there was no time for an encore and that he was trying to get Linda Gail Lewis to go on stage? Apparently she said she wasn't going on after that Elvis show. The crowd were still chanting for me and she flatly refused to take to the stage. By this time she was giving me dirty looks as if id done something wrong. I was so disappointed, I wanted to meet her and have a talk about her brother Jerry Lee who I admired so much. She wasn't for having anything to do with me so as we passed her walking out of the green room I said "Follow that, I can see where your brother gets it from" Jerry Lee Lewis had always insisted on performing last.

Anyway it was such a let down. It took her about thirty minutes before she started her set and Ive got to say I wasn't impressed especially after all the commotion she caused.

Phil called me one morning and said he had an enquiry to be resident in a hotel in Spain. Five shows a week for six months plus free accommodation, free food and drinks and £1200 nett per week in my hand. It sounded fantastic but there was two reasons why I couldn't do it. The first and most important was I couldn't leave Ben for six months, Donna had let him down on so many occasions, I was his one constant in life. And I certainly couldn't pull him out of school and take him with me, six months without school was too much. Secondly the contract didn't include my sound man/woman. At that time I didn't think I could do the show without Pete or Lesley, both of them had gotten in sinc with me on stage which made the show very slick.

So I turned it down. Phil didn't understand at first he thought it would give me a definite income for six months and a great experience. I told him residencies are not how they sound. Its hard work concentrating every night in the same venue. When your on tour its alright because every night is a different venue and different people so it keeps it fresh and keeps you on your toes. Eventually he agreed it was wrong to take Ben out of school for that long.

One residency I did take that year was for me and the band to perform at The New York Club in Southport every other Fridays and Saturday. The money wasn't great but it gave us the exposure I was looking for with the band. Also it was like a paid rehearsal. One massive downside was the stairs, four flights we had to carry all the speakers, drum kit and amps etc. I had bought bigger speakers especially for use with the band. They were excellent for Theatres and large corporates and they were on wheels, but wheels were no good with four flights of stairs, they were a killer.

It was a late night venue the punters came in after the pubs closed at 11pm so you can imagine what it was like. But I had assurances off the owner Johnny Ball that everything would be alright and I would have two security fellas just in case. This one night the security dissapeared and one bloke kneeled down in front of me pretending to give me a blow job. We were doing "The Wonder Of You" then this guy went to bite me so without missing a beat oi sang "Thats the wonder.......Whack...I gave him an uppercut..........the wonder of you". The band thought it was great they were all laughing.

I got a call to perform with my band at a wedding in Cheshire. It was really posh at Shrigley Hall Hotel in the village of Pott Shrigley. We set up and did the soundcheck and then found the bedroom suite we were given to get changed in. I popped downstairs to ask the best man something. When I returned I couldn't believe my eyes, Neil (keyboards) was jumping from the bed into the open wardrobe and back again. He was doing it for at least ten minutes The rest of the band were cheering him on. As extremely talented as Neil was he was always acting the goat. One night in a theatre I was taking a drink of water and he played a sample on his keyboards of gurgling water which came out of the speakers, the audience was in stitches as was I.

Neil, daft as a brush we missed him when he left. He's now a tutor at a university.

While I was at Phil's office one day he took a call from another agency with view to me and the band going to Hong Kong for two weeks. I felt like two weeks was reasonable with regards to Ben. But when we looked into it, it wasn't viable it would have meant, after expenses, me and the band splitting £120 per night between us. Bass player John told me not to take it, he thought it was way too low and he wasn't prepared to go all that way for peanuts. He was right, so Phil called the agent back and declined. Instead he sent the Beatles tribute show. I spoke with them at a showcase later and they told me it was in a rubbish karaoke bar and it actually cost them to do the gig. Apparently it cost the equivalent of £6 for a pint of Guinness, at that time Guinness cost about £2 a pint. Food wasn't included so I can only imagine what the costs were. Glad we didn't do that one.

Erica from Big Foot Events called me direct one afternoon, which Phil wasn't best pleased about. Anyway she said Bob Carruthers had asked for me personally to do a show at his house in Stratford-upon-Avon. My fees had risen by now to £600+ per night so I was happy to go and do it. Secretly I wanted to see where this down to earth millionaire lived.

Pete Bond couldn't do it for some reason and Lesley would be getting in from her work and virtually jumping in the van. So I asked my old mate Darren Lyons if he would drive, I paid him of course and he laughed and said "the last time you paid me to do a show with you was at Langley Labour club and I got £2". This time I paid him the same as Lesley £70.

When we arrived at Bobs house all three of us just stared at it, it was huge. Bob told me he had bought it off John Thaw the actor for four million! It was truly stunning. One of Bobs staff showed us to a room for me to get changed in. Then we had a little look around this beautiful property. This young lady latched on to me showing us around. I found out later that it was Bobs psycho sister. She kept making a play for me but she wasn't my type and besides it was clear to see that she was on some sort of medication. Lesley and Darren kept taking the mick out of me, they reckoned I would be rich for life if I got with her. I made a hasty retreat after that.

As usual the show went down excellent. When I made my entrance, which was on a huge patio, Bob and his guests made an arch for me to walk through. I thought I hope his sister isn't at the other end! She wasn't and the show went on, I got them singing "Happy Birthday" to Bob and then we rocked the night away. After the show they served food and Bob being Scottish of course it had to be Haggis. I had never tried it before but it was really nice, Darren liked it but Lesley pulled her face.

It was such a special night, Bob had invited us into his private sanctuary and to me that meant a great deal. I really felt part of his family!

New Years Eve 1999/2000 and all the tribute acts were booked into venues at three and four times their normal fee as it was a special year. Phil had me booked into a restaurant in Bolton, solo for £2000. Talk about milking it, everyone thought they would get a huge fee. Normally New Years Eve was double money so to charge four times that amount was just greedy and I told Phil so. He literally had pound signs in his eyes.

Has we entered into December more and more tribute acts were reporting being cancelled. They couldn't sell the high priced tickets to cover the artistes fees. I was no different, the restaurant in Bolton had tried to sell the tickets at £75 each. Phil called and told me they had cancelled. I was a bit gutted not because of the money but all us artistes loved performing on New Years Eve it was a really exciting night. I took it on the chin and prepared to spend my first ever New Years Eve not working.

I decided to spend it with Ben at Pete's house with the rest of Bens cousins. Donna had promised Ben she would phone him at midnight. Then I heard on the grapevine she was going to Tenerife and would be away for New Years Eve. Still she promised she would call Ben from her holiday.

As I suspected she never did call. Ben was devastated, he was only seven years old. He clung to me all night until it was time to go home. He was extremely upset and cried himself to sleep yet again! Donna eventually called him on 10th January, her birthday. Again Ben was upset and confused and I had to pick up the pieces, I was beginning to be mentally exhausted as well but I could never let Ben down.

Eventually I got Ben into see a child psychologist which helped him a bit. But Donna caused him more upset and confusion and later on he had to see the psychologist again. The poor boy didn't know which way to turn, we all think we can rely on our Mothers unconditional love, Ben couldn't. At least not until a few years down the line, and even then it wasn't Donna.......

Chapter 13

2000-2002......LET IT BE ME

Sunday 8th January 2000, Elvis' birthday, me and Steve were in The Woodman pub as usual. During the week I'd mentioned it was my birthday as a joke. Everyone knew my birthday was 4th July American Independence Day. So everyone came in the pub with cards and wishing me happy birthday. I was a bit gobsmacked. I had told Steve earlier it was a joke. His wife Pauline turned up with a card and was most put out when she realised what had happened. She didn't speak to me for a week!. I wouldn't mind but she had given me a birthday card back in July. I thought it was funny but I couldn't believe my in-laws lack of mentality and sense of humour.

On 17th January Phil had arranged his Lookalike Ball. It was at Patrick's new place in Bury. It was a sit down meal and rather than have a disco he had brought in a karaoke, he reckoned we would all sing a couple of songs each. I arrived with Lesley and Jacqui. Lesley had kept telling me in private that Jacqui really liked me but I wasn't sure. I had always looked at her and her sisters as my little sisters, I felt a bit nervous.

It was very surreal being in the same room as Robbie Williams, Abba, Blues Brothers, Cher, Diana Ross, Tom Jones, Neil Diamond and many many more. The respect I seemed to be getting, said to me I was on the same level as them in the top bracket of the tribute market.

We sat with Cher and Jacqui sat next to me. Lesley kept giving me the eyes to make a move but I chickened out and got up to sing a song to a massive applause.. After I finished singing I went to the men's room to freshen up. When I came out Jacqui was stood right in front of me and gave me a sensual kiss. Lesley had been right! I kissed Jacqui back then we went back into the room hand in hand and sat down. Lesley had a great big grin on her face and I told her that Jacqui and I were an item. It was the beginning of a real relationship.

We kept calling each other after she had gone back to Wales. It got to the point if she was a few minutes late calling me I would get the jitters. But I understood it was awkward for her, she had to end her failing marriage to her husband Steve. After a couple of weeks she invited Ben and I to stay at her house for a couple of days. It didn't sit well with me but she eventually convinced me that it would be a break from the madness that was my life at home.

Jacqui made a make-up bed for Ben and I had the single bed in the same room. Her then husband Steve was at work quite a lot so it gave us time to spend together, the three of us. Avril lived just around the corner so we visited her a couple of times, she had no idea what was going on. She just thought that Pete and Ben was visiting one of his little sisters. We also went to Conwy Castle just down the coast and one of my favourite photo's Ben took of us is one of my favourites. I have it on my desk in my office. At that point I didn't know what would happen in the future I just went with the flow.

Meanwhile I did a show with TJ Slater (Tom Jones) at Oulton Hall Hotel in Yorkshire. It was pretty high end, it was The Law Society Ball. TJ went on and went down fantastic as usual. When he came off he warned me the atmosphere was ready to bubble over. That was like a red rag to a bull. As my helicopter intro was playing and the voice-over said "Elvis Is In The Building" I could hear the crowd erupting, you would have thought the real Elvis was coming on. When I walked on it went ballistic as I started the show with CC Rider. All these posh lawyers in monkey suits bowing down to me. At first I thought they were taking the mick but after fifteen minutes I realised they were genuine. Then the inevitable happened. A big fat guy with John Lennon glasses jumped on stage and tried to take the microphone off me. I remembered what TJ had said, " never give your microphone to anyone its your show". So I politely said no to him, he got very uppity saying he wanted to do karaoke as well! KARAOKE! What an insult, at that point I moved the microphone away from my mouth and said to him " Get off my stage F**k off "! (sorry for the bad language) He looked at me in astonishment and asked me did I know who he was? I replied " I couldn't care less who you are I'm being paid to do this show and this is my stage so get lost ". His face was a picture I don't think anyone had ever stood up to him like that before. I glanced over to TJ who was stood in the wings, he was in stitches laughing and applauding me for standing my ground. The rest of the show was brilliant all the lawyers and their wives were a fantastic audience. Afterwards I was backstage with TJ and he asked if I knew who that fat guy was? "I dunno why? " " it was Judge Lord Pickles" he said! I just mumbled " he could be The Queen of England for all I care no one interrupts my show, insults me and gets away with it, its my stage, my show and no one will ever ruin it "

TJ was still giggling and then told me I was learning fast, well done!

Talking about TJ Slater, I went to see his show at Patrick's new restaurant The Church Inn in Birtle, Lancashire. I went to see him backstage he was on his mobile phone and he beckoned me over " Elvis say hello to my new girlfriend " so I went along with it " Hi Honey this is Elvis", she was tickled but seemed very nice, I gave the phone back to TJ. He said his goodbyes then turned to me and said he was seeing her and she was the real Tom Jones current girlfriend! Wow I asked if she had a sister and he burst out laughing. I couldn't believe the balls he had. He went on stage and smashed it.

It was a big learning curve being in the top bracket of Tribute Acts and TJ was my mentor. I learned a lot from him. He was a real force of nature that's for sure.

John Ford Productions was a prestigious company and they booked me to do a show in London, again for The Law Society. I must have done something right at Oulton Hall Hotel. It was in the biggest marquee I'd ever seen, it held 2500 and it even had stairs leading to a Mezzanine Suite. I was contracted to perform five songs for the fee of £650, could this job get any better! The one thing I found a bit strange was John Ford got in touch with Phil and asked him to get me to send my five songs to him so he could get them to the band? Band! What band? I'm performing on backing tracks. The story was, there were five other tribute

179

acts on and they had sent their songs to the band. The band were set to learn the song versions and mime to the backing track! I couldn't believe it why would a client want that? I never really found out but when when it came to me I walked on to a huge reception and started of with Suspicious Minds. I turned to the drummer and he pleaded with me could he play his drums rather than mime. I sad " no problem you can all play live if you want ". They did and we brought the marquee down. John Ford was non the wiser and the audience had no idea whatsoever. It was a strange one though but I did enjoy watching the other five tribute acts, Robbie Williams, Madonna, Cher, Tom Jones and Kylie Minogue.

One band gig that Phil got us was in Saundersfoot in South Wales. The money was ok and I arranged accommodation for the band. However it was in the summer and I couldn't find anywhere for the rest of the crew, me, Ricky, Lesley and John Clews. John came along to help Lesley with the driving. He said he knew how far it was to travel there and back in one day. He was right even I had misjudged the distance. It took us about six hours non stop. The gig went really well. It was in a nightclub so we didn't get finished till around 1am. As you can imagine by the time we got home it was around 8am and I was thankful John had offered to drive for me. I was so appreciative to Ricky, he worked his socks off that night.

We were still playing at Johnny Balls New York Club, Fridays and Saturdays fortnightly. I got to know Johnny pretty well. I had heard rumours of him being a gangster on Merseyside but that didn't matter to me as long as he treated me with respect which he always did..

His Mum was always sat on the front row and asking for her favourite song ' My Way ' which we always did towards the end of the show. A few years later Johnny asked me to do a few songs for his mum in her hospice, she was dying of cancer. Lesley and I set the small speakers up and tried to be as quiet and respectful as we could. They wheeled his mum out and her face lit up, she didn't know I was coming. I did about forty minutes and thought that was probably enough considering where we were. John came chasing after me with my wages. However he said " I'm not paying you unless you sing my mums favourite song ". I said are you kidding but he was deadly serious. So knowing his reputation and being close to losing his mum, I went back out. I gave his mum a scarf and a kiss and then I sang My Way......and now the end is near....... that was pretty hard!

Off stage my life seemed to be improving. Jacqui and I phoned each other every day. She desperately wanted out of her marriage to Steve who wasn't squeaky clean himself. He asked her if they could go to see a marriage councillor so she agreed to it out of respect. But she had already made her mind up, she wanted to be with me. We spoke of all the logistics and decided it would be best, eventually, for her to move to Manchester and move in with Ben and me. However she was struggling with how to do this so I suggested she spoke with her sister Michelle, I knew she would be helpful, she was one of my Little Sisters. And to Jacqui's surprise she was helpful and was also there for her for moral support. After all that the hardest thing was to tell her mum Avril. Jacqui and her sisters always thought of their mum as being fairly stern, which she could be at times. However I knew she would come around to the idea of Jacqui and I being together. But it wasn't me that had to tell her.

At Phil's office we had been arranging another showcase for Phil's agency Ambassador Promotions. We decided I would get the prime slot for my fifteen minutes. Although it was solo and not the band. Phil hired The Willows Cabaret Club in Salford. I had never been there before and I was suitably impressed with the place. Just before I went on stage Ricky came and told me an old friend was sat at the back, Mick from Maxine's had brought a minibus with him. I went down really well and Phil got a few bookings for me off the clients. When I had finished my slot I got changed and made a beeline to the back to greet Mick. It was like no time had passed between us, he complimented me on my show. He said he was so pleased to see me singing live. I just wish he could have seen me with my band but it wasn't to be. I asked him if he was going to book me at his new venue Oakfields Caravan Park in Towyn (the same one I used to perform in) but

181

he said Phil had quoted too much even as a solo tribute. I told him I'd see what I could do about it. We had a few drinks and then Phil called me over to meet someone. I said goodbye to Mick and thanked him for coming. It was great to see him again.

Johnny Peller gave me some bookings with my band at Jumping Jacks Nightclubs and Yates Winelodge's nationwide, along with our residency at Johnny Balls New York Club, I was kept busy with the band. Johnny Peller also gave me loads of solo contracts to appear at Arena Pubs again nationwide. I wasn't sure at first about playing in pubs again, I knew all about the negative things they could throw up. However Johnny and Phil convinced me and in any case they were all £500 solo bookings so who was I to turn my nose up!

I had the opportunity to put my live band on at The Cairndale Hotel in Dumfries. I had got Phil the contract to supply the hotel every Friday and Saturday nights. I had done the very first night as a solo tribute and it was an electric atmosphere and went down extremely well.

The live band night was fantastic, I really enjoyed the audiences in Dumfries and continued to play there for many years to come.

The owners of The Cairndale Hotel had agreed to stage one of Phil's showcases. Phil was trying to get more bookings in Scotland for me and other tribute acts. When we were doing soundchecks I phoned Jacqui and said " listen to this guy he's awesome " and held the phone up for her to hear. She thought it was the real Neil Diamond! And there started a lifelong friendship with Rob Leigh, quite simply the best Neil Diamond look and soundalike in the business. As the years went along he became my best friend in the business until his untimely death in 2020.

After the soundchecks I went to the front desk to get my room key and they said they didn't have one they were fully booked with the showcase! Phil had arranged accommodation for all fifteen tribute acts apart from me! I couldn't believe it, I went in search of him. His excuse was he thought I'd be travelling home the same night. I hit the roof, I always stayed over at The

Cairndale so why was tonight any different? He was full of apologies but I was so annoyed with him he was supposed to be my manager, he was supposed to give me priority surely!

The hotel had made available a meeting room for all the acts to get ready in so I hung out with them all. It was here I first met Glen and Dean who played John and Paul in the Beatles band. They seemed nice fellas and we remained friends even up to today!

Come time for my fifteen minute set, I was so wound up I went on stage and completely smashed it. I was like a man possessed, I wanted Phil to remember just who he was managing! Jed Stone (the compere/comedian) didn't know what to say after I finished and that was odd because he's a Liverpool comedian and we all know they're never short of a word.

Me and Pete Bond travelled home in his car, very disillusioned.

The following day Phil phoned very apologetically saying it was a misunderstanding and that The Cairndale wanted to book me and The Beatles for a gig on the same night in a show called ' 20th Century Legends'

So I thought great both bands on one night! But no the hotel wanted the full Beatles band but just me solo! What was wrong with people they had previously booked my band and it went exceptionally well. The answer was it was down to finances. So I took it on the chin, until......

On the night The Beatles demanded to go on last because they were a band. Normally Elvis would go on last because he was the bigger star. However I relented and went on first, blew the audience away and The Beatles refused to go on until the audience had calmed down. Eventually they went on after half an hour and they went well apart from the audience chanting "We want Elvis"

Lesley and I stood at the back and smiled. From that day on they refused to go on stage after me and always insisted I closed the show. It wasn't a case of one-upmanship, they were a great band, it was simply the case that people expected Elvis on last and I had perfected a high octane non-stop routine that won audiences over every time!

183

I did another showcase this time for Johnny Peller in Yorkshire. The prize was gigs at a chain of five star hotels across eastern Europe. I performed solo and when me and Lesley was in the dressing room we got to know some of the other acts. The nicest of which was the 60s band The Dakota's and Steve Steinman as Meatloaf. In fact Steve Steinman scolded his bass player who was taking the mick out of me looking like Elvis. I'll never forget what he said " Pack it in idiot, don't you know who this is, its Lewis Gates so keep your trap shut ". I was a bit taken aback but I thanked him and he replied " were all top draw tribute acts especially you " I was so flattered and instantly he had my respect.

I never got the gig, Steve Steinman did so I was pleased for him. I spoke to him on the phone sometime after and he told me if I get to do anything in Europe or further afield make sure you use your live band. People are more impressed with a live band rather than solo with tracks. I took it onboard he seemed to be successful with his band, doing theatre tours with his Meatloaf Tribute and Vampires Rock Show.

I got a call to do a 21st birthday party in Manchester one wednesday night. It was in an underground nightclub beneath the Manchester Olympic Swimming Pools on Oxford Road. We got there and it was empty but the DJ was helpful and showed us where to set up and get changed, it was a bit like The Cavern in Liverpool. I got ready for the 10pm start time and when I came out it was bouncing with 100% females! Oh my God they were rowdy, they had their hands all over me but I wasnt complaining, perks of the job! After the show I knew I had to keep a low profile or I would never get away alive. The DJ agreed to help Leslie to load the car. Then Leslie came to fetch me from the dressing room. I thought i'd got away and I was on the phone to Jacqui when I heard all this screaming. I turned around and to see thirty to forty women charging towards us. I looked at Leslie and said run for it. So we were chased down the corridor and up the stairs and out into the car park. Leslie got the engine running really fast and we sped off. Phew! That was a close call I said to Jacqui who was still on the phone and listening to it all, she couldn't believe what she was hearing. I couldn't, I just loved my job!

184

Jacqui and I were constantly on the phone to each other and we became serious. Avril was furious with Jacqui, I think she thought that I would let Jacqui down as if I was still seeing other women as I had years ago in Summer Seasons. Jacqui tried explaining that I wasn't like that now and I was a family man, which I was.

Finally the day came when I would be happy once more. May 1st 2000 I hired a van which Lesley offered to drive down to Kinmel Bay to pick up Jacqui and her things and move to Manchester to be with Ben and I. I couldn't believe my luck, a second chance at being happy. Once she had settled in she phoned her mum and explained what was happening. Avril went berserk and told her to choose between her or Pete! She chose me and Ben I'm thankful to say although she was extremely upset. Apparently Avril said she was washing her hands with her. Which seemed a bit childish, she knew I was a good trustworthy person. However we found out later why she was being like that, but more of that later......

I told Jacqui to call her sister Michelle and see if she could smooth the waters. She was brilliant, as she was at the beginning of our relationship. She got Avril to see that it was the best thing for Jacqui, Ben and me.

Avril phoned two days later and apologised to Jacqui and they made up. Jacqui was really pleased, she was very close to her mum and she hated the thought of not seeing her again.

But a big thank you to my "little sister" Michelle, we both love you loads.

So we started to make a new life together as a family, I couldn't believe I was getting a second chance at happiness. Jacqui couldn't have children but she bonded with Ben instantly! He had already asked about her moving in with us so he was really made up. Right out of the blue he asked if he could call her mum, we were both taken aback. We had hoped that one day he would ask but not as early as this. Of course Jacqui agreed. I suppose having his biological mum Donna rejecting him and letting him down, he just wanted to be loved and have some stability.

As you can expect it didn't go down well with Donna who insisted he call her Jacqui when he was at her house. He asked her could he call her Mum Jacqui and Donna lashed out at him screaming absolutely not!.

Ben was upset about this, as any child of eight years old would be. Jacqui and i comforted him and told him just to do as Donna asked, it wasn't a problem with Jacqui or myself. Eventually the tears stopped and he called Jacqui his Mum.

Life was very different for Jacqui coming to live in a big city from a small seaside resort. One of the things I thought was funny was when she and I joined Steve Grayson in The Woodman one Sunday night. The first thing was she couldn't understand any of them at all because we spoke too fast for her. She thought we all talked Chinese! I suppose Mancs do talk quick amongst themselves but she caught on in the end. The other thing was she was adamant that the welsh could out drink anybody. How wrong she was, she couldn't keep up with us so I slowed down, Steve called me a wuss and laughed!

We got on with starting our new life together with a few subtle changes we made. We had our usual Sunday dinner at Lesley's and when we got home Jacqui said we would never have Sunday dinner there again. She said the gravy was full of grease and the veggies were overcooked. Who was I to argue. The next Sunday we had dinner at home and my God what a difference, Jacqui could really cook and from then on we had Sunday dinner at home. Lesley was a bit miffed because she had lost the £3 off me that everyone had to pay for their dinner.

I really couldn't believe my luck, Jacqui's cooking was on another planet!

Sometimes Jacqui would come with us on the shows and Ben would stay with his cousins and his Nanna Ann. Sometimes she would babysit Ben at home. Occasionally Lesley would show Jacqui how everything worked and how I wanted things done on stage. Jacqui took to this pretty well but we didn't see what came next.......

Lesley started being horrible and awkward saying Jacqui was trying to take her job. When in reality Lesley had encouraged Jacqui to learn it all!

Then one night at Patrick's new place The Church Inn in Bury, Lesley started insisting that I organise a free ticket for Donna! Donna of all people. I just didn't understand where she was coming from. There were times when Lesley had taken me and shown me support when I was at court with Donna. And let me tell you there were lots of court dates to do with Donna acting erratically over Ben.

I just couldn't understand why Lesley was being like this she had said many times she hated Donna for what she was putting Ben and i through.

Lesley, Jacqui and I arrived at The Church and started setting the gear up. Again she demanded I get a ticket for Donna. I told her it was sold out but even if I could she would have to pay like any other customer! Why would I bow down to Donna?

Personally I think Donna had seen how much Lesley and Pete had helped me over the last year and she poisoned Lesley's mind, with the blood is thicker than water thing.

So without further ado she promptly decided she was finishing and left Jacqui and I with all the equipment and went home, with my van!

We had no choice but to do the show, Jacqui hadn't done a show on her own before but she did brilliantly. I was so proud of her. After the show Pete turned up with the van all apologetic and embarrassed about Lesley's behaviour. We all loaded the gear and Pete took us home.

The next morning we went to see Lesley for some answers. She said that she thought Jacqui was trying to take over her job which was ridiculous and I told her so. She didn't believe me and said she wouldn't be doing anymore shows from then on. This left me in a bit of a position, Jacqui still had her L plates on and Pete decided to take Lesley's side which I understood. He didn't want any strife off her if he was to be loyal to me. I understood Pete's position totally. So that was that, almost two years of travelling the country and entertaining audiences was over, it was such a shame.

The following week we went to see Lesley to see if she would change her mind but she made it very clear that she didn't want us visiting any more. And Pete was finishing as well!

To this day I don't think she realises that Donna had played her. Families, I just don't get them at all.

So in one fell swoop I had lost my drivers and sound/light techs and babysitters. Jacqui wasn't up to taking the reins just yet so I called Phil. He suggested I ask Gary Mac. I knew Gary from when he was a DJ in Middleton. I phoned him and he was very interested, he didn't mind picking the hire van up and dropping it off so I took him on. Jacqui was fantastic looking after Ben while I was out working so everything seemed rosy again, phew!

Gary knew a lot about sound and lighting so it made setting the equipment up so much easier. He knew about accoustics and how to avoid feedback so it was a real bonus.

We did a show for the BMA (British Medical Association) up in Edinburgh at the five star Intercontinental Balmoral Hotel. When we pulled up I went in to find out where we were supposed to unload and set up etc. When I came out to tell Gary, there was an old Scottish guy dressed in his kilt and whacking our van with his walking stick. Of course the van had a Manchester name and number on the side so he decided he wanted to resurrect the English / Scottish wars! I couldn't believe it, I would have to pay for any damage. Gary got out of the cab and shifted him away. We both looked at each other and burst out laughing, you couldn't make it up. The old guy shuffled away shouting to himself, we couldn't understand a word.

The show went extremely well, so much so that Gary had to stop the music half way through because the audience had swamped me on stage and the stage was about to collapse. I asked them to calm down which they did and the event ended up being superb.

The BMA gave us a room to change in and I looked at the room prices. Oh my God £500 a night. After the show we went into the bar, got a drink and sat down. Then in walks the comedian Brian Conley with his wife. Neither of us would approach him for his autograph we were in awe like two little kids back in Middleton. When I look back now I had a ball with Gary Mac Rest in peace my friend.

Then just when everything seemed rosy Jacqui got tonsillitis and had to have them out. When the day came Ben and I went with her to provide support. It was going to take about an hour. After the second hour I went up to the desk and asked for an update and they couldn't give me one. Third and fourth hour the same response. When it came to five hours I was really beginning to panic but trying not to show it for Bens sake. I kept reassuring him that everything would be alright. I had only just got together with this wonderful woman and I thought we were going to lose her, lose our second chance of happiness. I called Jacqui's mum Avril and told her what I knew and she should come up to Manchester, fearing the worst.

Almost six hours after Jacqui going down for her operation an annesiathist came and spoke with me. She said I shouldn't worry and she knew the operation should have taken just an hour. But they had lost a swab inside her lungs and took a while to find it. In doing so her lungs had flooded and they had to correct it. However she was alright now and everything was good. Good! I shouted, my son thought he was going to lose his mum and me my future! She calmed me down and said there was no need to take it any further. What she meant was for me not to sue the NHS. She nearly died but I was just so relieved Jacqui was alright. Maybe I should have sued, people had sued for far less. The biggest prize I had was Jacqui healthy. Avril, Ben and I saw Jacqui on the ward, she was still very drowsy but seemed alright. Avril drove us home and the following day I got a taxi and picked Jacqui up to come home, Phew!

The show carried on, being a success and Jacqui, Ben and I were enjoying being a family. Until, you guessed it, Donna reared her head once more by letting Ben down countless times and trying to cause trouble in general.

It was as if she didn't want Ben and me but she wouldn't let us be with someone else! I'd had enough, it was confusing Ben all the time. So I got in touch with social services and asked for some help. They spoke with her then came to our house and spoke with me then spoke with Ben separately. Then at the end when we were all sitting and talking, Donna called, shouting and swearing on the phone. Jacqui asked her to calm down for Ben's sake but she just got louder. The guy from social services looked shocked, we could all hear the verbal abuse Donna was spouting. He made his excuses and left. I was sure something would get done to stop Donna from putting Ben through this, he was only eight years old.

Absolutely nothing was done, the social services report read that Ben needed to see his biological mother. What a joke, he was eight, of course he wanted to see her. I didn't want to stop her I just wanted her to respect her own son and be reliable for him.

At one point I was out gigging when she turned up an hour late to pick him up and rather than knock on the door she just kept her hand on her cars horn for an eternity. Jacqui went out to find out what was going on but Donna just dismissed her and kept her hand on the horn. By this time Ben was getting really upset so as a last resort Jacqui called Donna's dad and asked him to come and speak with her. He turned up five minutes later and talked her into stopping upsetting Ben and to leave.

Gary and I carried on gigging nationwide. One venue I remember was John Browns Nightclub in Clydebank near Glasgow. It was on the top floor and we had to load the gear up three flights of fire escape stairs and obviously afterwards down again. It was a killer but the crowd were excellent. We did it quite a few times.

We also did a wedding up in Northumberland at one of the Devere hotels. Now Gary always insisted that he went in first to find out loading details and to get our room key. This time there was no room key! I was sat in the van and I'll never forget Gary ripping the receptionist apart " You want Lewis to get changed in the disabled toilets!! Absolutely not, Lewis Gates is an international tribute artiste, get him a room or we go home! ". We got a bedroom to get changed in and the wedding guests had a fantastic time. At one point I was leading the conga while singing Viva Las Vegas. Gary's face was a picture, he was loving it.

Another venue we did was at The Brooklands Hotel in Yorkshire. It was with my band and it was a sell out! I decided to do my theatre show which included some costume changes. Half way through the first set I went and got changed into my black jumpsuit. I was playing to the audience and the loved it. Then I went down on my left knee on the parcais dance floor. The pain in my knee wast excruciating. I carried on and I could feel the blood trickling down my leg. Finally the interval came and when Jacqui looked at my knee she knew it was pretty bad. I finished the show to great applause but it was the beginning of years of knee pain.

While Gary and I were gigging around the country, on our days off I started to show Jacqui the ropes with the mixing desk and lighting console, just in case. She was pretty fast picking everything up which I was pleased about.

Just as well really because Phil phoned me and said I would have to let Gary go? I asked him why and he said he wanted him to work in his office. He told me to tell him it was a personality clash. I didn't know what to do so I thought how much Phil had accelerated my career with high class bookings, I decided to go along with it. We were doing a show at The Fiveways in Hazel Grove on a thursday night and after the show I told him, he was gobsmacked and hurt, quite rightly as well. I told him to speak with Phil but he was distraught and I felt so sorry for him. Years later I'm pleased to say we made up and I told him it was Phil's fault. He was ok with that and we still talked occasionally on the phone.

And so it started an eighteen year adventure for Jacqui and I touring the UK and Europe, it really was a rock n roller-coaster ride that I wouldn't have missed for the world........

Chapter 14

2002....THE FAIR'S MOVING ON

2002, we came in from shopping and had a message on the land line, it was Lesley. There was so many expletives I couldn't possibly share with you. Although the worst one was she said Jacqui would never be Bens mum because she could never have kids. This is the worst possible thing one woman can say to another woman. I had accepted Jacqui not being able to have children when we got together, and I had told Lesley in confidence, I never thought she would be so vicious. It really was a case of they had left the gravy train, they didn't want me but they didn't want anyone else to have me! This just sealed their fate, I would never see any of that family ever again!

We woke up one morning when Jacqui went out she discovered two tyres had been slashed. Straight away I knew who had done it, that family was toxic.

We got the tyres sorted out, it was a Saab 2000 so it was quite expensive. Two days later and the side windows were smashed. The following week all four tyres were slashed. In the middle of all this Donna had arranged for one of theses 'cash for houses' companies to come and value the house for a quick sale. I threw him out unceremoniously. Then two days later we awoke to find a For Sale sign in the front garden. The guy was just leaving when I uprooted the sign and told him to leave in no uncertain terms. Donna had no right to put the house up for sale it was a joint mortgage. In any case it was effectively making her own son homeless, what kind of mother does that? Obviously we wouldn't make Ben homeless we were trying as hard as we could to try and find another house away from that horrid place. I just couldn't comprehend how Donna could do that to Ben, I still cant to this day. I'm convinced she had had a breakdown of sorts because the Donna that I knew would never have done that to Ben or me for that matter!Bullying me and Ben out of our home, how low could she go?

Somebody had a grudge against us and it didn't take a rocket scientist to figure out who. We installed CCTV cameras in the hope of catching them. The police had suggested this as without proof of who was doing it they couldn't do anything. The following morning I went through the CCTV footage and saw what looked like a male in a hoodie slashing the tyres and smashing the windows again. It was hopeless because we couldn't tell who it was and to our dismay we found out that side windows were not insured nor were the tyres. Obviously the perpetrators knew this and was knowingly costing us a lot of money every week. Later on we found out it was Donna and Leslie that had paid somebody, that shall remain nameless because he probably will get his comeuppance. Talk about being bitter, I had done nothing wrong apart from trying to get on with my new life.

We came to the conclusion we had to move quick! So I spoke with my new friend Stuart Kean and he said he would see what he could do. He could see the mess we were in, it was costing us £200 - £300 a week which was totally unacceptable. He had even lent me some cash at one point to do the repairs because I was running out of money.

We had been looking for a new house anyway, new relationship, new life etc. We had found a place in Heywood that ticked all the boxes and even had a granny flat in the back garden which we had earmarked for Ricky the DJ (he'd had enough of Langley as well). The downside was it wasn't available until October and we were only in July. It was such a shame but we had to move pretty quick we couldn't afford to maintain the weekly car vandalism. I felt so sorry for Ricky, life deals you horrible cards sometimes.

Stuart came up trumps with a two bedroom weavers cottage in Littleborough which was on the other side of Rochdale. It was ideal albeit a little small but you cant have everything. It was owned by Paul and Clarke Topham who owned the main garage in Rochdale. Paul told me not to worry if my ex-inlaws found out where we lived, he would stop any nonsense. Paul and Clarke were both ex-boxers and both 6ft plus and built like Tyson Fury. I was so grateful for the safety net. The one stipulation was we had to cut ties with absolutely everyone on Langley. I couldn't even tell Ricky which I was extremely upset about but I had to keep my new family safe.

So we hired a van and to my utter surprise my Father helped us move. Now I realise he was just making sure we actually moved away from him. Anyway we moved into Frederick Street in Littleborough and got to know some of the neighbours. Living either side of us were elderly people, Barbara and Ray and to our left was Mary. All three were lovely people and we would remain friends for life.

We awakened to our first day in our new house and the relief of not facing our car being vandalised was palpable. We felt as though we could breathe again having left everything behind. I decided to go for a newspaper. It was just a small walk into Littleborough village and I couldn't believe how nice the locals were. Everyone was saying good morning, they didn't even know me! It was like taking a step back in time to the 1950s, we had struck lucky through the help of Stuart Kean and I'll never be able to thank him enough.

Phil had more prestigious events booked and he had booked a tour in August for the thirty fifth anniversary of Elvis passing.

Jacqui took to the sound desk and lighting desk like duck to water. We went to the Isle Of Man to perform at The Hilton Hotel & Casino. I had done this before with Lesley and by now they were treating us like royalty. Each show was booked by various businesses (Scottish Widows, Aviva, Lloyds Bank, Barclaycard and many more) summer balls or Christmas party nights. We had a ball ourselves and they always gave us the wedding suite.

Jacqui's first proper gig with me and the band was The American Motorhome Show at Billing Aquadrome near Northampton. We were in a marquee which held about 1500 all standing. We did the sound check and everything sounded great. Then later it was showtime, the band started the 2001 theme and when I walked out the whole place literally exploded with noise. I turned around thinking someone famous had come on, but no it was all for me. What a fantastic crowd, there was crash barriers at the front like they have at all the festivals and a good job there was, they got really rowdy and I was loving it. When I started Love Me Tender I threw my first scarf into the crowd and there was a big scramble for it. I turned around for Jacqui for more scarves but she was stood rooted behind Guy and his drums. Guy told her to go give me more scarves but she was frozen, she had never been involved in a show like this so it was understandable. I knew what had happened straight away so I walked behind the drums and took the scarves off her and gave her a kiss. The audience saw this and all the women now wanted a scarf and a kiss, Love Me Tender must have lasted ten minutes, it was disorganized chaos!

We had two songs to do when some idiot pulled the plug on the generator. I must have kissed somebody's wife and he wasn't best pleased. And at the age of nineteen but like an old pro Guy did a ten minute drum solo, what a drummer! We finally came back on and finished the show to rapturous applause.

We did a solo show at Carnforth British Legion. I didn't like these shows, I had done them years before and they always had a cantankerous chairman/concert secretary or compère in control mode. At this one it was the compère. I had told him we had an helicopter intro and just to say its showtime when Jacqui gave him the nod. Jacqui also reminded him of this five minutes before we started. Well he just had to have his say introducing me. Jacqui gave him the nod and he ignored her so she started the helicopter with the security guys speaking as if they were in the helicopter. Then he started waffling on and it was ruining the intro so Jacqui aimed the smoke machine at him and flooded the stage with smoke. And what did the idiot do but to turn his microphone up. We were working with a 7.5k sound system back then so Jacqui whacked it up and drowned him out. He conceded defeat, the complete fool. I was backstage laughing my socks off! Well done Jacqui!

We used to do a lot of Hilton Hotels back then. One of them that sticks in my mind is the one in Coventry. It held 400 in the function suite and was always sold out. On the fourth time it sold out and I stayed on stage for 1hr 20min instead of an hour. As an artiste you know when to leave them wanting more and I felt that was about right. The place was bouncing! When I came out of the dressing room the duty manager approached me, I thought he wanted to discuss more bookings which was usually the case. He said and I quote " You'll never play here again " I asked him why " because you were booked for an hour and you did an hour and twenty " I was shocked and told him I wasn't charging him extra and he replied " while your on stage longer were losing out on bar sales ". I couldn't believe what I was hearing and I was stuck for words! We never played there again, the agent Erica at Big Foot Events couldn't believe the mentality of the Hilton Management.

Phil got me and the band a strange booking at Kelvin Art Gallery and Museum in Glasgow. It was for Glaxo Smith Clyne, their summer ball. But the sound was awful, we had to play in the main atrium which was great apart from the roof was a hundred feet tall. I didn't use any effects on my microphone, it was too much echo I sounded like I was singing in a church. And as for the band the bass guitar and bass drum were both booming off the walls. It went well despite the sound and we got paid which was the main thing. I vowed never to play in a museum ever again!

Meanwhile Ben decided he wanted to see Donna again, we never ever tried to dissuade him. It was always his decision. He was ten years old by now so he called her himself to arrange it. The weekend he went we were in Scotland so we dropped him off at what used to be our home. Donna had moved in and was now paying the mortgage. Jacqui gave Ben my mobile number along with our new neighbours numbers, Barbara and Ray and Mary.

We dropped him off on the Friday afternoon. Jacqui and i were a bit on edge because Donna would have known we were travelling a distance. We didn't hear anything until Ben called at just after midnight on Saturday night. We were on the M8 just outside of Glasgow on our way home. Ben was in a state of panic saying Donna had kicked him outside telling him to get lost back to his Dads! We were about three and a half hours from home so I tried to calm him down and we pulled onto the hard shoulder. Jacqui called Barbara and explained the situation. Barbara and Ray were brilliant they told Jacqui they would send a taxi for Ben and bring him home to her house. We hadn't been their neighbours for long yet they were willing to help like this. I told Ben that there was a taxi coming to pick him up and taking him back to Barbara and Rays and because it would be between 4am and 5am when we got back we would knock on Barbara's in the morning for him. He calmed down somewhat but I think she deeply upset him, he decided he didn't want to see her again which was fine with us we just wanted him to be happy like any child should be. My God what kind of woman does that to her child. I shouldn't have been surprised though after she had bullied us into leaving our family home and technically leaving her son homeless!

Not long after that episode Phil sent me a contract to do a gig in Ayr in Scotland. Scotland again! It was a nice hotel gig we didn't have accommodation included but we did have a bedroom to get changed in. So we decided we would take Ben with us. The first of many shows he came with us, I think that's where he got the rock n roll/showbiz bug.

We arrived at 5pm with plenty of time to set up before the guests arrived at 7pm. However when I asked for the manager he came out to greet us with " I called Phil three months ago to cancel, has he not told you?". I was in shock, I asked him was he sure he had, he said absolutely he did. So I called Phil and told him what I had been told and he tried telling me he had never had a cancellation phone call. So I asked him what should I do but he didn't seem that bothered so I slammed the phone down on him.

The Hotel Manager came up to me, I must have looked stressed. He said we were more than welcome to stay overnight for free. I gave a huge sigh of relief. He gave us a double room with a foldaway bed for Ben. I thanked him profusely and went to his restaurant and had a meal. Afterwards he came over again to see if we were alright, Jacqui and I had calmed down by now and we thanked him again. What a lovely man.

We were contracted to a show at The Cairndale Hotel in Dumfries three days later which was about an hour and half south of Ayr. So I called Phil and told him our predicament which was caused by him and that we would be staying at The Cairndale until it was the day of our show. He was well in with Matthew Wallace the owner of The Cairndale and seeing as it was me that got Phil dozens of contracts for other tribute acts for The Cairndale, he didn't really have a leg to stand on. He reluctantly agreed to sort it out.

We said our farewells to that lovely Manager in Ayr and proceeded to get in our van. By this time we had bought our own second hand van it was cheaper than hiring all the time. Jacqui tried to turn it over and nothing. She tried again and nothing at all. The manager came outside he could see we were having problems and had a look. I didn't know much about engines but he told us our radiator had frozen......aaarrrggghhh! We called the RAC and they got us going so we headed south to Dumfries. About half way there we broke down again. Another RAC man came and towed us to a garage in Dumfries that he knew well. They told us what was wrong and it would take a day or two to fix it. That was alright with us as we were stopping at The Cairndale for a few days anyway. We got a taxi to the hotel and went to check in only to find out that Phil had not even booked us in. Could this week get any worse? Luckily the receptionist knew us well from previous shows and she checked us in to a family room. The following day Phil called so I shouted at him about the Cairndale not knowing anything about us staying and he hung up on me. That was like a red rag to a bull, but I would sort him out when I got back to Littleborough.

We went to the garage after not hearing anything for two days and they said it would definitely be ready in the morning the day of the show at the hotel.

We picked the van up at a cost of nearly £300 and went back to The Cairndale to set up the equipment. It was a sell out again with just over three hundred attending. As usual it was a huge success. After we had loaded the van we went back to reception to hand our key in and thanked them once more. We just really wanted to go home now. So we headed for home hoping the van didn't break down again, which it didn't thankfully!

The morning after I phoned Phil to have it out with him and as usual he was full of apologies. But that didn't cut it for me, I told him to get his act together or we were through, which surprisingly he did for a while......

Phil had booked me into the prestigious Met Club in London for a private party on the Friday and then moving on to Lampeter in Mid Wales for a wedding on the Saturday. We finally found the Met Club but there was yellow lines everywhere so we quickly unloaded the gear and Jacqui went to try and find somewhere to park in central London!

I set up the gear, did a quick sound check and asked where I was to get changed. A lovely man led me to a side room where I met a Mind Reader act who was on after me. The function suite wasn't big but they crammed over a hundred guests in there. I had twenty minutes before showtime and still no sign of Jacqui. I asked this guy if he could start my disc, I showed him what to do which was literally pressing play on the mini-disc player and I went to get changed. Still no sign of Jacqui! The guy came backstage and asked if I was ready and he went to press the play button. I came out to a huge ovation and still no sign of Jacqui. If anyone reading this has seen my solo show, you'll know that I need someone on the sound and lights for it to be successful, it leaves me to concentrate on being Elvis. I just let the disc continue into each song, I couldn't see the buttons with my poor eyesight. Finally Jacqui appeared looking a bit annoyed. She had to park about twenty minute walk from the venue so she wasn't best pleased but we did the show and it went down a storm. And Ive got to say the management and guests treated us like royalty they were brilliant!

We stayed at a Travelodge overnight then headed for Wales at midday. We stopped at a services on the M4 and while paying for our coffees somebody recognised me. I didn't recognise this lady but I stepped into Lewis Gates mode and spoke with her while Jacqui paid at the till. Jacqui's face was a picture, she couldn't believe someone would recognise Lewis Gates this far from home. I think this was when she realised that Lewis Gates was national and not just in Manchester.

We got to The Best Western Hotel in Lampeter at around 5pm. The duty manager came out and told us the wedding was running late and we would need to wait until after the meal and speeches. So we thought not a problem it was still early.

Another van pulled up, it was the lady DJ. I explained what the situation was, she wasn't best pleased but had to accept it.

At 7.pm there was still no sign of the meal finishing let alone the speeches!

8.pm and still no sign. I was due on at 9pm so it was cutting it a bit fine. All this time we had to sit in our vans and it was getting cold by now. The duty manager said he didn't have a room for us to sit in. At 8.30pm I went inside again and pulled the manager. I told him my contract stated I was to perform at 9pm and it just wasn't going to happen at this rate. It usually took us about thirty minutes to set up for a solo show. Once again he sent me outside to the cold van. At 8.45pm he finally came out to tell me and the DJ we could set up our equipment to start at 9pm, unbelievable! We had been made to sit outside for almost three hours in the cold van so we wasn't about to start rushing. We didn't even do a soundcheck and that's not good when you're booked as a soundalike. I couldn't be bothered by then we just wanted to go home. The DJ started at 9pm but it was about 9.30pm before I came on. We did just the minimum of sixty minutes that was on the contract. The guests were loving it and when it came time for me to finish they were all cheering for more including the bride and groom. I just left the stage, normally I would do another fifteen to twenty minutes but I was so annoyed at how we had been treated. We took the gear down, loaded the van and said goodbye to the DJ. From arriving to leaving the bride and groom had not said a word, not even a thank you. Normally we would go and say goodbye to the bride and groom but I was incensed with their arrogance and bad manners. We headed for home after a very contrasting weekend!

Our private life was great during this period. Donna hadn't shown her face which was alright with me but after a while Ben started making small hints about missing her. We never ever dissuaded him from seeing her we just pointed out to him how she had upset him last time. He thought about it and said he'd leave it for now. He had started at Littleborough Junior school, it was his last year before he went to Wardle High School. He seem to flourish at his new school and he seemed so settled in our new house.

Phil called me and asked if I wanted to go to Malaga again. I thought about it and agreed. I decided to take Jacqui and Ben seeing as it was half term at school. We all looked forward to it even though I had to pay Jacqui and Bens air fare which took out a hefty sum from my three shows fees. But Tony Reddin was great agreeing for us to stay at his villa. It was our first holiday as a family, our relationship was relatively new and I kept telling Jacqui we were guaranteed sunshine! We got off the plane and you guessed it, it was raining, the rain in Spain! But we had a great week even though Tony cancelled one show again and only paid me half of my fee for the last one. Apparently the venue manager only agrees to pay in full if the venue is full!

We had been sunbathing on the beach on the day of the last show and later when we got to the venue I couldn't get my legs into my jumpsuit. There was a chemist nearby so Jacqui went and bought some spray aftersun. Tony came backstage and asked what was going on it sounded pretty rude out front. When he saw the aftersun he burst out laughing and he ribbed me all night, it was a great gig.

Back home we were doing some really high brow shows for several different Agents. We did one for Big Foot Events at The Village Hotel in Bury. I didn't have a clue what the event was for until the manageress explained it was for Bury Councils Christmas Party for people with living difficulties. There was around two hundred there, so I decided to do what Elvis would have done and brought them all into the show. They loved it and at the end I got as many as would fit onto the stage to sing and wave their arms to American Trilogy. I'd had experience with learning difficulties when I was with Mick at Maxine's Club in Rhyl all those years ago. For some reason Elvis was special to these wonderful special people. It was a brilliant night even the carers enjoyed it.

Another high end show we did was at The Monkey Island Hotel on an actual Island on the Thames in Windsor. It was a corporate event for Glaxo Smith Clyne. We arrived mid afternoon and discovered the only way to get the equipment in was on of those rope bridges you see in the jungle. The bass speakers were on wheels so we loaded as much as we could on to them and wheeled it in over this rope bridge. That was comical in itself, swinging to and fro.

We set up in the extremely posh function room and was told we had a bedroom for the night if we wanted it. We walked into this bedroom and it was like walking into a room at Buckingham Palace, it was very regal. It had originally been owned by Princess Diana's family but was now owned by a rich Arab. We checked out the room service menu, £19 for a bowl of soup, £32 for a sandwich. We didn't have to pay of course Glaxo would, but we didn't feel comfortable and went and found a garage and ate pork pies and a Ginster's pasty.

The actual show went down well and people were dancing. Afterwards when the room had emptied into the bar area we couldn't get over how many expensive bottles of champagne bottles had been opened and just left full. I suppose Glaxo staff were getting their moneys worth.

The bedroom we had cost Glaxo £500 for the night but Jacqui didn't want to stay she said she'd rather sleep in her own bed. So she drove the three and half hour journey home and I was perplexed about the whole thing.

The owners of The Midway Park Hotel were the Foy brothers (ex bookies and not to be messed with). They asked Phil if I could do one of their sons weddings. It was at a four star hotel near Wrexham and they wanted me to be at the ceremony but to sit at the back as inconspicuous as possible. When the ceremony was almost over and the bride and groom were signing the register and I was to sing Love Me Tender. My speakers had been set up prior so it was pretty easy. All the guests thought it was actually Elvis singing until the groom looked to the back and gave me the thumbs up. It was like one of those romcom movies, all the guests turned around at the same time it was so funny!

The Foy brothers asked Phil if I could perform at their other sons twenty first birthday in a nightclub in Manchester. I thought it was great that two young men appreciated what I did. I knew their dads appreciated me and I really didn't want to let them down but I was contracted to do a wedding in Birmingham. Phil said to cancel the Birmingham gig because the Foy's twenty first gig could open some doors. Apparently they had booked a girl band that were supposed to be hitting the big time very soon. But my morals dictated to do the Birmingham wedding. How wrong was I, the girl band was Girls Aloud and in a matter of weeks they were superstars! The irony was that Mr Foy had told Girls Aloud they would have to go on stage first because he wanted Elvis as top of the bill. Que Sera.

A funny gig we did was at The Cumbrian Grand Hotel in the Lake District. It was one of the first double headers with my new mate Rob Leigh (Neil Diamond). It was huge and the ballroom was gigantic. We used Robs equipment, his idea, he was always nervous using other peoples gear. Later on he used mine all the time. Anyway we decided that Rob should start the show and I would finish it. I suppose Elvis always had to top the bill, it didn't bother me when I went on but Rob thought it best this way and it always worked well.

There was a little corridor leading from the reception to the ballroom and when Rob was almost finished I stood there out of sight of the audience. I kid you not this actually happened, I was stood there with my white Elvis jumpsuit on and two little old ladies came scurrying out of the ballroom and said to me " you don't want to go in there the DJ is way too loud! ". I didn't know what to say so I just smiled. I couldn't believe it there was posters all over the hotel displaying VEGAS NIGHTS - Neil Diamond and Elvis with our photo's, I'm stood there with long black hair and sideburns in my studded Elvis suit and they just didn't have a clue what was going on. When I had finished my show and and walked through the foyer these two ladies said was it too loud for you as well my dear! Rob and I laughed for ages afterwards.

So we were making a new life for ourselves in this lovely little village at the foot of the Pennines. Our neighbours were only too willing to have Ben if we had to leave for a show early afternoon. One Saturday we had a night off, which was really odd. Anyhow we decided to have a pub crawl to find a new local pub for ourselves. Our house was directly behind The Dyers Arms so we started in there. It seemed a bit old fashioned but the Boddington's beer I had was spot on. We went into the village and tried nearly all the other pubs which were great, but we decided The Dyers was the best and less than sixty seconds away from our house. So we ended the night in there where we met Ryan, John and Breeda's (the owners) Grandson we also met Sharon, Brenda and Phil the hardcore locals. They were brilliant people and I would realise just how brilliant in the not so distant future, but more about that soon.

I didn't have many weekends off but I had the odd Sunday when we would spend the afternoon drinking and eating Brenda's food in The Dyers, it was so chilled and we both felt relaxed.

One afternoon John Bene (the Hungarian owner) came and sat by us and bought us a drink. Then he asked me about the show I did. I told him all about it either with the live band or Solo. He said obviously the pub was too small for the band but would I do a solo show for him. I explained the fee was out of his budget but that I would happily do a charity night at The Dyers if he wanted. He bit my hand off and was so grateful. This began a true friendship which we still have today. We did the charity which was for Springfield hospice the local hospice. We raised just over £400 but Springfield Hospice never even acknowledged our efforts, they didn't even acknowledge the cheque for £400 John had sent them.

I was a bit deflated about this as was John and Breeda. However I found out over the years that was just the way they were. I ended up refusing to do any shows for Springfield Hospice and I told people why, which by all accounts didn't go down well but the truth is the truth! A thank you counts for a lot in my book and besides its good manners.

We were doing a chain of pubs run by Watling Street Brewery. Again they were midweek gigs and the fee was a little lower at £350 but midweek bookings were a bonus. We were at The Coach and Horses in Wilmslow one night and after the show we met Ken and Julie. Julie was the Elvis fan and Ken just liked lively music. Anyway Ken was in the pub with some friends when he heard me singing. He dialled Julie and said listen to this as he put the phone in the air. Within twenty minutes Julie was there and they both enjoyed the show. Afterwards they said they had never heard an Elvis with a voice like mine. We spoke for a while, it was nice when someone appreciated my show, Ive always had time for the Elvis fans when they want to talk after the show. Ken and Julie became really nice friends and we have been out for several meals with them and they've been to several of our private parties we've had over the years. They are truly genuine people and we love them both dearly.

Later on when I used to put leaflets on tables explaining how to book my show, Ken did it for me once so I started calling him The Colonel.......

Meanwhile back in Littleborough we were mixing in with the locals and they all made us feel comfortable. In the summer months I would try a few songs out at home on my small monitor speaker in the living room Well the neighbours cottoned on to this as I had the back door open. I was getting applause after each song so I went outside to find that Barbara ,Ray, Mary and Jacqui sat in the sun drinking wine, it was a bit strange but in a really nice way.

Jacqui decided she wanted to try and make my Elvis suits. She'd only ever sewn buttons on shirts before but she was so determined. To our surprise she was a natural. We bought the

205

small stud machines and hot glue machine that were now available. In my mum's day she had sew sequins and stones on by hand. Jacqui got used to everything really quick and created an elaborate light blue Stone suit. She counted everything at the end and there was 2,500 silver Studs and Diamanties on it! God it was heavy to wear but I was so proud of her. She reckoned she'd had some divine help from my mum. I knew she was right.

Later on she would make me the dark blue Owl suit, the white Porthole suit, a white two piece Chainmail Suit, a Cisco Kid Suit and a black two piece Rainfall Suit. I couldn't believe how good she was and how lucky I was.

God works in mysterious ways......

That particular year Littleborough Cricket Club had asked if I would perform on New Years Eve solo. I did a deal with them that because they had let me use the cabaret room for band rehearsals I charged them £750 instead of the usual £1000 for New Years Eve. It was on my doorstep so no travelling and I thought it was great. I also said I would do the disco for free saving them about £200.

And what a great night it was the place was bouncing, I finished the disco at about 2am and headed for home when we saw The Dyers was still open. When we went in it was crowded and I got a big cheer. Apparently most of them had been at the cricket club. We finally went the fifty yards home at around 6am! Wow what a brilliant New Years Eve that was!

The second night I worked with Stuart Keans Ambassadors Legends show was at John Browns Nightclub in Glasgow. I had done this venue before on my own and it was great. However when I told Stuart what songs I wanted to do he completely refused and said " I normally pick the songs for Steve ". I was a bit taken aback and I told him again which songs I wanted. Again he refused, seeing as I was only to perform for seven songs I let it go. I thought he would tell me before he started each song. But he didn't, he thought he would test my Elvis knowledge, what a fool. I just sang whatever he put on the disc. Then I got into it and asked him to put on more songs but he realised I had won and put on the last song.

206

Its funny because he never asked me to be on his show again, he was a bit strange.

At home one night when we were in bed we heard the stomping sound of men's boots running up the street. We didn't know what it was till we asked our neighbour Mary the following morning. She laughed and said all the Littleborough firemen lived on our row so they must have been charging the hundred yards to the fire station. It reminded me of that programme when we were kids, Trumpton. In fact the whole village reminded me of that programme from my childhood, it was like stepping back in time, it was wonderful.

Then catastrophe hit. It was a Wednesday and we were booked into a restaurant in Worcester. Jacqui had a check up at Bury Hospital at 1pm so we loaded the gear all set to go straight from the hospital to the gig. We came out of the hospital and our hearts sank! The van had been smashed open and almost all the gear was stolen. After a few minutes of shock Jacqui called the police. They took the van to the station and searched it and questioned both of us separately. I thought hold on a minute they think we've done an insurance job. Problem was we were not insured. Stupid of us I know, hindsight is wonderful.

The Police were embarrassed when they realized they were wrong. They let us get our van and go on our way.

What was I going to do? I had lots of shows contracted even theatre shows, I thought it was the end of the road and I genuinely didn't know which way to turn.........

Chapter 15

2002-2003....IF YOUR LOOKING FOR TROUBLE

We were sat in our house when someone knocked on the door. It was Stuart, he had heard what had happened and had a solution for us. He had some JBL speakers and some small bass speakers and cases etc. we could have the lot for £200. The JBLs was worth £400 on their own. But we had no capital, we were waiting for cheques and bacs from gigs to go in the bank. He said just pay him whenever we could. What a life saver, I couldn't thank him enough. We were doing our theatre show that very weekend at Gracie Fields Theatre in Rochdale. My new home town what would it look like if I only had half a sound system. That night we went into The Dyers for a drink to calm us down when Shoney one of the regulars offered to lend us £10,000 and pay it back whenever we could, I was stunned, I told him we would think about it but what a gesture.

We decided to go to Altrincham to see my old friend Paul Tandy at Concert Systems. He didn't really deal with small shows like mine but I had been buying things off him for years. He always sold quality sound systems. I told him my predicament and he came good for me. He lent me a full sound system, amplifiers and radio microphone. He said if I liked it I could pay him back on a monthly basis, and if I didn't we could try out other sound systems.

So there was no need to take Shoney up on his offer but I thanked him profusely, what a guy.

Needless to say Concert Systems equipment was top draw, having said that he was regularly providing sound systems for The Manchester Arena for international superstars. I asked him later on why would he trust me not to just run away with his gear and he said he had known me long enough to know I was honest.

So in all he lent me equipment to the value of around £12,000. I must have a guardian angel. We did the Gracie Fields Theatre, it was a big success and Lennie Capuano the manager was very pleased and put another date in the diary for the following year.

Phil called and said would I like to be in a new television show and if so I would need to go to Manchester for an audition, it was for an Elvis singing part. He told me it was Peter Kay's Phoenix Nights, I had never heard of him then but I thought why not. When I got to the audition I was given a room to get changed into my suit and waited with the rest of the Elvis's. One thing that struck was they all looked awful with cheap suits and dodgy wigs. I was beginning to become a bit wary. Anyway they shouted my name and I went in to find a camera man and this guy who introduced himself as Peter Kay, he was extremely nice. He told me what the part entailed and that it was for a joke Elvis and he could tell I was a professional Elvis. He apologised and explained they had wanted a one legged Elvis singing and playing the spoons on his good leg. After having a good laugh about it I told him most of my work was as a soundalike, I sounded like Elvis. So he suggested that I was there now and I should sing an acappella song because everything was taped and put in Channel 4 TVs library and who knows I might get some work off it. I really appreciated his honesty and genuine kindness. I sang Blue Suede Shoes and Peter's face froze I think he was in shock, then he started clapping his hands. I finished singing and shook his and the camera man's hand and left. I never heard anything from Channel 4 but it just shows how Mr Kay is a true gentleman off stage in real life. As far as Phil was concerned I roasted him, he knew it was a comedy part and if he had told me I wouldn't have gone. I would never ever put Elvis down in anything I would do.
The cracks began to show with Phil.

Back in The Dyers Arms John, Breeda, Sharon and Brenda was organise a benefit night for me, for the equipment that was stolen. The only thing was Jacqui and I didn't know anything about it. They asked me to do a charity night for the Dyers kids Christmas party. When in actual fact it was for me. On the night The Dyers was hammered, and there was raffle tickets, football cards and Elvis quiz cards of which I had set the questions. How ironic. Halfway through the night Sharon came up on stage and said on the mic she would like to thank everyone so I stood to one side. She told everyone that all the pubs in Littleborough had chipped in via the Elvis quiz cards and that with everything else we had raised was £960. Everyone cheered then she turned to me and said " its not for the kids Christmas party, its for you and Jacqui because you lost all your equipment ". You can imagine that Jacqui and I were flabbergasted! We had only been in the village six months and for everyone to show they cared like that was very overwhelming. I gave Sharon a huge hug and asked John Bene if I could sing a bit longer. I think the second set lasted two and half hours, I was so emotional.

It didn't end there though. The Reid twins were well known in the village for doing charities and when they got word about my predicament they came knocking at our door. It was the first time we had met them but they wanted to do a benefit day at The Cricket Club. And could I get some of my tribute friends to do a spot. That wasn't a problem I asked Rob Leigh (Neil Diamond) and he just said yes straight away. I also asked Steve Sinclair (Tom Jones) and he said yes as well, i'd lost touch with TJ Slater my mentor who did Tom Jones. I said to the Twinnies to sort the artistes with some expenses which they agreed whole heartedly. On the day the club was jam packed, a lot from The Dyers from the week before, I was stuck for words. Twinnies and their Tug'O'War friends were circulating with raffle tickets and football cards and it was generally a great day. Alan and Louise came as did John Clews and his wife Donna, John had done the Dyers Charity night for me and was doing the odd disco there as well.

In the end Twinnies and the wonderful people of Littleborough raised £1400 on the day and a further £200 came in afterwards. So add to that The Dyers money raised and everyone had raised £2,400 for us. I thanked the tribute acts and all the people that was there and we went home on a crest of an emotional wave. These wonderful people of Littleborough that we had known for just six months had lifted our spirits and let us know that we belonged there amongst them, they were indeed real friends.

I got a call from Gary Marriott at Omega Promotions. He asked if I wanted to do a show at an army base in Germany. He told me he would be there doing his comedy show and he would work my mini-disc/songs. Jacqui drove me to Manchester Airport and we met Gary in the cafe. He told me more about the gig. It was at the Officers Mess in Padaborn near Düsseldorf. They paid me well and covered the cost of flights etc. The German promoter met us at Düsseldorf Airport and dropped us in town where Gary and I went for a beer. He had been there lots of times, Gary was a stand up comedian { Jed Stone } aswell as an agent and he'd entertained the troops many times. We finally got to Padaborn and sound checked. Our accommodation was in the barracks which was sparse but it was ok. We got ready for the show, Gary was on first then me and on last was a covers band. Finally I got on stage at around 11.30pm and did an hour and a quarter. Gary had given me a heads up about the officers probably wont get up and dance until they were told by their boss and they wouldn't take their jackets of either.

So I thought you live or die when your on your own on stage so I went at it with both barrels and rocked the place. They were all up dancing minus their jackets, Gary thought I'd get told off but I couldn't care less this was my show and this is how I did it! I had them all dancing on the tables, Gary just laughed and shook his head in disbelief. Afterwards the guy in charge stood in front of me with all his medals on his chest and said " Son I just want to tell you that was the best entertainment Ive ever seen for a very long time well done ". I thanked him and winked at Gary who had a smile as big as a Cheshire cat.

Later on some of the Para's tracked me down at the bar and wanted to know if I would do a parachute dive in the morning with my Elvis suit on! I declined which I regret now. Then they asked if they could borrow my suit to dive in it themselves? Gary got me out of that one by saying our return flight was at 9am. But my God they partied hard they had a champagne breakfast at 6am which was interesting because none of us could stand straight lining up with our breakfast plates. It was comical. We had an hours sleep when Gary woke me to get ready to go home.

What an amazing twenty four hours and it was midweek which was all the better. The following night I was in a restaurant in Manchester which didn't even compare but it was alright and the money was good!

The next time we went Germany I was going to be a support act for a Girls Aloud tribute band. Everything was the same apart from we were playing in a huge aircraft hangar. It was an event for The Sappers and there was around five hundred there. Nice big stage and huge sound system. I sound checked pretty quick and went to the green room. Showtime came and I blew them all away, everyone was up dancing and cheering for more. When I exited the stage this Girls Aloud band were complaining about having to go on after me. I just couldn't understand why people can't just do their show, I've had to follow very popular acts over the years.

When it came time to get on the minibus to go to the hotel, Girls Aloud had gone already, no minibus! Jacqui was fuming, we had no idea where the hotel was so she pulled this General to one side. Now if you can imagine this General was all of 6"7 and Jacqui was all of 5"4 and she was waving her finger at him and reading him the riot act. He looked frightened to death, it was so funny, my little Welsh girl taking charge. The General got one of his lackies and ordered him to get a taxi for Lewis and his wife at the Generals expense and take them to the Hotel! I loved Germany.

I had done shows many times at The Warehouse Nightclub in Penrith. The owner phoned Phil and wanted to book me for his wedding. It involved playing in huge marquee just outside Penrith. He gave us accommodation which was great and we went and sound checked. Ben was with us because I was on at The Cairndale Hotel in Dumfries the following night Ben came to both shows.

Jacqui went into the marquee to start the disc. By this time I was using my helicopter intro with security men talking over on it. It gave the impression Elvis was landing outside and that's what all the wedding guests thought. Most of the two hundred guests rushed outside to see the helicopter to find little old me stood there on my own. There was a collective sigh and they walked backed back inside. Talk about anticlimax, the intro usually built up the atmosphere not deflate it. However John Bowman the groom got up dancing straight away which helped and after four or five songs all was forgiven and everyone was up dancing and having a great time. At the end John Bowman paid me an extra £50 and said he thought the helicopter was excellent.

I played at his Warehouse Nightclub many times after that and it was always crammed with party people.

The gigs with the band began drying up. I didn't know at the time but I was told that Phil had purposely told prospective bookers that I no longer had a band. This was so that he could take advantage of my good nature even more so than he could with four musicians in the way. Anyway more about that shortly. We had a band gig at Northwich Memorial Hall but we'd not sold hardly any tickets. But the show must go on and with around thirty people in the audience we put out an excellent performance. Ben was with us, he was ten at the time so he was at an awkward age never mind the hassle Donna gave him. The management allowed him to use their lighting desk way up in the Gods. It was only one master fade slider and flash fader so it was easy. Until halfway through the second half all the lights just stopped working. He'd done really well all night until Jacqui went upstairs to find him fast asleep, bless him. That was when we realised he needed to have a permanent baby sitter. He came with us sometimes but mostly stayed at home with one of our neighbours.

It was in Northwich we first met Eileen and Steve Sharman. They were very impressed with our show and seemed to like Jacqui and I as well. Eileen had a brain tumour which was inoperable but not terminal. She did regular fund raisers in Northwich at The Bowling Green Club. She asked if I would do a night so I agreed to it. The first night was fantastic and they raised about £1500. Everyone was so pleased. Eileen then asked do I know any other tribute shows that would share the bill with me. So I suggested Rob Leigh as Neil Diamond we had not long started doing our Vegas Nights show. She took a chance on him off my recommendation. What a storming night it was they raised just over £2500 and Steve and Eileen were ecstatic. This started quite a few years of working for Steve and Eileen with our newly formed Vegas Nights Show! And a friendship that lasts up until today.

Phil called with a booking, he said the army want you for some top brass birthday bash. It was for an SAS Captain on the Outer Hebrides. I must have made an impression on the Para's in Germany now the SAS wanted me. You couldn't make this up. I asked Phil what was the transport to the island and he said about forty five minute sail so I just turned it down flat. I was scared to death of any sailing after that experience to the Isle Of Man with my mum years earlier. I asked him if they could fly me in a helicopter I would do it. He got back to them but they were not willing to do that. Phil was having kittens, he kept saying " but its £750 for a solo show "! They wouldn't back down and neither would I. It might sound foolish but when you've got a phobia about anything there's nothing you can do..

I also turned down about six or seven cruise jobs over the years, Caribbean, Mediterranean you name it I wouldn't sail and I still won't today.

In our private life everything was running smoothly. Donna had kept her distance from Ben and he was doing well in his new school. We were firmly embedded in our local village and when we had a drink with our new friends I don't think they believed stories I was telling them about our escapades on the road.

Stuart who had helped us move to Littleborough had disappeared from sight. Somebody told me he was like that, friends with someone and then dropping them. That made me feel better, I thought I had done something wrong. Good job I had paid him back the money for those speakers.

I took our show to The Gracie Fields Theatre in Rochdale again. I thought I would give lots of free tickets to our friends in The Dyers Arms. However only John, Breeda and a handful came which was a shame. I was soon to learn that they didn't really leave the village much, for anything. But that was alright because it was like living in an episode of ITVs Heartbeat set back in the 1960s.

A kids drama class called me about being in a film portraying Elvis. They had come to see my show in Radcliffe once and had suggested I try and do some acting because it was like I was acting during my show. So I called this number and it turned out they wanted two Elvis Impersonators for background work. It paid £175 a day midweek so I thought ok I'll give it a go. I called Stuarts brother, Steve, he did the Elvis part in their show and we both went to Blackpool for three days work. The stars of the film were June Brown and Penelope Keith and they were so down to earth. I thought June Brown would be genuine because of her role Dot Cotton in Eastenders, but I thought maybe Penelope Keith might be a bit snooty with her posh accent. However I was wrong she was so down to earth and spent a lot of time with all of us.

We were in background roles such as walking on the Pleasure Beach and on the Ferris Wheel. Which they got us to sing as we went around, then promptly wouldn't let us off and speeded up the wheel, that was so funny, you had to be there.

The main part me and Steve were in was on the train with a group of George Formby Impersonators. We had June and Penelope sat in front with us all around them. Then the director says ok this scene is where everyone is singing " Leaning on a Lampost "? Steve and I looked at each other and Steve said hold on we knew nothing about this we don't even know the lyrics. So the director suggested we just do a few " huh huh huh's " throughout the song. So we did, it was hysterical but just added to the comical scene. On the last day of filming I was to appear on the back seat of an open top bus on the Promenade kissing the Marilyn Monroe lookalike. It was for the closing credits. How lucky was I, kissing Marilyn!

We set off and got onto the M61 towards Blackpool and there was a really bad traffic jam, I didn't make it on time and missed out. Just my luck!

But the film was called " Margery and Gladys " and was released in 2003. That was my last attempt at acting. Too much standing around in costume freezing cold in Blackpool.

Then came the ill fated 25th Anniversary tour in 2002. It was twenty five years since Elvis had passed and I wanted to do a big tour with the band. Phil didn't! Probably too much hard work. So he placated me and booked a few paid shows and some ticketed theatre shows. It started at twenty four shows but dwindled very fast and we ended up with just fourteen. The first was at The Cairndale Hotel in Dumfries. It was a sell out, which it usually was at that venue, I had a good following there. Phil had insisted on hiring two dancers for the tour against my better judgement I agreed. They worked at The Cairndale and we never saw them again. Someone said Phil had tried it on with one of them. He probably scared them off. For the rest of the tour he was constantly reminding me to apologise for the absence of the dancers.

From Dumfries we headed south doing shows in the north west, the midlands and then found ourselves in a place called Chard in Somerset. It was a social club that was run by an ex-BBC producer who organized everything in minute detail. Of course when I introduced myself and apologised about the dancers he hit the roof. By this time I was pretty tired so I told him to call Phil it was his fault. We set up the gear and sound checked then this guy came over to me threatening to pay the fee minus the dancers wage which was £200. I agreed to this then I had Phil on the phone moaning about the situation. I told him about the fee situation and I also told him the dancers fee on this show would come off his commission. He didn't like that at all but I told him he could like it or lump it! I also pulled him about the accommodation. Jacqui and I had a guest house which was nice but he put the band in tents on a caravan park. They were quite annoyed when they found this out. All Phil kept saying was " but its summer everywhere is booked up " absolute rubbish he was trying to get the band to quit, I have no doubt about that. Poor Ricky ended up in a sleeping bag in the van.

The show itself went down extremely well and the ex BBC man was gushing afterwards. He also gave me some advice, he said I didn't need a manager like Phil. He told me to manage myself and I would get further in my career. Jacqui and I agreed with him. This tour was a hotch potch of gigs poorly planned and half of them didn't even have contracts.

We travelled from Somerset to Lowestoft in Suffolk to The Marina Theatre

for the last but one show on the tour. At last a proper theatre and it was sold out eleven hundred Elvis fans, I felt vindicated that what I was trying to create was actually coming true!

Stuart the promoter from Whirlwind Promotions was a lovely man. Nothing was too much trouble and he even put us all in a guest house for the night. The only thing he wanted was a mention for Whirlwind at the end of the show. That was simple I would have done that anyway.

What a show it was! Probably the stand out song was Bridge Over Troubled Water. You could hear a pin drop, I felt alive, the feeling of holding a large audience in the palm of my hands was exhilarating. It was a high I had never experienced before with such a large audience. When I first got the band together that was a high but this was a hundred times stronger. Everything just fell into place I just wish my mum could have been there........maybe she was.

We did the usual two song encore and the audience were going bananas. In truth we could have done ten encores and they would still have wanted more. We were all buzzing!

Stuart came back stage and booked us there and then for the following August . I told him that Jacqui and I had agreed to fire Phil when we got back to Manchester. So he said he would call me next week. Which he did and there started a good relationship with a great promoter.

The last show on the tour was a solo gig in a pub in Warrington. This was on the actual Anniversary night. I wasn't best pleased especially after the previous nights success. Don't get me wrong pubs are alright but on the 25th Anniversary I wanted something special. The band was not happy either sat back at home twiddling their thumbs.

The outcome was there was no more than twenty people in the audience and the landlord was obnoxious. I was glad the tour was over.

I found out later that Phil had booked another Elvis Impersonator, Liberty Mounten and his band, into the The Concorde Suite in London for the actual Anniversary night 16th August? For the fee of £2500 and there's me playing solo in a pub in Warrington for £500! What the hell was he playing at it should have been me and my band playing at the prestigious Concorde Suite!

I decided to not call Phil on the Monday, I needed to rest and get my energy back. So on the Tuesday I called him and told him he was fired. He managed me on a handshake so there was nothing he could do. He wasn't best pleased but I told him it was his own fault. He was spending too much time at the Bookies and the Casino, he obviously had a gambling problem. Well he wasn't gambling money that he had scammed off the top of my fees any longer. The phone call was brief, he was threatening all sorts of things and he said he wanted commission off any future bookings I had that he had booked. Which you would normally think was right and proper, but if I told you he owed me just over £4,000 when I added it up. You'll understand why I told him to get lost, he'd had enough of my hard earned money!

For God's sake I ran his office for two weeks while he was on a Caribbean cruise and made plenty of bookings and commission for him. I ran it remote from my house and I must have spent over £100 in phone calls to London,Scotland and Wales etc. His payment to me was a bottle of Jim Bean! I don't even like the stuff. I was too soft with him but hindsight is a wonderful thing.

I knew I had to act fast with regards to future bookings for the diary. I put an advert in the Stage Newspaper stating that I was no longer associated with Ambassador Promotions and Phil Hughes. It was quite strong but I had to stand up for myself. I put my phone number at the bottom hoping some agents might call me direct. Oh my God! The following day the phone never stopped ringing! Johnny Peller called asking what had happened so I told him, I was completely truthful with him. He told me I was better off managing myself and said he would book me direct with the terms he used with all acts. Other agents that called were Omega Promotions, Henderson Management, Big Foot Events,

Vegas Entertainment, Essex Entertainment, Shout Promotions, MBA, Quality Promotions, John Ford Productions, Bob Crossland Agency, The Edge and a good few more that I cant quite recall. I told them all the same thing I had told Johnny Peller. All of them reacted in the same way, they were glad to be dealing with me direct!

I had always wanted my Dad to be proud of me, all children do especially sons. I had got him to come to The Gracie Fields Theatre earlier in the year. He came backstage afterwards to meet the band but then left abruptly. So I tried again by offering two free tickets to come and watch my solo show at The Birch Hotel, literally two miles from his home. He said he wasn't sure but eventually agreed. Phil Hughes was also there, it was a venue he supplied tribute shows to, he was after his commission? The tickets cost me £25 each and they included a meal and my show. I was so pleased that Dad and his wife Ann were there. I pulled out all the stops to impress so he would be proud and also to show Phil what he had lost!
But alas Dad and Ann both left straight after I finished again. He knew it only took me five minutes to get changed and to come and mingle and sign autographs etc. That was the night it really hit home that he really didn't care whatsoever about his only son. I was quite upset.

As for Phil he was stood near while I was signing autographs and having my picture took with people. I just gave him a look, "if your looking for trouble" look, and he exited the building rather rapid. I swear to God I would have punched him right in the face if he tried to talk to me. He had some cheek to turn up, maybe he wanted commission from the gig. He had no chance of that or indeed of any future commissions.

Young Paul at Johnny Pellers Agency called and asked would I travel to Carlisle on a Wednesday night for £500, absolutely! He said it was Carlisle Working Men's Club and there was a band on as well. I got to the venue and saw the poster for the event, I was support act to the sixties band The Fortunes. I thought wow this is going to be great. I walked into the club at 5pm to set up and sound check only to find there was absolutely no room on the stage for me. So I thought that's alright I'll play on the dance floor. But there was still no room onstage for my speakers etc. so I asked one of the Fortunes could I possibly link my mixing rack into there's, all that was needed was two channels in their 32 channel mixing desk. His reply was " It'll cost you £60 " I was a bit shocked. In the tribute world we always linked into each others mixers if there was two or three tributes on the bill. I was quite angry to be honest, I told him no problem I'm on before you so I'll set up my small speakers up on the dance floor in front of theirs. I made a another attempt to get on with them backstage, but they seemed to think they were still stars and acted like it. They looked down their noses at me and were pretty rude so you know me it was like a red rag to a bull!

I went on stage/dance-floor and ripped the place apart. I really gave it everything to show these obnoxious has been's a lesson. The audience were on their feet and stomping on the tables when I finished " WE WANT ELVIS ". I walked passed The Fortunes dressing room and they all stood there with their mouths wide open in shock. I just said " your turn boys "

The organiser came back stage to pay me and told me The Fortunes had refused to go on stage until the audience had calmed down. What a bunch of narrow minded fools.

Jacqui and I decided to watch there set and lo and behold a few of them were miming with vocals and instruments. We stood at the back and could see their sound man tweaking channels apart from the channels that were used for miming. Why would they mime they were sixties legends. I found out off the organiser that their fee was only £750 and out of that there was five musicians and two sound engineers/roadies to pay. This organiser had only gone and told them what my fee was so they were miffed that I was getting more than them individually and I was only a tribute act not a proper act like them! This explained the nastiness at the start of the evening but to me that was totally unprofessional. Whatever show your doing you just do it and don't worry about other acts!

Rob Leigh and I had become close friends by now and we promoted each others shows to venues and agents wherever we were appearing. One job that Rob got me was for a Tribute set at a Sixties Weekend in Ayr. It was at the old Pontin's campsite now privately owned. The promoter phoned me with the details. I was being paid £600 for an hours set at two in the afternoon. All I needed to take was my minidisc and myself. This was the first time Jacqui had worked a 32 channel mixing desk on her own. She did magnificently the sound was great, the audience was great and we were back home by teatime for chippy tea.

One bad note was we met Herman's Hermits and they were just as grumpy as The Fortunes. I was beginning to see a pattern but I wasn't bothered we were laughing all the way to the bank.

I got Rob quite a few gigs over the years and him me.

That December I was really busy doing the Christmas Party nights at hotels and Restaurants etc. One of them was at The Van Dyke Hotel near Chesterfield. I usually did this venue three or four times a year so I was very familiar with it. It was a sell out as usual and before I went on stage the manager came and warned me about a group of women on a hen night. He said they very rowdy and had been drinking all day. So as I walked out on stage I clocked where they were and was prepared for anything. What I wasn't prepared for was when I had my guitar on singing CC Rider, one of the women walked straight up to me and took her top off revealing everything. Its not often I get stuck for words but I honestly didn't know what to say. I was blushing while laughing! I just carried on singing and after a while the audience started booing her so she left me alone and everyone cheered. I joked with them asking who's next?

New Years Eve found us in Leicester in a refurbished Town Hall. I was on with a Madonna Tribute act who I had worked with before. Whoever thought the two would mix had surely been on something. She was really nice and went on first. By this time word had spread about not going on stage after my show. I had worked with Marie Lloyd the Uks best Cher Tribute act and she flatly refused to go on last. She said to Phil that " there was no way she was going on after Lewis ". Anyway in Leicester the

221

show went down extremely well and I had been paid extra to play some music afterwards. Not to be a DJ just to play some dance music. After I had changed I came from backstage and Jacqui had the place bouncing, everyone was on the dance floor. It was 11.30pm so we decided to keep it going until midnight then I would bring the New Year in on stage and sing some rock n roll songs to keep the atmosphere going. It was one of the best New Years Eves we did. At around 1am we slowed it down with me singing Queens " We Are The Champions "! Wow what a reaction everybody had their arms in the air singing it with me! It was great!

As 2003 dawned we had a full diary and life was good. Ben had moved up to Wardle High School and he was happy, as were we.

I had purposely left two weeks empty in the diary, we had booked our first proper holiday as a family. We went to the Greek island of Rhodes and it was fantastic. We hired a car and covered most of the island. One of the highlights was at the very south of Rhodes we saw the two oceans meet, it was a bit surreal. We loved the old town area and had many meals in the tavernas.

We got back all refreshed and ready to go! Then our neighbour Mary knocked on and said she had brought the washing in for us? We had only left a few towels on the line and left the back door unlocked. Two weeks with the door unlocked, unbelievable, it really was like stepping back in time to when people trusted and looked out for each other.

We had truly landed in place of yesteryear, humble, kind and genuinely nice people!

First Band Publicity designed
by my Manager Phil Hughes

After a show at Leeds University 2002

Second Band Publicity
designed by me in 2003

Jacqui & me in Florida our favourite place

Jacqui and i after Phil Hughes
Showcase at The Willows, Salford

My Good friend The Legendary TJ Slater
(Tom Jones) at New York Club, Southport
Support Act to Me and the band

Corporate Event in London
in nightclub opposite The Ritz Hotel

My right hand man and friend Big John

My showbiz Dad Alan singing
for me at my 40th birthday party

Jacqui's surprise 40th birthday party

Our great friends Ken & Julie at Jacqui's 40th

My best mate Buddy

Our fantastic neighbours in Littleborough
Mary, Barbara and Ray, they were the best

The movie i was in with June Brown
and Penelope Keith, both were so nice

Barclays Corporate Event
Devere Grand Hotel Brighton

Circus Casino Stoke-on-trent 2007

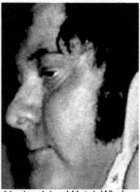

Monkey Island Hotel, Windsor

Our Wedding 2008 Above Jacqui, Lydia & Sophie
Top Right: Jacqui & Me...Mid: Jacqui, Ben,
Me & John...Below: At the Hungarian Club...
Bottom right: My good friends Joe & his mum
Betty

ROR Publicity 2010

On stage at The Gamecock Inn, Bury 2011

On stage with ROR, Ben on
drums, a dream come true!

**Plank
Ben
Quo**

Backstage Tommy Slash
and Iain Van Halen

Our Publicity

My good friend Rob Leigh R.I.P

Some of the clients we worked
for with Vegas Nights and my
solo & live band show

At Warners Thoresby Hall 2008

Elvis Kitchen opens in 2012

Jacqui's Front of House team
Jade, Jacqui, Jess & Rosie

The ELVIS Chef...David Elliott
with my best mate Rob Leigh
after his Neil Diamond show

On stage at Elvis Kitchen
C.C Rider 2013

My old friend Denis Williams
proposed to Bev at EK

Jerry Talks about Elvis on EK2s
opening night, a true gentleman

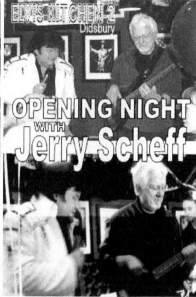

Jerry telling Elvis stories

Singing with Elvis' Bass Player
big highlight of my career

The RCA Band with Jerry Scheff
Kalvin, Me, Jerry, Ben, Liviu & James

My best friend of over 45 years
Steve McKay when he came to EK

One of my favourite pics of Ben and me
taken after one of his gigs in Manchester

The Final Farewell
18th March 2018

Jacqui & Me at home 2023

Chapter 16

2003-2004....ANYWAY YOU WANT ME

As 2004 dawned the band and I were booked into a huge Social Club in Wrexham for the Elvis Presley Fan Club. I had tried without success to get bookings with various Elvis fan clubs. I have no idea why none of them took the bait. I had always offered my show for free, I wanted to see how we went down with real Elvis fans.

Todd Slaughter the head of The Official Elvis Presley Fan Club of Great Britain sent me a very derisory letter stating that they didn't advocate Elvis Impersonators and then went and booked Big Jim White? I tried him the year after and he didn't even reply?

Anyway the Welsh Fan Club took the gamble and I was really pumped up for it. It was a sell out with 400 people crammed into this Social Club. We absolutely stormed the place, the dance floor was full and they were stood on their seats and tables cheering for more. It was a very satisfying concert, knowing that true Elvis fans did approve of what I was doing. It was after all a 100% tribute to The King!

Ben had come with us on this gig and he was very inquisitive and annoying about everything. To the point of being a pain. After the show the adrenaline was high throughout the band and Guy and Neil decided to teach Ben a lesson and put his head down the toilet and flushed it. It was hilarious, Ben was finally quiet! However the next thing that happened was Neil jumping off the toilet cubicle onto the toilet which then smashed into pieces. We all packed up our gear quickly and made a hasty exit. We never got pulled for it but I did have a word with Neil to calm down a bit, it could have cost me a lot of money.

The Official Elvis Fan Club Welsh Branch Leader that had booked me was over the moon and said he would be in touch for a booking the following year. You guessed it no phone call came, so I called him. His response was pathetic, if you can believe this......" You sang Wooden Heart in a white jumpsuit and Elvis never did that so Ive been told I cant book you again!". WHAT! What a load of nonsense, Elvis did indeed sing Wooden Heart in Las Vegas in 1975 in a white jumpsuit? I've got it on video. But more to the point who had told him he couldn't book me? He said Todd Slaughter!!

This Todd Slaughter guy was beginning to get on my nerves. Here I was performing free of charge for the true Elvis fans and because for some reason he had taken a dislike to me I was blocked, I wasn't allowed to perform free of charge for Elvis fans? He had never even met me?

Well more fool him, he was missing out on a quality authentic Elvis Presley Tribute Show. What a complete fool.

I never played for an Elvis Fan Club again, not by choice I might add.

Later on something happened with Todd Slaughter which made me smile, but more about that later.

I got a call to do a show at a nightclub in Cleethorpes. Well I say a nightclub, it was a dump where people would go after the pubs closed. The contract from Big Foot Events stated to perform two forty five minute sets between 10pm and 12pm for £500. When we got there and set up nobody seemed to know what was happening so I thought I'd start at 10pm then go on for the second set at 11.15pm leaving me to finish at midnight. The first set went down really well with the few that were in and as I was about to go on at 11.15pm the Manager came running into the dressing room telling me not to go on until midnight. Absolutely alright with me if you pay me nightclub money an extra £200. He flatly refused and told me my contract said the fee was £500. Yes £500 is hotel and restaurant prices, nightclub prices and times are more. I told him to call the agent at which point he said "You'll never work at this venue again", I thought that was so funny, as if I needed a crummy pick up joint in Cleethorpes. He came back and said he couldn't get hold of the agent so I told him I could go on now but if you want me on at midnight he'd have to pay the extra and up front. He stormed off again and then sent his underling to tell me he wasn't paying me at all! So I sent him a message back saying that was ok The Musicians Union would take him to court for my fee. The message returned telling me to go on stage now and he would pay the fee.

I did the second set and it was getting a bit lively with the drunks from the pubs coming in. Amazingly he told the security to not help if it got rowdy. It did get rowdy but I handled it.

Later when Jacqui went to get paid the manager had gone home and left an envelope with my fee made up of all five pound notes.

He must have been from the same company as Todd Slaughter......Idiots Are Us!!

The following week Big Foot Events called saying this nightclub wanted me back? I politely declined and explained what had happened, and not long after Big Foot Events stopped supplying to the venue.

We knew we had fitted in with the locals in Littleborough when Ryan (John and Breeda's grandson) walked straight into our house without knocking and plonked down on the sofa. " Hiya Pete ", " Hiya Ryan ". Let me just say that Ryan has learning difficulties and he only ever walked into peoples houses without knocking if he felt comfortable with them. I was a bit emotional but we watched television for a bit then he just got up and said " I'm off now Pete bye " and he was gone. Ryan was one of my biggest fans. Especially when I let him sing at The Dyers one night, I could see he was itching to sing but Breeda had told him it wasn't karaoke and that he wasn't allowed. That was enough for me, I got him up and he sang a couple of songs and finished with a duet with me. The audience was cheering very loudly!

Johnny Peller called me for a gig with my band at Bath Racecourse. This was before all the big racecourse events they have today with the big stars. We set up our gear in what I can only explain was a stage, situated right next to the track, with a bouncy castle upside down above us, it was weird. The event organizer asked us to start at 7pm. At 6.55pm he came back and asked to change it to 7.15pm. Then he came back and asked if we could start after the final race at 7.30pm. With his direction of when the band saw the horses pass the stage to begin the show.

235

So the horses came and the band started up 2001 Theme. It was so loud the horses heads were looking around to see where the loud noise was coming from, it was comical.

Then it started to rain but the audience really enjoyed it while we were all freezing cold.

Worcester Racecourse got in touch next but this time it was a solo show with a couple of dancers I was using at the time. We got changed downstairs on an open topped bus which we were to perform on upstairs. When it was time we started on top of this bus which did a right turn driving around to the front of the Grandstand, it was very cool. There was about 2000 left in the Grandstand I kept it all uptempo and they all joined in singing and dancing with me. It was a great experience and the organizers were superb.

This Rock'n'Roller Coaster I was on was a wild ride!

I got in touch with Arlene Heyman, Adam Carters manager, his show encompassed three Elvis era's but his best was the fifties and sixties of the Elvis period. I was looking to put together a theatre show together with the two of us and my band. So we went to The Tickled Trout Hotel in Preston where Adam had been performing the night before and had quite a good meeting about how I thought the show should flow etc. To my surprise Arlene and Adam agreed with virtually all of my ideas. Arlene had a reputation of being hard to deal with but I found her to be alright.

I started working on some artwork for the new show and with a few tweaks she was happy with it. Arlene had a few connections in theatre land and she said she would make some enquiries However she drew a blank, she even tried The London Palladium but the hire costs were too expensive.

I had done a show near Chester and the hotel manager passed on my details to his friends at Clear Channel in London. The hotel manager had given me a brilliant reference so they were curious.

I arranged a meeting in Rochdale with two of their AnR men and showed them my plans for the show. It wasn't going to be a run of the mill Elvis show, I had plans for each segment to be introduced by having Elvis on a huge screen video montage. Adam would do the 50s Rock n Roll Era and the 68 Comeback

Special, I would be doing early 70's and The Final Concerts 1977. Then we would both finish the show with An American Trilogy.

The AnR men were very impressed with the layout plan the only thing they were sceptical about was the costings. They thought both Elvis's should get a bit less and the band too. I couldn't believe my ears, I had put a very reasonable breakdown together with me and Adam down for earning £300 each per night, that was a lot less than our normal fees. So I decided to play my ace card, I asked them to listen to our demo CD, I asked the manager of the restaurant could he just play the first two songs on the CD. Up first was Adam and they seemed impressed with him. Then came me singing Hurt and they had wary smiles on their faces. They asked me was it really me singing or was it the real Elvis, I told them it was me. They asked if they could take the CD with them and they would be in touch. I was quite hopeful.

A few weeks went by and I'd heard nothing so I gave them a call, the number was not recognised. So I got in touch with the Chester hotel manager that had originally put us forward to his friends. He said to leave it with him. This would have been a big game changer for my career so I wasn't best pleased when I tried to call The Chester manager back and he had left the hotel permanently! I desperately called Clear Channel's office in London. The secretary explained that the AnR men had said I had tried to con them with Elvis real voice on the demo CD! I pleaded my case but she wasn't for listening and just brushed me off. I tried the week after but I got the same response.

So that was that, an other avenue blocked!

About a year later John Tremayne (my bass player) was at in my house having a coffee when who comes on the TV but a below par Elvis act explaining what his theatre show was about. It was exactly the same as mine and guess what? It was promoted by Clear Channel! I was learning very quickly who to trust and who not to trust. And to make sure I copyrighted my ideas. I suppose them thinking my voice was Elvis real voice was a big compliment but I never saw it like that at the time.

On to some people that are nice. I got a call from a guy called Martin who lived in Croston in Lancashire. I told him my price for the midweek event and he agreed. We arrived at this pub and it was tiny, I was wondering how Martin could afford it. When he arrived he told me there would be thirty five people attending and they had all paid £10 each, which added up to my £350 midweek fee.

What a great night we had, they were all real Elvis fans and were shouting requests for rare songs which I normally never got to perform so I gladly obliged.

This started a great friendship with Martin, his wife Angela and Jackie and Neil. In fact they even came to our wedding in 2008.

These people gave me back faith in mankind!

Now that I was managing myself I discussed with Jacqui about putting some theatre shows on ourselves. I felt that being on a theatre stage was where I was born to be. She agreed but advised to doing just a few to start off with. Of course I had my annual theatre show at The Marina Theatre in Lowestoft but I had ambitions to do more.

My band were very excited about the prospect so I booked three theatres. Gracie Fields Theatre in Rochdale, Heywood Civic Center and The Longfield Suite in Prestwich, Manchester. I spaced them apart so we had three or four months to promote each one.

At The Gracie Fields I left twenty free tickets behind the bar at my local The Dyers Arms. Alas only six turned up on the night, maybe they weren't theatre types. We didn't sell many tickets to the public either. We had put posters all round town and advertised in the local paper but in the end we only had sixty seven in the audience. Not many for a theatre that seats almost seven hundred,

At Heywood Civic they had actually paid me a guaranteed fee so it wasn't such a gamble. It was less than I would ask for with the band but at least I wouldn't lose any money. It sold out, six hundred, I couldn't believe it! It was a brilliant night and the band were really hot, we all had a great time and afterwards I even had a queue for autographs.

Then we did The Longfield Suite. It was a huge room with a huge theatre size stage. We had put posters up all around the area and in the venue. Two weeks before the event I phoned the box office only to be told they hadn't sold one ticket?

This was really strange because I was popular in the area. I smelt a rat. So I got my old friend John Clews to call the box office, they told him the event was Sold Out and no tickets were left? Something funny was going on and I was determined to get to the bottom of it. Firstly we went to all the shops, chippy's and taxi ranks we had put posters up and you guessed it, they had all been taken down. Then I headed to the venue and spoke with the assistant manager, a young guy who had been to see my show and liked it. He told me about this other Elvis, Elvis Williamson who played at the venue regularly and apparently gave some of his fee to the General Manager to make sure he was the only Elvis to play at the venue. This was shocking, when I originally met with the General Manager and signed a contract to appear there, he told me that no other Elvis was playing there?. I made an appointment to speak with the General Manager. I asked him why the box office was telling everyone the event was sold out? He denied this so I told him about Johns phone call and told him it had been recorded. We all went downstairs to the box office and he told his staff off. By this time we were one week before the event! I told him it was too late to be telling his staff off when clearly they had been instructed to say it was a sell out and no more tickets were available. He pleaded with me to not cancel the booking. I was undecided, I spoke with John Tremayne about what had happened and he advised to do the gig and afterwards to sue the venue for loss of earnings. I decided to go along with Johns suggestion and do the show.

We had about ten people in attendance in a room that held three hundred. I felt humiliated but John kept lifting my spirits. He even presented me with a painting of my mum that he had painted, He was a painter in his spare time and I was overwhelmed with it. It did cheer me up with all the shennanigans of the tickets.

I got to the bottom of everything that went wrong with the event. Elvis Williamson had been tipped off by Phil Hughes that I was performing at   The Longfield Suite and urged him to take all the posters down around the town. He had also, in conjunction with the General Manager, conspired to cancel my show through the box office! Of course I couldn't prove this but some time later one of Phil's friends told me everything.

The Longfield Suite was owned by Bury Council so I started proceedings to sue Bury Council.

When the day of the court case arrived I was told by the usher that Jacqui could not enter the court with me. So I was on my own when I walked into court to find that the Longfield Suite had three people on there team. We both got to say our versions and the Judge said that both parties would receive the verdict by post.

About a week later I got the letter and the verdict was in favour of me. Phew I had won the case and the judge had awarded me £2000 and also Bury Council would pay my costs.

Two weeks later I got a letter saying Bury Council was appealing the decision and a court date would be allocated soon.

When I got to Bury Court for the appeal the same thing happened again, I was the only person allowed into court and they brought a barrister and three people from the venue including the young assistant manager who couldn't look me in the eye. It was a different judge which I didn't mind but a strange thing happened, this barrister spoke at length about my unprofessionalism and that I was unreliable and therefore the case should be squashed? The judge had his say and he was clearly on their side. Then he made his decision that there was no case and Bury Council had won their appeal. I got up to speak my case and the judge said I wasn't allowed to say anything as this was an appeal? I couldn't believe it, I had been shafted! The original case was so black and white and Bury Councils Barrister waffles nonsense and I don't get to reply? To say I was angry was an understatement, I got up and told them all what I thought.

240

Then I looked straight at the judge and told him he was bent and how much had they paid him! I stormed out and Jacqui drove me home. I was fully expecting a letter telling me I had to pay Bury Councils court costs. I did get a letter saying the case was closed, I wasn't allowed to appeal it and I had no court costs to pay? Are you kidding me? The loser in a court case almost always covers the cost. All I could think was it was the judges guilty conscience, it had to be. What an absolute joke!

I needed to get back on stage. Luckily enough we had a full diary so I didn't have to wait too long. Colin the infamous ABBA Girls manager called me and gave me some bookings, commission free. I got him a few bookings in return. Anyway one gig he got me was an Indian restaurant near Cambridge, Wednesday night £450 nett in my back pocket. To be fair they treated us well, it was a big success and they sent us home with a big bag of Indian cuisine. We ended up doing the venue twice a year until the recession hit in 2008.

Another gig Colin got us was for the learning difficulties which was held at Cheltenham Town Hall. We were in the smaller function suite that held about one hundred. It was a strange one this because they wanted me on stage at 10am – Noon, two sets and we were home by teatime with a wad of money in Jacqui's purse. The organizer was disabled himself, he used to be in a band so he was interested in all the acts that were booked, he was lovely.

As for the audience, they were brilliant. I had them up on stage with me, I thought it would collapse at one point. But they were all so polite and respectful. It gave me back faith in human beings after the court trial.

They all wanted their photo's with me afterwards which I was more than happy to do. I loved doing those gigs.

Bob Carruthers secretary called again with some gigs. One was at a restaurant in Wandsworth in London, which went down a storm. Another was at a small hotel in Stratford Upon Avon where Bob lived. It was his movie company's Cromwell Productions Christmas Party. We set up at the venue, Bob walked in and paid us prior to the gig and made us feel comfortable paying for a bedroom for us. He knocked on the bedroom door and when Jacqui opened it he said " I forgot earlier, here's a little something for your Ben for Christmas " £50, I was stuck for words. I guess he classed us as part of his work family. The show went really well, Bob introduced me as coming from Macclesfield again! He did this every time. I have no idea why, perhaps he didn't like the sound of Rochdale? Who knows, I was just happy to be earning good money off him. It was always a pleasure doing Bobs gigs. He treated us like family every time!

Despite Phil Hughes efforts my band were still just about working. The only way I could think of to keep them busy was to offer them to other Elvis impersonators when I was doing solo gigs. I kept a duplicate diary so I knew when they were unavailable. It meant I missed out on a few gigs but at least I knew the quality of the band when I needed them and I was overloaded with solo gigs anyway.

One show I did with the band was for Barclays Bank at Ragley Hall in Cheshire. It was a venue they owned and they had several balls there throughout the year. We went down that well they booked us to do another summer ball at The Devere Grand Hotel in Brighton. The same hotel that the IRA had bombed back in the eighties. By this time I had a long wheel base transit van so all the bands gear and all of us could travel together. I had it partitioned off with seats built in.
On the way down Jacqui said to the band feel free if anyone wants to take over the driving. Jonathan (keyboards) offered and on our way we went. After about an hour unbelievably we ran out of petrol! Jacqui hit the roof why didn't Jon say we were low on petrol? So we're stuck on the hard shoulder about an hour away from Brighton. Chris (guitarist) set off to the nearest petrol station with a jerry can. Eventually he got back and we got to the petrol station to fill up.

We got to the hotel with just thirty minutes to sound check which would normally take about an hour. Anyway we got it done just in time. The show went down a storm and they were all

242

jokingly bowing before me at the end. I didn't care I was just relieved to have got to the hotel in time.

After the show I positioned myself near the bar so I could be seen if anyone wanted to speak to me. TJ Slater taught me this, he said the more your seen after the show the more chances people might approach you for a private booking etc. So this guy came up to me and started asking me intelligent questions about the show. He was very complimentary and then he asked " how much are you charging us? ". I was a little hesitant but I told him £1750. He then blew me away and told me he was the Managing Director of Barclays and we should be charging them at least double that amount! I tried not to look shocked but inside my heart was racing. As he walked away another guy came up to me (TJ's wise words were paying off   ) he asked if they paid me extra would me and my pianist Jonathan play and sing in the piano bar for an hour. He said they wanted a sing-a-long. Having just been told it was alright to charge Barclays £3500+ next time, I said to him to keep the beer and wine flowing we didn't need paying extra. So that's what we did for about an hour or two. Barclays had already paid for our accommodation at the hotel so we just partied. At one point the Managing Director stood next to me singing whatever Jonathan was playing, it was a great night.

We did several shows for Barclays that year at The Belfry and some Hilton Hotels which were all in the same vain, they treated us with the utmost respect and we always had accommodation if we wanted it. Then around a year later I was reading the newspaper and the headlines were all about high level corruptness at Barclays. It turned out that the Managing Director who told me to charge them more had been found fiddling millions of pounds off Barclays and had fled back to the states where he was from. There was a photo of this guy in the paper and I thought oh my God no wonder he was encouraging me to charge more. I was on peanuts compared to what he was scamming!

I was regularly doing five star hotels and restaurants and while I was doing one in the midlands I saw this tall Elvis looking guy sat in the front row. He was very polite and applauding me

243

during the show and afterwards he came backstage and was very complimentary. He said he had always wanted to see my show again, he had seen my show years ago in Rhyl when he was a kid and that I had blew him away. He said his name was Rocky and then corrected himself saying RockE was his stage name. I used to get crackpots coming backstage all the time telling me they could sing better than me! But this RockE seemed different, apart from being six foot five and having a better resemblance to Elvis than I did.

We became friends and he came up to Rochdale a couple of times, John Bass Player took me down to his house in the midlands and we had a jam session together. He did a few gigs with my band and they seemed to like him. They all said he couldn't light a candle to my voice but he was very imposing and impressive with the audience.

Then one day he called me and asked if I wanted to do a show together. Not just any old show, he wanted to do a theatre show with me. With the experience of Clear Channel still fresh in my memory I trod very carefully.

He paid me a visit and outlined his ideas which all sounded very good. I put my input in and we both agreed it would be a great show. We didn't have the capital to fund a nationwide tour so we booked three theatre shows in the midlands near to where he lived, he said a lot of people would attend because he was very popular in his home town. Of course I had a following in the midlands as well so it seemed a good idea.

I went ahead and booked Dudley Town Hall and Stourbridge Civic Centre, RockE booked a very large social club in West Bromwich. We had to put deposits down on all of them and like a fool I put the money up, RockE said he couldn't afford it. Anyway it came to a total of around £400.

I got to work on the video intro's we were going to use similar to the Clear Channel debacle. RockE got to work on stage costumes and getting that authentic look. The final part of the show was me playing Elvis in his last concert. RockE gave me an authentic Electrovoice microphone and wind shield and authentic scarves to throw to the audience. I'd not done this since for a while and i was very excited about it all.

Dudley Town Hall was the first show and they had Sold Out 1100 seats when I called about how many we had sold. This was three weeks prior. Two weeks prior I called RockE and I couldn't get hold of him, I tried him two or three times a day for a week. Obviously his bottle had gone and he wouldn't speak with me. At that short notice I wouldn't be able to get another Elvis in and the band learn the different keys for the new guy. But the main thing was if I could have pulled it off there would have been a backlash by the RockE fans that would have attended. He was so popular and I reckoned about three quarters of the audience would have been there for him. I couldn't give them there ticket money back I had overheads and it would have meant I would have lost money.

So I called Dudley Town Halls box office and told them what had happened. They were not best pleased at all, which I totally understood but I was in dire straits at this point. I cancelled Stourbridge Civic Center, they had sold about fifty percent of the tickets but were very nice about it. I left the social club in West Bromwich to RockE to deal with, after all it was his venue so to speak.

That was the end of that show and it was a great shame because I know we could have got it off the ground and toured with it. It wasn't going to be like the usual Elvis theatre shows, we had some really special touches to make it unique. And because RockE bottled it I was left out of pocket to the tune of around £900 (Posters, Venue Hire, Radio Advertising etc.,).

I kept trying to call him but he wouldn't answer. So if your reading this RockE, for a very tall imposing man you have the heart of a mouse and I have lost all respect for you!

I was booked into The Village Hotel in Whiston. I had been there a few times but this time the Manager warned me about the new sound limiter. You could see the limiter on the back wall. With this in mind I sound checked and it was alright. When I came on stage later I was only on my fourth song when the power went off. I got Jacqui to turn it down a little while the Manager reset the limiter. This went on for every other song until I got completely annoyed, I gave Jacqui the microphone and sang accapella The Wonder Of You. Of course the audience who were by now all on the dance-floor, joined in, and lo and behold the limiter went off again, I didn't stand a chance I shouted to the audience what was happening and I had to finish the show. The Manager came to my room afterwards and apologised profusely but I told him I wouldn't be coming back unless he got rid of that limiter. He said he couldn't and had to follow orders from head office.

It was just embarrassing, the audience must have thought my equipment was faulty. They had these limiter boxes in the pubs and working mens clubs that I played in twenty years ago and you just had to put up with them, you needed the money. Fortunately I wasn't in that position now so when the agent asked me to go back to The Village Hotel in Whiston I politely declined.

The Americana Festival in Lincolnshire was our next stop. The band and I were booked as support act on the tribute stage just before Jerry Lee Lewis' sister Linda Gail Lewis and her tribute to her brother. There was about 2500 people watching our set and we really rocked. When we finished the crowd were chanting for Elvis, it was great. I always left audiences wanting more just like the King did, when we went backstage into the green room, Linda Gail Lewis stood there with a frown on her face. The promoter came rushing in trying to cajole her to take the stage. She was adamant " I'm not going on stage after that Fxxxing Elvis ". I just looked at her in disbelief! I was honoured to be her support act, she was a well known artiste in her own right. I guess she just carries the same diva blood as her brother.

We got changed and went out front to watch her show but she didn't come on for about thirty minutes, she was obviously letting the crowd calm down. The funny thing was as we stood at the back they were still chanting for Elvis, and they did all the way through her set. I felt a little sorry for her but she had told the promoter she was top of the bill and would be going on last so I suppose it was her own fault!

Another festival we did was The American Motorhome Festival in Thame near Oxford. This time it was in a giant marquee. The show went brilliant, the audience were very vocal and loved it. Afterwards when we had loaded the van we got stuck in the sloppy muddy field. The band had all toddled off in their cars so the event organizer arranged for a local farmer to drag us out with his tractor. Elvis slowly left the building!

By now Ben had moved to Wardle High School near Littleborough. He liked it very much and had discovered music. He had had some drum lessons off some of my drummers and was really focussed on being a drummer. Wardle High School had other ideas. They were well known for producing musicians, unfortunately it was of the brass band genre of musicians. Ben went along with this thinking he would get a chance on the one drum kit they had. They gave him ' the Triangle' ? I thought he was joking but he told me not to make a fuss so I didn't Then came the day Wardle High School Brass Band were to perform at The Bridgewater Hall in Manchester as part of a brass band festival. Jacqui and I paid £8 each only to see Ben play the triangle a couple of times. My blood was boiling, surely they could have let him have a go on the drum kit, even if just in rehearsals. But Mr Cooper wouldn't advocate any genre of music only brass band style. Ben was totally at that level then. I felt so sorry for him on that stage stood at the back. Memories of me being told I was tone deaf at school came flooding back!

We went to Bens parents evening and we were very pleased with his progress. Then we met his music teacher who promptly told me you don't need to read music to be a successful musician! What! Was he having a laugh I told him. He squirmed in his seat, I told him a few home truths and his head pointed down to the floor in embarrassment.

After this Ben started having private drum lessons with Mr Cooper but didn't seem to be learning either the drums or music in general. So I asked John Tremayne could he give Ben some music lessons. What John didn't know about music wasn't worth knowing. So Ben started learning in depth about the rudiments of music. He was invigorated!

The Rotherham Real Ale Festival was next for the band and myself. By all accounts it was quite prestigious. It was held at a large college in Rotherham and we were top of the bill in the main hall. It was pretty big with about a thousand standing. The show went brilliantly and we got several ovations. Afterwards when we got backstage I noticed something very wrong. Two of my Elvis suits had been stolen! I always carried three with me to every show. I was stood there in my white suit in disbelief! The organisers were distraught. They looked through the CCTV footage and saw someone walking out with both the red and blue suits over his arm. However the organisers were a bit unsure what to do because they knew who it was. I insisted on calling the police, they came and looked through the footage and told me to leave it with them. They gave me a crime number and left. Jacqui and I felt numb, she had made the suits herself it had taken dozens of hours painstakingly making the exact replicas. On the blue suit alone there was over 2500 stones and studs.

The police called me a week or so later saying they had no leads? The exact response I got off the organisers? Obviously they all knew who it was off the CCTV footage and they were just trying to brush it away. So I sent a very strong worded letter to the organisers and the college stating I wanted paying for my suits. To buy a suit from America it usually cost around £1500 - £2500 but seeing has Jacqui had personally made both my suits I said I would accept £1500 for both. This would cover the cost of making two more new suits with not much left over. Eventually they sent me a cheque for £1250 and I thought fair enough I didn't feel like arguing over £250 and I accepted the money.

I think they were more embarrassed than anything else. Who in their right mind would steal two Elvis suits, they were fitted exactly for my measurements and wouldn't fit anyone else properly. But hey that's the British public for you if something's there they'll take it.

July 4th 2004 and It was the big 40 for me. We had a party in The Dyers and all our friends came from far and wide. John Clews had offered his services as the DJ as a present for me, which I really appreciated. What I didn't know was Jacqui had arranged for the best Everly Brothers Tribute Act to perform for me. I had worked with them in Derby and thought they were excellent. It was a fantastic night and all our new local friends had a great time.

The only bad thing that happened was my Father had sent me a birthday card and on the back of it he said Aunty Joan had died and if I wanted the grave papers for my mums grave I should ask his second wife Ann for them after he had died. Apparently he had decided to get cremated rather than be buried with mum. Who in their right mind puts that on the back of a birthday card? Normal people would phone up and say it, but I guess I shouldn't have been surprised by his spinelessness.

Ben had been complaining about being left out while at Grandpa's in favour of Annes grandchildren for a while by then. They had bought a caravan and it was never his turn to go, it was always these other kids turn. There was also other small things that had happened that made me realise he was mentally abusing Ben now. For Gods sake Ben was his only Grandson you would think he would want to spend as much time with him as possible. Especially as Ben was having a torrid time with Donna's twisted treatment of him. So enough was enough and I wrote him a letter detailing everything that was wrong. I figured if he didn't respect or love me enough to pick up the phone about Aunty Joan and Mums grave papers then I would no longer respect him either. I told him a few home truths and said goodbye to him for the final time. I couldn't have all the negativity and mind games and when I realised he was doing it to Ben that was the final straw. He never called to ask why I had sent him the letter, mind you everything in the letter was true so he could only have apologised which I knew he would never do.

Ive never heard from him since and its been eighteen years now. He's missed so much of mine and Bens life but obviously he doesn't care. Against my better judgement I let him back into our lives and that was a mistake. When people have hurt or upset me over the years Ive learnt how to just cut them off dead and move on with my life, for my own sanity. This is what Ive done with him, as far as I'm concerned he died when my Mum died in 1988.

We had many high class venues to perform at through the end of 2004 but 2005 would change my life yet again, for the good......

Chapter 17

2005-2008....VIVA LAS VEGAS

2005 opened with a big bang at The London Hippodrome. I was hired by Avis Car Rental, they were promoting their introduction into the USA car rental market. They had flown in travel agents from all across North America. We arrived to find no car parking spaces anywhere, we eventually found an NCP in China Town. £60 for four hours! Good job I didn't need any equipment. Jacqui found the event organizer and she explained what she wanted me to do. The place was huge and our dressing room was backstage up twenty flights of stairs to the tiniest dressing room you could imagine. It must have been for the bottom of the bill in the olden days!

Avis had an American theme running all day. They even had artistes on stage portraying Thelma and Louise with a huge American car as the centre piece.

They only wanted four songs from me at the end of the event. I could pick whichever three songs I wanted, preferably up tempo. As long as I used Viva Las Vegas when I walked on stage and changed the words to Viva Las Avis! I thought ok I can do that. They had hired eight Las Vegas Showgirls mixing and mingling throughout the day and they were to walk on stage with me singing Viva Las Avis. The stage was huge so I had four Vegas showgirls on either side of me for the four songs.

I whipped it up a bit after Viva Las Avis with Suspicious Minds, Jailhouse Rock and finishing with The Wonder Of You. The audience (all travel agents) were going bananas, I had to keep away from the edge of the stage, their arms were outstretched trying to grab a piece of me. It was brilliant and Avis were very pleased.

" Viva Las Avis " at The London Hippodrome, so funny. But hey I can still say I played at that iconic venue.

Also in January I was booked into a nightclub in Southend in Essex. When we got there I thought oh great the carpet was all sticky from stale beer. Anyway I thought lets do it. The manager was great and showed me where I would be performing......a podium that the pole dancers usually used. It was tiny with a pole in the middle, I almost fell off three times. They had about four of these podiums and when I was singing they had girls on the other podiums dancing sexy routines! I was in my element, the place was mobbed with around six hundred 18 – 23 year olds. I was booked to perform for ten minutes and they had asked me to sing ' A little Less Conversation ' as the first song. No problem with that, I fitted another four songs in and the crowd was going bonkers, good job the security was on the ball it took four of them to get me to the stage and back afterwards. I felt like the real Elvis getting mobbed. All this and I got paid £750 for ten minutes work. This Rock'n'Roller coaster I was on was getting faster by the week but it was great!

I got a strange call one morning in February asking to book me and the band for her husbands fortieth birthday party. It would be a daytime set and she would bacs the fee to me beforehand as long as I sent her an invoice. She gave me her address then told me who her husband was. It was a guy called Steve Morgan, I'd never heard of him but she explained his background. He was the man responsible for all the Devere Hotels and he was in the process of buying Liverpool Football Club!

They flew in from Jersey where they lived and Steve had no idea about me and the band until we started the show. He was sat there in his Liverpool football shirt and loving every minute.

Our drummer Chris couldn't make it so he put in a dep called Spencer. It was all last minute but he told me he knew all the Elvis music, he had done it many times before with 'Rockin on Heavens Door' theatre show. Even so I was a bit nervous that it wouldn't sound right, we hadnt even rehearsed. But Wow! What a drummer! When he played the 2001 Theme and then into the drum intro it was like a wall of sound, he was exceptional. It was an unbelievable afternoon and Steve Morgan was made up.

We had been going out for lunch sometimes with our good friends Ken and Julie. We would go to Hollingworth Lake restaurant or we would go over to Cheshire where they lived. It was at The Beach, Hollingworth Lake that Jacqui doubled over in pain, we left the meal and went home. Jacqui was clearly in a lot of pain so we went to Rochdale Infirmary where they concluded she needed her Gall Bladder removing. The only thing was it would take a fair few days to have it done in Rochdale so they sent her to Trafford General. I was stuck at home, Trafford is about thirty minutes away by car and I can't drive but I kept in touch with her on our mobile phones. They did the operation the following day and we thought everything was alright even though she was still in pain we were told it would fade in a day or two. She was still in great pain the following day but they sent her home in a black cab of all things. She was still bent over in pain, they could have sent her home in a normal taxi, it would have been less painful.

Anyway she was home for a week and she wasn't getting better so we went to our doctor who promptly sent her straight to Rochdale Infirmary, she had an abscess on her lungs so no wonder she couldn't breathe. She stayed in hospital for three weeks while they drained all the fluid away. I couldn't believe Trafford General Hospital sent her home knowing she had an abscess on her lungs.

I cancelled all my shows for two months until she felt ready for us to go back on the road again. She's not been the same since with only certain foods she s allowed to eat but I thank God she s still with us!

And on the road again we certainly went with new venues in the diary all the time. I had tried to get bookings with Warner Leisure Hotels. My little sister Michelle worked at the one in North Wales, Bodelwyddan Castle. She said that Warner Hotels would be ideally suited for my show and they paid decent money.

Erica at Big Foot Events eventually came up with a booking with my band at Warner's Alveston Hall in Cheshire for £1500, I was over the moon and determined to make a good impression.

253

There was fourteen Warner Hotels and there was a real prospect of playing at them all if we did well.

We went down a storm and the management was backstage afterwards praising all of us. This meant a lot because we had been working towards this level of venue for a long time. I had been playing at prestigious venues with my solo show but not too much with the band. Erica called on the Monday and gave me all fourteen Warner Hotel bookings into my diary. The hotels down south we were given accommodation. By that time I had a long wheelbase Transit van so the band fitted all their equipment into the van and they travelled in one car to save on petrol.

By this time Neil on Keyboards had decided to stop touring and start his teaching career. I was a bit upset but you can't hold back peoples dreams and we parted on good terms.

So I needed a good keyboard player that new all the Elvis material. Chris Wharton on drums said I should call Jonathan Davies in Wales, Chris had played with him a few times and said he was just what we needed.

When I called Jonathan he said he would love to join my band but it would have to be in a couple of months as he was tied to a contract with another Elvis show.

Jacqui and I went to see one of his shows at Stockport Plaza and we were blown away. Not only with his piano and keyboard skills but also with his fantastic backing vocals. The Elvis he was working for was'nt that great but at last I had found another brilliant pianist who knew the Elvis material like the back of his hand. And also he could sing as well!

Eventually he came on board and he fit like a hand in a glove. His knowledge of Elvis' songs was huge and we set about doing songs I had only ever dreamed of performing. Getting the other musicians to learn new material was pretty easy but whenever I had asked Neil he wasn't over keen on learning new songs. Now Jonathan was with us the sky was the limit. I even got to sing Danny Boy at Heywood Civic Centre for my showbiz Dad Alan. That was Jonathan's idea and we did it just me with him on piano, you could here a pin drop and Alan was in tears.

We had a wedding to perform solo at in London, Barnet, North London to be precise. The Groom had asked if we would set up and be ready from 3pm. Apparently he was in a band called The Hothouse Flowers, who if you can recall had a few hits at the time. Anyway we were set up and ready to go when the Groom came into our hotel room and asked ever so politely would I mind going with him and his bride into an helicopter tour of London and when we arrived back the guests would be there. He asked Jacqui if she could play our helicopter intro as soon as she saw us arriving back. So I got into my Elvis suit and went with them in the helicopter. What a trip it was I saw all the sights and a few football grounds. They sat me in the front seat with the Bride and Groom in the back. When we got back the pilot who was ex RAF wanted his picture took with me and his helicopter for his website and I had pictures taken with everyone. Then we went inside and started the show which went down a storm. All of his band were there and they were so respectful and appreciative of my show. You couldn't make it up could you!

Life was great and it got even better when Erica called and asked would I like to perform at Warner's as a solo act as well. I didn't hesitate she got me £550 per booking spread out over all fourteen hotels.

Later on when my best friend Rob Leigh and I put a show together called Vegas Nights Live, Warner's bought that show as well, Elvis, Neil Diamond and Andy Wood as Tom Jones on stage in one night, there was no band unfortunately we were all solo on playback but it was another fourteen bookings!

It got to the stage that I started to get a following at Warner's There brochures were sent out to the punters to choose which weekend they wanted to book. Ours was usually the Elvis weekend or 70s weekend. We started to see a lot of the same faces in the different Warner Hotels and when they spoke to me after the shows I found out they were travelling long distances for these weekends just to see our show. It was amazing!

At their flagship hotel on Hayling Island I was doing a solo show. It was a full house four hundred. Nearly all Warner Hotels were built like the old style cabaret clubs where the seats were

255

layered and everyone could see the stage easily enough. I knew I had the audience with me this particular night, you could hear a pin drop when I was introducing a song or talking to the audience. I tried a new song out, new for me anyway. Help Me Make It Through The Night, not your normal Elvis song but he did record and release it and I told the story about it. All my audiences appreciated the little anecdotes I put in about the songs or about Elvis. And this night was no different they loved it. At the end of my show I got a full standing ovation it was superb.

On the Monday morning Erica called and said there had been three complaints, I couldn't believe what I was hearing. She said that one had said I looked nothing like Elvis, another said Elvis didn't even sing Help Me Make It Through the night and lastly one complained I didn't sound like Elvis. Erica had trouble saying the last one without laughing, we both knew it was a load of rubbish. But according to Warner's rules she had to pull me about it. She could tell I was offended and kept telling me not to be worried it wouldn't affect the bookings I had with them. The following day she called me back and on behalf of Warner's and apologised for any upset it may have caused. That was nice but surely Warner's could have phoned themselves. Three hundred and ninety seven people gave me a standing ovation and three complained! Unbelievable!

One of the Warner venues I seemed to perform at the most was Thorseby Hall in Nottingham. I got to know the Entertainments Manager Stuart quite well there. He would help me do the sound check with the band and set and work the spotlights for me. This particular night I was doing it solo and he had told me the previous time not to bring my mini disc player as Warner's had bought him a brand new top of the range Denon mini-disc player. We started the show and everything was going great up to the third song when the disc just stopped. I joked with the audience while Stuart and Jacqui were frantically trying to get this disc player to work. Something had told me to take my disc player/rack with me so Stuart and Jacqui rushed out to our van and came back in speedily trying to get it connected. By this time I had sang three songs accapella, wished some people happy

256

birthday and generally made a clown of myself! Finally Jacqui got my fourth song playing and a huge cheer went up, we finished the show to another standing ovation and I think the audience really appreciated me entertaining them with and without the disc player. I was waiting for a call of complaint on the Monday morning but I didn't get one. Phew!

2005 and we were flying high, inundated with gigs. In August the band and I made our annual trip to The Marina Theatre in Lowestoft. Stuart from Showtime Productions had booked me direct after I had left Phil's management and he was always very helpful. We had done a show in Somerset the night before and we arrived a little late so Stuart was panicking a bit. We sound-checked pretty quick and everything was perfect.

As I stood backstage while the helicopter intro was playing Stuart introduced me to this young girl would would be operating the smoke machine from the wings. This girl was really blowing the smoke on stage and into the air. What neither of us knew was the smoke machine was leaking oil. So when I walked on stage my legs flew into the air and I landed on my back. I couldn't get up it was as slippery as frozen ice. I turned over onto my stomach and gradually got up, I was so embarrassed, the audience were in stitches of laughter! The funny thing was the band who had ripped into CC Rider actually slowed down while I was on the floor and then speeded back up when I got up. It was a bit surreal it all happened in slow motion.

When I look back now I think it was hilarious but back then all I could do was carry on with the show. Five minutes later in typical Jacqui fashion a mop appears at the side of the stage curtain, I was saying my good evenings and the audience burst into laughter again. When I saw it I couldn't help but burst out as well. Stuart filmed the concert and the following day he called me and said all you could see was half a mop coming out of the curtain drying up the mess. When I finished the first half of the show I said to the audience I would be back in the second half with my full Norman Wisdom act!

So we were travelling the country Wednesdays to Saturdays and then on Sunday afternoon you could find us in The Dyers Arms with our friends just chilling out. It was a family friendly pub so Ben could come in when he wanted to but he was a teenager now and wanted to do his own thing. He had gotten into Hip-hop big time, he liked Eminem and 50Cent. Jacqui took him to see 50 Cent at Manchester Arena and then I took him to see Snoop Dog at the Arena. Actually to my surprise Snoop Dog was really good. As Ben went through his teenage years his taste in music changed slightly. He got into Heavy Metal and Jacqui took him to see Slipknot at the Arena. She came home and couldn't hear anything for two days!

But all the while he was listening to different types of music and still had a deep yearning to play the drums. So we got him a cheap drum kit and got him some lessons locally once a week. After talking to his drum tutor he said Ben was improving very quickly and had a natural rhythm inside him. I called my drummer Chris and asked if he could give Ben a lesson and evaluate where he was at.

So we went to Chester, Chris had been employed as the drum tutor at the prestigious Kings School during the day as well as gigging with my show in the evenings. Chris spoke with me alone after Bens lesson and told me Ben was a natural. He still had a lot to learn he was only fifteen but he had a natural feel to his playing. Jacqui and I were so proud as parents and especially me being an entertainer.

In October of 2005 the band and I were booked into Warner's Bembridge Hotel on the Isle Of Wight. I didn't have to take all my equipment just my mixer rack for the band to plug into I would then link into Warner's 20k sound rig, it was a great sound system. John Tremayne offered for us to travel with him in his jeep to save on petrol. What I had to take fitted easily with his bass guitar and amp. Just before we set off for his house in Bury I whacked my head on the boot of our estate car. Yet again there was blood everywhere, London repeating itself.

We got to John's and he asked what had happened. He said he could fix it and promptly put a load of white pepper where the cut was. It stopped bleeding almost immediately.

As I was getting ready to go on stage I was wondering wether to blow dry my hair as usual or not now I had all this pepper on my head. I got it to look okay as long as I didn't bow down on stage because the audience would see what now looked like a sand pit on my head!

We got about halfway through the show when John whispered to me he needed the toilet. I said he should have gone beforehand but there was no toilets backstage at this Warner's they were at the back of the cabaret room. I was introducing the next song when John came running past me and said for me to talk for a bit he needed the loo. He went running to the back with the audience in stitches. I didn't know what to say then it came to me. The old Fawlty Towers line " Don't mind him he's from Barcelona......he goes back on Monday " the crowd roared with laughter and I talked a load of nonsense until he shuffled back towards the stage with the audience giving him a huge applause. I then said to the band "Should we do Bridge Over Troubled Water? ". The crowd roared again and then we finally rocked the house.

I did a funny gig in September of that year in Kirby Lonsdale in the Lake District. It was a private party in a huge house. Mark Owen lived next door and I wondered if he would be there. The host was really nice and hospitable, nothing was too much trouble. When I came on everyone thought Mark Owen was coming home in his helicopter, but it was just little me. I was singing in the back garden whiched backed onto a farmers field with lots of cows. When I started singing I could see some cows sauntering over to the dry stone wall. Then during the second song Burning Love I turned a watched in disbelief as three cows were moving their heads from side to side in sinc. It was like the advert on tv, I burst in to laughter as did the guests. I started conducting them and they followed my direction while the music played. It wa so funny and just made it a great party!

259

In November of 2005 we went on holiday to America. I had told Jacqui all about it over the last few years, we went for three weeks. We changed planes in Atlanta and in Atlanta you get off the plane, get onto a monorail to the terminal, clear customs then get on the underground railway to the next terminal. Jacqui's face was a picture, she couldn't believe how big the airport was. We took the short flight to Orlando. When we got out of the airport in Orlando it was about 8pm so it was dark and Jaqcui had to negotiate driving on the wrong side of the wide road, the darkness didn't help. She got us near to International Drive and insisted we stop for something to eat and a rest. She did really well getting us the ten miles to Orlando so we went to IHOP (International House Of Pancakes). I knew she'd like it there. We all ordered burgers and when Jacqui's came I've never seen her eyes so wide open in amazement. Of course it was huge and she couldn't get over how nice the waitress was. Ben and i knew all about the American way but to her it was a big culture shock. She just kept saying " wow I know what you mean now".

We hired a villa in Kissimmee close to the theme parks. It was a lovely villa and on Jacqui's first morning in the states, while she was still in bed. Ben and I kneeled down on one knee, woke her up and I produced an engagement ring! We were over the moon when she said yes. I still can't believe Ben kept the secret all that way on the plane. But he had a new better mum and that was incentive enough I suppose. I couldn't believe it either, I got a very emotional, we all had tears in our eyes, Ben and I was getting a second chance at happiness!

So on our first morning in Orlando and we went for breakfast. When we got to the car there was frost on the windshield! It was Spain all over again, Jacqui said she was cursed and we laughed. I had told her how warm it would be even in the morning. The week before Florida had had the coldest November week in fifty years, we got the tail end of it. But it warmed up mid morning. At breakfast at The Ponderosa Jacqui's reaction was much the same as the night before I think she was a little overawed.

We didn't do much the first day so that Jacqui could acclimatise etc. Second day we went to Sea World to see the

260

dolphins, Jacqui had always loved dolphins and she loved being up close and stroking them, she was so relaxed and happy it made my heart warm.

Two days later we went to The Magic Kingdom, my favourite place. As a kid growing up on Langley estate I could only ever dream of meeting Mickey Mouse. Of course Ben and I had been before so Ben was acting as Jacqui's personal tour guide. We all loved it!

Over the next three weeks we went to the usual theme parks, Animal Kingdom, MGM Studios, Universal Studios and Busch Gardens. We also went to Daytona Beach a place I fell in love with years before. Jacqui loved it too. It was funny we were wearing shorts and t-shirts, it was in the mid seventies but the locals thought it was cold they all had on their sweaters and coats.

While we were in Kissimmee we had arranged to meet our friends Ken and Julie who were in Florida at the same time. Jacqui told them I had proposed and we should find a little chapel like in Vegas! But I wanted to plan it properly at home. It was pretty cool all of us going for a meal three thousand miles from home. We went into this place where the deal was all you could eat steak for $10. Ken challenged Ben, I cant remember who won but they both had tummy aches afterwards. We then went to Old Town and Ben saw this big bucking bronco and reckoned he could stay on it. So it started and then it got faster and faster. Ben came off it and was desperately holding onto the reins while his body was flying around and around on the wooden floor. It was hilarious. Jacqui, Ken, Julie and I couldn't stop laughing. When he got off he couldn't walk straight but he wanted another go and I said absolutely not I didn't fancy a trip to hospital.

Too soon it was time to go home and Jacqui had fallen for the whole USA experience just like I had before. On the way back she asked when we could go back again, my heart felt content.

Ben was coming along strong with his drum lessons each week but his other lessons seemed to suffer a little. Ben wanted to go to Music College when he became sixteen and they told him he would need ten GCEs including music. He was so focussed on getting in to Manchester Music College he got his head down and really worked hard. I couldn't trust Mr Cooper to pass Ben with a music GCSE so my right hand man, John the bass player, offered to give him free theory music lessons. John called me the day after Bens first lesson and was so annoyed with Wardle High School. He said they mustn't have been teaching Ben anything at all, he was at the bottom level. However he said if Ben worked hard he might be able to get him a GCSE pass. I was so grateful to John for doing this. It proved successful in the end, Ben got his GCSE in music as well as in nine other subjects. He would be going to Manchester Music College after all, despite Mr Cooper! We were so very proud of Ben it was his first step to becoming a musician. The next step would be University but he had to pass his exams at college first over the next two years.

We carried on touring the country and one call we got was from William Lees Jones the Managing Director and heir to Lees Brewery. It was his fortieth birthday and he had organized for a huge marquee in the garden of his mansion near Oulton Park, Cheshire. He greeted us at the door himself and was so pleased we could make it. He was a true gentleman and welcomed us into his home, which was even bigger than Graceland! He made coffee for us and said to ask if we needed anything. He pulled out his DVD box set of Phoenix Nights for us to watch and said he'd be back in a bit. Another millionaire looking after us and me just a kid from Langley! Sometimes I had to pinch myself, Jacqui just took it all in her stride, making more coffee in a kitchen bigger than our whole house back in Littleborough.

William came back and said I would be on stage in half an hour. So I got ready went on stage and blew the place away. All these posh people were up dancing and chanting for more Elvis at the end. William asked if I'd do another couple of songs so I thought why not he had treated me like royalty. Afterwards I got changed and we went back into the marquee and stood at the bar with William and his friends. It was a free bar of course and when the time arose I asked him why he didn't have any of his Lees' beer there. This was his exact reply " I'm not having that crap at my party" he was so funny and we got to know him pretty well. I think he liked my candidness.

We got another call off William Lees Jones. This time it was to appear at the Area Managers Christmas party to be held at his newly acquired Midland Hotel in Morecambe. It was a lovely hotel and again he greeted us in the foyer and showed us to the function suite where the party would be. The one thing I noticed was there was no bar in the function suite, it was in another room. This could potentially be a problem I thought, but we got on with setting the gear up and then we were shown to a bedroom that William had reserved for us for the night. He had even put a star on the outside of the door with Elvis on it, he had a great sense of humour.

When I came on stage I was into my second song Burning Love when one table got up and walked out. That was strange but I thought its their party and they might not like Elvis, it happens. Then each song I did one by one all the tables emptied until there was just William and his wife left. I asked him what did he want me to do, I was quite happy to sing to an empty room after all I had already been paid my fee. He showed his class and to his credit he asked me to sing just one more, his favourite Suspicious Minds. That was weird without an audience, it was an audience participation song. Afterwards William was so apologetic he knew I was in the top bracket of tribute acts, he was so embarrassed. So I jokingly said "come on I'll buy you a beer " knowing that it was a free bar. He laughed and we had a beer together.

I thought I had engaged quite well with him in fact I knew I had. However to this day he has never been in touch and I have no idea why. Maybe he was too embarrassed how his staff had acted, but hey as they say 'that's Rock n Roll'.

Young Paul at Peller Artistes was always calling with bookings this time he called and asked if I would be willing to do my show in Arena chain of pubs? He said they were paying £500 for Friday nights, some up North and some down South. He said there would be around twenty gigs a year. So I agreed, I could always pull out if they were a bit rough.

The first one was in central London, it was a sports pub with TVs everywhere even in the stage area. We were setting up the gear and I completely forgot about the TVs, stood up quickly and whacked my forehead on the bottom of one. There was blood everywhere, it wouldn't stop bleeding and I had to go on stage soon in a white suit. Jacqui did her best to stem the bleeding which it did for a while. Then when I started the show the adrenalin kicked in and you guessed it the red stuff started trickling down my face again. Jacqui gave me a handkerchief so I did the rest of the show holding it to my forehead. The audience just didn't care as long as they could dance. They wasn't disrespectful they were just being typical Londoners, self important.

I got a call from a new agent asking me to do a show at Stockport County FC. When we walked into the function suite we were so surprised, it was huge. It held at least six hundred. The show went down really well and afterwards the management asked to book me direct, they were dropping the agent. I squared it off with the agent and we did it a few times and I worked it out that the football club made a profit of around £10,000 each time I was on. Everybody was happy. Apart from Adam Carter (Elvis) that is, who was setting his equipment up when we arrived one time. It turned out he was supposed to be in the small room upstairs doing a wedding for sixty people. When I had sold over six hundred tickets downstairs. So he had to drag his gear down and upstairs. He wasn't very happy at all but that wasn't my fault. At the end of the night I purposely went to say goodnight to Adam to show no hard feelings but he just drove off into the night.

On that particular night when I walked on stage, the noise was deafening, and when i put my guitar on about twenty women charged and dived on top of me breaking the guitar. I hadn't even sang a note! I was loving it but Jacqui had to stop the disc until order was restored.

I did offer to supply top tribute shows to the management of Stockport FC but they turned me down flat. I told them that they would all be as good as me and they would make a good profit, but they just said no!

When I called for another booking they told me they were stopping all the tribute shows! No reason was given and I lost another venue. They did carry on with tribute shows, but they were all the cheaper ones. Talk about bad management. Apparently everyone was complaining and eventually they stopped tribute nights altogether.

Later on Stockport County FC found themselves dropping down the leagues and struggling for income. Now I might be wrong but £10,000 profit off one tribute night was good. Just imagine what it could have been over twelve months on Friday and Saturday nights. It's not rocket science but it seemed it was for Stockport County FC.

We did more shows for Barclays at a string of Hilton hotels nationwide and we also did shows for Bob Carruthers. Notably at The Hilton Hotel in Edinburgh where I tried to plant a seed in his head about doing some kind of big show in 2007, the 30th Anniversary of Elvis passing. I suggested he used me with my band somewhere. He hadn't seen me with the band and I knew he would love it, it took my performance up a few notches with the band.

A few weeks went by then I got a call to do another party for him in Stratford upon Avon again. The show went well and afterwards he told me his ideas about an Anniversary show. Apparently his brother owned Murrayfield Stadium in Edinburgh and Bob had promoted some big acts over the last few summers, The Who, Bryan Adams etc.

Anyway his idea was to do it similar to the EPE Production with the big screen and Elvis original band playing live to Elvis voice and image on a huge screen. He thought we could do the same thing cutting Elvis' voice out and having me on a small podium doing the vocals on stage with my band. He even said he would hire a full orchestra. This was going to be hard for me because I had to watch Elvis on a small monitor screen like a hawk so the lip sinc would look right. I had mimed to Elvis all those years ago but this was a whole new ball game. The band

265

were over the moon and thought we might just make some inroads in the business onto bigger stages etc. I thought the same so I started getting a set list together mainly using the Aloha From Hawaii Show from 1973.

Bob outlined his plan, to make sure it succeeded he was going to book the Who on the Friday night, they always sold out at Murrayfield. Then on the Saturday he was going to promote the event as Tribute Party On The Pitch with Björn Again (Abba) QE11 (Queen) and finishing the night with Elvis! He was going to do a two day pass to try capture some of Fridays fans of The Who and a day pass just for the Saturday. It all sounded a bit surreal at first but I had got to know Bob pretty well and he knew how to promote things. Along with his movie company he also owned Classic Rock Magazine so he knew all the rock bands on first name terms. He estimated there would be an audience of around sixty thousand! It was a dream come true!

I had negotiated the fee with him by email, four musicians at £500 each and £1000 for my fee. I felt I was being fare with these figures as I knew Björn Again would be charging at least £5000 and after all Bob had given me some fantastic gigs in some very highbrow venues and I trusted him.

I trusted him that much that that I didn't even contract the show which I should have done but I had always worked for him on a handshake.

Everything looked extremely exciting. Jacqui and I even took a holiday in June 2007 to Egypt for some sunshine and rest so we would be prepared for the biggest show of my life in August.

Marsa Alam in Southern Egypt was just what we both needed, a complete rest. We fell in love with the hotel with its own beach and mile long jetty. Anyone that's been to Egypt will tell you its Hot, Hot, Hot! When the plane doors opened it was like a heatwave rushing throughout the plane. I thought America was hot but this was something else.

The nearest hotel to ours was five miles further down the coast so we had total privacy. We had our own cabana on the beach and we lay in the shallow Red sea while tropical fish swarmed around

266

us. In truth it was the most relaxed we had ever been. It truly felt like paradise and we both felt rejuvenated and ready for the big challenge ahead of us in Scotland.

Chapter 18

2008-2010...POCKETFUL OF RAINBOWS

We arrived back at Manchester Airport from Egypt all refreshed and raring to go. I gave Bobs office a call to confirm everything was alright for August 16th at Murrayfield Stadium. But there was something wrong? His secretary was very hesitant and said she would get Bob to call me. My heart sank! Surely the show would still be on?

I heard nothing in over a week so I called again and I got an answer machine. I left a nice but concerned message for someone to get back to me, the show was only six weeks away.

We did the warm up gigs at Warner Hotels and the band was extremely tight so all was looking good from my end. I even watched the Aloha Show at home without the sound but with it playing on the CD so I could lip sinc to Elvis.

Four weeks to showtime and I called Bobs office again. Again his secretary was just putting me off. That was the last straw, I told her to get back to me and tell me if this huge show was going to happen or not. If it wasn't going to happen I would need my band to be paid their fee of £2000. I told her because Bob had always done right by me I wouldn't need paying as long as he would carry on booking me solo in the future, I reiterated about paying my band.

The following week the news finally came through that Bob hadn't been able to get the copyright license off The Elvis Presley Estate in time and the show was called off. I was distraught, angry and sad at the same time. He also said through his secretary that he would not pay my band as he said we didn't have a contract. Which was true but I had emails confirming all the details so in my book that served as a contract. I got in touch with The Musicians Union and they completely agreed with me!

Bobs answer was he offered free flights and accommodation to his St Lucia villa in the Caribbean for a week. As tempting as that was I would still be liable to pay my band the £2000 fee outstanding. I turned him down. The same offer came in a week later and I turned him down again. His secretary couldn't understand why I shouldn't take a holiday in St. Lucia while my band lost out on their fee.

A few days later I called in a last vain attempt to make Bob see sense but all I got was the answer machine. I tried twice more without success. Obviously he had told his secretary to ignore my calls.

What had happened was a massive thing for me and my band. I would probably never get the chance to perform in front of 60,000 people ever again. So I instructed The Musicians Union to start court proceedings for the full fee of £3000 (mine included). I was adamant I wouldn't let my band or myself down. They went over the details and said they knew of Bob Carruthers and his dealings with well known bands, apparently he had a reputation of not fulfilling his end of the deal. The MU said I had a very strong case and started acting on my behalf.

It took about six months to get to court which was held in his home town of Stratford Upon Avon. When the day arrived. Jacqui, John (bassist) Chris (Guitarist) my MU solicitor and I attended. I was allowed my solicitor and one musician in court for support. Bob flew in from St. Lucia armed with his Barrister. A Barrister for a small claims court! Unbelievable!

The judge heard my side of the case. My MU solicitor wasn't allowed to speak up for me which was strange, even she was shocked. Then Bobs Barrister started to verbally rip me apart. He even denied there were any emails? The were in black and white in front of us and the judge? He said I had doctored them and made them up. I was truly shocked that a Barrister would perjor himself in court. I just stood my ground thinking the truth would out.

At the end the Judge made his decision that I had been ' Bamboozled ' with the idea of such a large show? I had been in

269

the business for twenty three years at that point. I think I was a bit too experienced to be ' Bamboozled '. I just wanted to be treated fairly. After all I had offered to forego my fee as long as my band was paid. I couldn't have be more honest.

But the judge was adamant and even said I had no case for appeal. This just stunk to me, something was very wrong. As we exited the court Bobs Barrister came over to me and apologised for what had just happened. He said he knew I was in the right but he was just doing his job that Bob was paying for. He apologised again and left! When does that ever happen!

When I think about what was done and said in court I'm convinced Bob had the judge in his pocket and I was stitched up big time! Why would his Barrister apologise to me afterwards? Because he knew I was totally in the right.

Bob sloped off looking very sheepish. And all because he couldn't be seen to be beaten by the small guy. He's a multi-millionaire, my fee was a drop in the ocean for him.

Yet again I had lost a court case and the powers that be had stitched me up. Ive never seen Bob to this day and I don't intend seeing him, maybe if he apologised but we all know that powerful business men don't do apologies!

We were all left dejected so I knew we had to focus on something positive. The diary was looking good for 2008 so Jacqui and I set a date for our wedding on the 20th September.

We didn't have much family in fact by now I only had Jacqui and Ben. Ben was sixteen and I asked him to be my co-best man along with John Clews. Jacqui's sister Michelle had emigrated to Australia so that just left Jacqui's mum Avril, sister Pamela and nieces and nephew, Lydia, Sophie and Jacob. We got married at Rochdale Registrar Office and when Jacqui walked in to the strains of me on CD singing Pocketful of Rainbows she just blew my mind, she was stunning in a beautiful dress that was just perfect. I had never seen her look so beautiful. Everything we had been through just melted into obscurity, I was even more in love with this incredible lady.

John Clews didn't make it to the ceremony he had been in a car accident the day before. He was ok though and came to the reception for a while. I drafted in John (bass player) to help Ben with his best man duties. Which I was incredibly grateful for.

Our VIP guest was Joe and his mum Betty. We first met Joe at a show I did at The Gateway a place for learning difficulties. Joe has learning difficulties and always got up on stage with me in his Elvis suit, my heart melted. He turned up in his Elvis suit to the wedding and I was so pleased he did. One of the best wedding photo's we have is of Joe, Betty, Jacqui and myself. They truly are a family with a pure heart.

We had invited other friends from all over the country and they all turned up which was amazing. We had our reception at The Hungarian Club, thanks to John Bene from The Dyers. We didn't want a posh hotel we had seen how it worked in those places so often before and instantly disliked the contempt the staff usually had for the guests. We just wanted a normal down to earth party. We booked The Avengers (Steve's 60s band) so everyone could have a ball, they were excellent. We also had a DJ we had worked with that we knew was very good and he was. I started to do a small speech and for the first time I was lost for words with so much emotion. Chris stepped forward and suggested we do Jacqui's favourite Elvis song he had learnt " Young and Beautiful ". So she sat on a chair in the middle of the dance floor and you could hear a pin drop as Chris and I played and sang the song, it was so romantic, Jacqui had a tear in her eye. When it finished the guests went bananas it was just like being at a show.

Jonathan my keyboard player got up on stage and we proceeded to sing Elvis songs for ages. I suppose it had to happen but everyone was really enjoying themselves and singing along. After that we all had a ball and danced the night away!

On the way from the Registrar Office to the club David Elliott had surprised us with an American fifties Cadillac for the journey, complete with a fifties dressed driver. We were in the car talking everything fifties with this fella and I totally forgot my little surprise wedding present for my new wife. So when we got to the club I took her into the dressing room for some privacy and gave her my invitation for a three night romantic break to Paris. We had already booked our honeymoon to the states but I wanted to give her something a bit special. She had told me she had been when she was small and loved it. So the day after the wedding we flew to Paris and Ive got to say it was stunning. We had a lovely hotel near The Arch De Triumph so most things were within walking distance, it was very romantic. The locals were so very polite and helpful which was a bit different from Nice and Cannes in the south where they were a bit obnoxious.

We went to all the major tourist places and when we got to Notre Damme Cathedral Jacqui lit a candle for my mum, I had a lump in my throat, mum would have loved that, it was like Jacqui knew it.

We got back from Paris and we had a month to wait for our honeymoon because yours truly had messed up with some bookings which we had to contractually fulfil.

It seemed like ages but we were finally on our way to America once again. A place I felt completely at home with. Even my asthma was 100% better over there, I never had to use my inhaler at all.

This time we went to Nashville, Memphis, New Orleans, Tallahassee, Daytona Beach and finally Orlando. It was heaven. We both fell in love with Lower Broadway in Nashville with all the diverse music bars. Along with country music you could literally walk in to any genre of music in any bar and it was all played live, no backing tracks! Our favourite places were Legends Bar and The Stage where we came across Johnny T. who just blew us away with his original country rock music, his band were electric. I still buy his new CD when he releases one.

We did all the tourist places like the Country Music Hall of Fame which was awe inspiring, there are no words to describe it. Then we went to Studio B which is still a working studio but was where Elvis had recorded most of his hits. Again it was awe inspiring to me to think I was stood in the same place that the king had stood recording over three hundred songs.

We didn't want to leave Nashville we had been lucky with getting a suite at The Hilton Hotel just off Broadway so everything was within walking distance.

But leave we did and headed for Memphis four hundred miles west. We stopped halfway at Casey Jones Village near Jackson. I knew there was a native American jewellery store there, Jacqui wanted a wedding ring made by native Americans. She found the one she wanted and was made up it was beautiful. However I couldn't find one for me but I had my mind set on one in Memphis!

We arrived in Memphis late afternoon and it was lovely and balmy. We had booked into The Days Inn Graceland which was around two hundred yards from Graceland so it was really handy. It still had a guitar shaped swimming pool like the last time I was there but it had a lot more Elvis things around the hotel which was quirky. We took a walk to the Graceland gates for Jacqui to see them then we went for dinner.

The following morning we were awoke to Elvis singing Shake Rattle and Roll very loud on the tannoy system at 8am. Wow that was a shock, Jacqui wasn't best pleased. They didn't do that the last time I was there. The Elvis music played non-stop till about 11pm.

We had breakfast and headed for the EPE Plaza opposite Graceland to get our tickets for the mansion, air-plane and car museum. We got on the bus and with our headphones on we went through the gates and could hear Elvis singing "Welcome To My World", it was very poignant. As we went through the front door I could still feel his presence, Jacqui said she could too. Yet again it was very emotional. As we toured the mansion we could feel Elvis showing us around it was a feeling of extreme love he had for his fans, we were both feeling it!

When we got to the Hall of Gold in the Trophy room I just stopped in amazement. The biggest collection of Gold Records in the world right in front of us. I was awestruck as I was the first time, Jacqui's eyes just widened in amazement. Then we went outside and believe it or not there was a call box so we called Ben from Graceland, he thought we were kidding him but it was true.

From there we went into the racquetball court where there was Albums of Gold Records from the floor to the ceiling along with some of the jumpsuits and many awards he received. I was really interested in the Sundial suit (the one he wore on his last tour). To get up close to it was magical, I know there was three identical ones made for him so they could be cleaned while on tour. So there was no way of knowing if it was the actual last suit he wore on June 26th 1977 at The Market Square Arena in Indianapolis, but at least he did wear this one at some point on the 1977 tour.

We headed backwards to look at the pasture. Somebody in Elvis close circle had told me that when they moved Elvis body back to Graceland they didn't bury him in the grave in case of another kidnap case. Apparently they buried him in the pasture with a tiny marker that only the family would know about. They supposedly buried Rising Sun, his horse next to him. Your not allowed into the large pasture so there's nothing to confirm all this. However when you look at the gravesite it just doesn't look right. Surely Vernon would have buried his son next to his wife Gladys but he isn't? There's more proof than just this but I wont bore you with it. I'm 100% convinced Elvis is buried in the pasture!

The following day we explored Downtown Memphis and went to Sun Records where it all began for Elvis. Sun had become more commercialised since I was last there but it was good to experience that 1950s feel. We both very much enjoyed it. Then we headed onto Beale Street and discovered a whole new feel to Memphis with its cobbled street, restaurants and bars. We had something to eat at BB Kings club which was cool. Then we had a beer at the oldest bar in Memphis – The Beer Tap.

The following night we decided to go back to Beale Street in a taxi so that Jacqui could also have a drink. We called into Blues City Cafe and I had the best ribs Ive ever tasted. There was music coming from the lounge that was connected so we drifted in. It was a trio doing a tribute to Johnny Cash. This guys voice was uncannily like the Man in Black but he looked like Jerry Springer it was surreal. He told stories as he went along and apparently he had part owned Sun Records in the 1980s and was responsible for bringing it out of administration. We got talking to him afterwards and told him we were on our honeymoon from the UK. He was a lovely guy and even gave me his guitar pick for Ben.

We also had a meal the following day at Alfred's on Beale St. I gotta say the rib-eye steak was the best ever and I definitely recommend going if you're ever in Memphis.

On our last day in Memphis we took a stroll towards the Elvis Cafe on the Plaza. There was an Elvis tribute act advertised and we thought we'd take a look. As we were just passing the Graceland gates a Geordie accent shouted " As I live and breathe Lewis Gates fancy seeing you here ". It was only two ladies that had seen my show in Middlesborough two weeks before! What were the chances especially opposite the gates! We had a little chat and told them we were going to see this Elvis tribute. They warned us he was rubbish but we decided to have a meal and watch the show. The two ladies actually came and sat on the opposite side to where we were sat. They was right he was rubbish but I know how it feels to be up there on your own so we stayed. Then it started, these ladies were shouting to get Lewis Gates up to sing. So much so it was a bit embarrassing, I felt sorry for this guy he knew what was happening but he soldiered on till the end. I wont name him because that wouldn't be fair, suffice to say he's still within the Elvis scene in Memphis.

The two ladies asked why I wouldn't get up and sing so I explained and they understood, they seemed to have a lot more respect for me after that.

We left Memphis and headed south to Mississippi. I'd found the address for Jerry Lee Lewis' ranch before we left England so we tried to find it. Which we did, it was on a normal country road and pretty secluded. We pulled up to the gates which were almost identical to Graceland's gates but with piano's on them. Unfortunately the ranch was closed to tourists, sometimes he would open it to fans but our luck wasn't in.

After Jerry Lee's residence we headed south towards New Orleans or as the locals call it Nawleans. It was about a six hour drive and we arrived at 5pm. We drove past all the suburbs that

275

were still flooded from hurricane Katrina two years before. It was awful seeing how many lives it must have ruined.

We parked up near the river and went to look for an hotel. It was going dark by now so we settled for The Westin Hotel which was really nice until we checked in and found out it was $300 for the night. I didn't have the energy to back out looking so we ended up being posh.

We went out for something to eat, God knows the prices at the hotel were expensive. After we ate we went exploring and ended up on the famous Bourbon Street.

The first bar we went into there was a great band playing Cajun music. We got two Budweiser's at the bar and the bartender gave us four bottles? When I told him we only wanted two he replied it was two for one. So we settled down to enjoy the band, When we left about an hour later there was a guy with an A Board advertising four drinks for the price of one! It was surreal.

There was another guy dressed up as a big green grenade selling huge Grenade Cocktails so Jacqui had one. She only got halfway down the cocktail and she was gone, I had a sip and it really was like dynamite! I more or less had to carry her back to the hotel. Jacqui was well in the land of nod so I switched the TV on and watched the hotels info channel. I found out that Bourbon street was owned by one business man and you were allowed to take your drinks from bar to bar. That made sense to me now I couldn't understand why people were getting away with it.

The next morning we decided we would check out,we couldn't afford another $300. We had breakfast at a cafe in the heart of the city. We both had Po Boys which simply put are huge muffins with whatever filling you wanted. They originated from the slavery days when orphaned kids would beg at the back of cafe's and the staff would give them whatever they could.

We had a good look around the French Quarter where Elvis had made King Creole. We even stood on the balcony in the exact spot that he had stood and sang "Crawfish". We bought a few souvenirs from the voodoo shops, looked at the riverboats on the mighty Mississippi river and then headed out of New Orleans east towards Tallahassee in Florida. After driving for a couple of hours we came across a place called Bay City and we decided to take a look. It was beautiful, lying directly on the Gulf of Mexico. We checked into a small motel and the owner and staff definitely had that southern charm, they were so welcoming. We went to get something to eat from the gas station, I had an unbelievably tasty Gumbo it was sensational.

The following morning we headed for Tallahassee and checked into our motel. This was a place Jacqui had always fancied going to ever since I used to sing the rock n roll song " Tallahassee Lassie ". Alas it was just like any other US city so she was a bit underwhelmed. I thought it was great but I'm a bit biased.

From there we headed south east towards Daytona Beach, Florida. My favourite American beach resort. We found the The Sands Hotel right on the beach. At $40 for the night it was the opposite to the Westin hotel in New Orleans but just as nice in style and class and our balcony look straight out over the Atlantic ocean. I showed Jacqui why I loved this place with its beautiful beach and old fashioned pier.

In the morning we headed for our final destination Kissimmee near Orlando. We had booked a private villa recommended to us by one of my fans. It was only an hour from Daytona Beach and when we arrived I couldn't believe the size of it. It was even bigger than Graceland, it was huge and beautifully decorated. The owner had left a wedding congratulations card and a bottle of bubbly for us. How nice was that. It was also nice and secluded which was perfect.

We had our last seven days at the villa and we hand picked which theme parks we would go to. With Jacqui's love of dolphins we had to do Sea World first. It was terrific as usual and Jacqui got to feed the dolphins. After the Shamu show, Shamu came right up to us in his tank as if he were trying to talk to us, it was fantastic.

We did a water park for one day then we went to Universal Studio's and The Spiderman ride which was spectacular as were all the other rides, we had a brilliant experience.

I would say the whole three week honeymoon was perfect, Jacqui had fallen in love with the south and where we had been. We both decided that if we ever got the chance we would live in America in a heartbeat.

We flew home and the following day disaster struck! I woke up on the Tuesday morning to a call from Erica from Big Foot Events telling me that Warner's Hotels had cancelled all fourteen shows I had with them. She explained it wasn't just me, they had cancelled everyone because of the international financial crises. Crisis? What crisis? We had been away for three weeks and the the world had spun on its axis! Other agents had also cancelled some shows. My heart sank, what was I going to say to Jacqui? We had just lost over twenty gigs in less than an hour! She took it pretty well considering and told me to focus on the gigs that were still in the diary. Which is what I did, I also used the internet to find venues that were still booking live entertainment. I got a few shows booked but the venues were now in a stronger position and were insisting on paying less. So rather than refuse the bookings I took quite a few at £300 - £350 after all something was better than nothing.

This continued over the next few years and my income dropped by about a third. I could actually feel the apathy in the audiences towards the mess the country was in. So I worked a bit harder to try and cheer people up and on the whole it worked, I was going down a storm!

However there were some shows that were a lost cause. I remember working in a pub in Wolverhampton. Wow how the mighty had fallen. It used to be five star hotels and restaurants. Anyway we set up and started the show at 9pm. The landlord did warn me the audience would be watching the football on the several screens around the room. My God they were ignorant. They watched the football on silent screens while I tried to entertain them. They just sat there staring at the screens with blank faces. In the interval I went to the landlord and said " its clearly not working can we call it a day I didn't want paying we would just go home". He wouldn't have any of it he insisted I do the second half, he was very apologetic and we felt sorry for him so we did the second set. Same thing again, no reaction. So I started changing the words of the songs so it was insulting the audience. Still nothing but me and Jacqui had a good laugh with it. When I came to sing American Trilogy at the end they all stood up and applauded shouting for more. That was surreal. I gave the mic to Jacqui and said to her tell them to Fxxk Off were done. Unbelievable!

Ben had passed his exams at Manchester Music College and had been accepted at Salford University he was going to study Music and Studio Recording. After all the stress he'd been through with Donna he had finally found his niche in life.

Ben had always wanted a dog and now he had left home for University we got one? I know it doesn't make sense its just the way it happened. All three of us went to Manchester Dog Rescue. While Jacqui and Ben were looking at the puppies I came across the only dog that wasn't barking. He was a beautiful three year old Golden Labrador called Beau. He just sat there wagging his tail and smiling at me almost saying " can we go home now". We all agreed he was meant to be with us. We changed his name to Buddy and he became my companion for the next nine years.

We did quite a lot of weddings during this period but the apathy was there too, I couldn't believe how it could be like that on someone's special day.

We did one at The Mecure Hotel in Rochdale. The bride and groom had seen me before and were fans. However they insisted I do two sets so I begrudgingly agreed. I had done this in the past and realistically just one set was enough at a wedding. Anyhow the first set was good most of them were dancing. Then it came to set two and I kid you not everyone vacated the room to the bar. Leaving just the bride, groom, me and Jacqui. How horrible and disrespectful towards the happy couple was that. I asked them what did they want me to do, I had only got five minutes into the set. Bless them they didn't know what to say they were completely embarrassed. So I asked them their favourite Elvis songs and did requests for them for the next forty five minutes. I think it made their night and they were full of thanks at the end. At least the sheep didn't win that time!

I also did a few funerals. One of which was for a vicar that had passed in the village of Ellesmere near Oswestry. The vicar had been to see me quite a few times at Mike's pub The Red Lion. So Mike called and asked me if I could do it. I'd never done a funeral before so I wasnt sure if they would want full on Rock n Roll. I started off with some slow songs and even a couple of Gospel songs. The the vicars brother came up and said the vicar would have wanted the usual Rock n Roll set. So I did and we had it bouncing, what a fantastic wake.

Another funeral I agreed to do was for our dear neighbour Ray, Barbra's husband. She asked me if I could sing Amazing Grace and I'll Remember You during the service. I was very nervous, especially looking out at a packed Church. I got through it and Barbra was so appreciative but it was very emotional.

I took a call from my old sound tech Gary Mac, he was running his own entertainments agency now that he had left Phil Hughes at Ambassador Promotions. I think he found Phil out too. Anyway he was begging me to help him out, a tribute act had let him down for Legends Nightclub in Batley, Yorkshire and the fee was £350. It was a Thursday and I asked him when it was for? He said tonight! It was 7.30pm and the venue was forty minutes away. I haven't had a shave I told him " it doesn't matter just get on stage by 9pm.

So we got there and the management were very pleased that I had turned up. I explained to them I hadn't had time for a shave and my roots were coming through I looked like a badger! They weren't bothered they told me I was covering for Rob Lamberti (George Michael). Great I had been conned, Rob Lamberti didn't go out for less than £500 even midweek.

I did the show and went down really well considering they were all coming to see George Michael. The management said it was great and they would have me back again through the agent. I had been trying to get in that venue for a while but they had their own Elvis. So I was very pleased with the outcome.

I never went back there again. I asked Gary and he just kept giving me the brush off. Just shows you when you help someone out they don't always reciprocate.

I got an email off Carol Crossley. Carol was a waitress at The Harbour Hotel from the old days in Rhyl. They were having a reunion at the pub across the road from The Harbour and would I be able to do a show for them. They asked if I could bring a DJ so I took John Clews, he'd been doing the odd wedding with me.

It was great to see all the staff again, although a bit surreal with them all being older! But so was I, you just don't feel it do you. It went down a smash but the odd thing was no one even mentioned that I was singing live? Don't forget the last time they had all seen me at The Harbour I was a mime act. That felt really strange, it wasn't like my vocals were off, I made sure they were spot on. You cant figure some people out so I did my show, talked a bit afterwards while John did his DJ set and then went home with a surreal feeling.

A year later Carol contacted me again asking if would do my show at Natalie's wedding. I took the booking it was on a Saturday night and bookings were pretty tight. But this was even more surreal than the reunion. Natalie hadn't been at the reunion but she wanted me at her wedding?

We went and did the show but I wasn't sure what to expect. While I was waiting to start I was in the side room where the buffet was I noticed Natalie looking at the food. There was no one else there and I was tempted to apologise for what happened years before. But I decided not to, I really didn't want to spoil her special day. I heard the intro playing so I turned and went on stage.

When we had packed up and ready to go we said our goodbyes to everyone then Natalie came to thank us. She couldn't look me in the eye and I knew there was still some hurt there. I felt terrible but there was nothing I could do. We headed for the motorway and home.

I took a call from David Elliott asking me to do his and Dyans wedding at The Sandygate Hotel. What an event that was. We spent most of the time upstairs in his flat with Uncle Kevin and some others watching Elvis and Johnny Cash on his 50 inch television. The actual show brought the house down. I did Dave's favourite Elvis songs and everyone was up dancing. Come closing time we all went back upstairs and carried on watching videos of Elvis. I think Jacqui and I got to our bedroom at 5am. What a day!

When we had got back from the states Ben had given me an idea that he had to start a different kind of band. The gist of it was we would mash Elvis hits with Classic Rock Anthems. Not only that, we would all dress up as Classic Rock Legends. Obviously I dressed as Elvis, Ben would dress as drum legend John Bonham and then we started auditioning. We didn't get a great response because I think some musicians didn't get the vision we had. However the first to auditions was Iain who was a great guitarist and he agreed to dress as ACDC guitar legend Angus Young. Next came Tommy and straight away I was praying he could play well because he was just what we were looking for, Guns and Roses legend Slash. He was the actual image of Slash and his playing was unbelievable so Tommy Slash was born! The last one to audition was a guy called Plank (his actual name) he had come to try out for the Slash part but he had seen Tommy outside and conceded the part. Now Plank had played guitar for some well know rock bands so I asked him if he could play bass. He said he could so I asked if he fancied auditioning on the bass for the part of Lemmy. He quickly agreed to this to my relief, we hadn't had anyone apply for the Lemmy part. It would include him dressing as Motorhead legend Lemmy. He played exceptionally well and his attitude was spot on for Lemmy,he got the job hands down.

So we had the line up......myself as lead singer Pete Presley (I wanted it to be different to Lewis Gates). On drums Ben as Benjamin John Bonham. Tommy on lead guitar as Tommy Slash. Iain on lead guitar as Iain Angus Young and Plank on Bass as Plank Lemmy.

There was a band in America called Metal Elvis and they were really good they rocked up a lot of Elvis songs and mashed a few as well. I wanted to be like them but better in I different way. I wanted to mash most up most of the set. So we rented a rehearsal room and all five of us put our heads together to try and create something special. It took us twelve months of creating and practising twice a week to finally be able to perform two forty five minute sets. Ive got to say these musicians were so clever, they actually got and was excited about what we wanted. Ben came up with the idea of using the Graveyard Theme intro with mist all over the stage. This would give the musicians time to get on stage and get ready. Then he came up with the idea of Lemmy starting the show singing Motorhead's "Bow down to the King" for two verses then I would walk on when the band started Paranoid mashed with Burning Love. When it was all timed right it went down a storm, the audiences loved it and we were only on the first song! Showmanship always works and I'm so proud that Ben came up with these ideas.

It was a struggle getting venues to book us though they just didn't get why Elvis was the lead singer. They said if you was dressed as a classic rock lead singer they would book us. These were all rock clubs and pubs. So I thought lets try the smaller normal pubs. We got a few bookings at these pubs in Rochdale and Manchester and we smashed every one of them. They all rebooked us. There was a place in Preston that had us on every other month, we gained a bit of a following. In fact we filmed a set there and its on our DVD.

We did a venue in my home town of Littleborough and it was there I me Trem Feighery and his brother Trim. Trem was a massive Elvis and Classic Rock fan so Raised On Rock was right up his street. Trim was a rock fan. They both loved the idea and Trem said we could really go places as he hadn't seen anything like it before. He also offered to come and video our show a few times free of charge. It was his hobby filming and photographing things. Wow I thought this was great, it would have cost us a fortune to have our show filmed. They were both very nice and unassuming people. They fit right in to our Raised on Rock band. In fact they came to all our shows and were very much important members of our crew.

Iain Angus Young got us a gig at a posh schools summer fete in Cheshire. Everything was going well until Plank Lemmy said to Tommy Slash " is that the wet coke or the dry white stuff"! His microphone was on and everyone heard it. Jacqui quickly turned his mic off. There was 150 kids asking their parents what's white coke? I couldn't believe it, we finished the show but we didn't get a rebooking. In the dressing room we all burst out into laughter. We only took the afternoon gig because we were short of gigs. We didn't need to be playing summer fete's anyway. We needed rock clubs!

We played regularly at The Gamecock Inn in Bury. The landlord John had a very open mind and he really got what we was trying to do. It got overly full whenever we were on and we gained a large following, it was great. I never in my wildest dreams thought I would be fronting a classic rock band. But there I was and loving it. It was totally out of my comfort zone but it made me work hard to produce the goods and that was a good thing. I had been doing my Lewis Gates shows on autopilot I had got into a bit of a rut. Don't get me wrong every show I did I gave 100% but it had all become the same every show. So Pete Presley's Raised On Rock was refreshing my career.

Even so we were struggling for gigs, people just didn't get the concept and yet when we did perform we brought the house down. I looked through the Bands and Venues website for inspiration. I came across an A&R company called Stringbean International based in London. I called them and they were really interested in our concept. Stringbean told me he was mainly into Reggae bands but was always on the look out for original and fresh ideas. I sent him our demo and left it with him. A few weeks later he called and said have you seen your YouTube page its gone ballistic. I had a quick look and couldn't believe the amount of hits we had. He also told me he had got 152 American radio stations playing our demo and the phone lines had lit up with interest. He sent me a list of all the radio stations. They were all on the east coast, Boston, New York etc. He said the next plan was to set up a small tour of rock venues in the vicinity of the radio stations. I left him to it, I could visualise him eventually becoming our manager.

Then tragedy struck. Tommy Slash decided to quit for no reason whatsoever. I was deflated we would never be able to find another Slash character he was the epitome of Slash. He was even friends with Slash's guitar tech so he knew any changes and what amp settings were needed.

The day after Iain Angus Young quit as well for personal reasons, everything was falling apart. We took a guy on called Quo to replace Iain. He had played with The Gutter Band (Gary Glitters Glitter Band) for years and he always dressed as Paul Stanley from Kiss. I could work with this, Kiss were legendary and everyone would know who he was. We set dates for rehearsals.

Before I had chance to go and try and talk Tommy around I got a call from Gavin one of his friends telling me Tommy had committed suicide! We were all in deep shock. Apparently he had hung himself but to this day none of us know why. Jacqui, Ben and I were in shock! He must have had his reasons, but why! Such a great shame and waste of a great talent.

We went to Tommy's funeral and it was very emotional, Tommy was such a big character and a big part of life. His Les Paul guitar stood next to his coffin and we said goodbye. I was devastated he was only twenty eight. Ben was devastated too, Tommy had been like a big brother to him, he always looked after him on the road. Ben was nineteen and it shook our little family to the core!

I spoke with Stringbean and told him what had happened and also told him we would try and get another Slash. Deep down I knew we wouldn't but this guy was trying his best to set up a small tour of America for us so I owed it to him to try. We auditioned a few people but there was only one and he wasn't fit to lace Tommy's boots.

We gave it a go with him and with Quo (who was extremely good on lead guitar and stage presence). We fulfilled some gigs that were booked but it just didn't work with the new Slash and the band split. I notified Stringbean and that was the end of me fronting a classic rock band and the dream of an American tour!

Then we got the terrible news that our friend/fan Pauline Fellows from the Midlands was terminally ill with cancer. I spoke with her daughter Debbie at length and we decided to put on a benefit night to raise enough money to send her and husband Brian to Memphis. Pauline had never been to Graceland and she had always wanted to go. Debbie organised a social club and I did a show there for her. I also asked John Clews if he would do the disco and auction for free which he was happy to do, he had met Pauline and Brian at some of my shows.

Somehow Debbie got lots of shops to donate gifts and vouchers she also got football shirts and footballs from their team West Bromwich Albion. The auction raised quite a lot I cant remember exactly but at the end of the night it was around £2,500. It was more than enough to pay for the trip.

Pauline was speechless she couldn't believe how many people cared.

Debbie had the plane tickets booked for January to Memphis but Pauline died a week before they were to fly.

We were all heartbroken. Pauline and Brian had started following me from all the way back to The Harbour Hotel days in Rhyl.

Brian asked me to sing Love Me Tender and Memories at her funeral Memories was very hard, I had sang sat next to her at the benefit night and many other times. There wasn't a dry eye in the church.

The show must go on and I did quite a few Lewis Gates shows at David Elliott's hotel over the next couple of years. Then he called me and said they were leaving The Sandygate Hotel and moving to a restaurant in Hazel Grove in Cheshire. Not only that, he was taking my advice and calling it Elvis' Kitchen and having Elvis themed meals and cocktails etc.

At long last I was going to be resident at a genuine Elvis venue. I had hinted to him through the years he would do really well with an Elvis place and now he was finally taking the plunge.

Now while David Elliott was a good chef he wasn't very artistic with anything else so I set about helping to decorate the walls with Elvis albums and memorabilia. I lent him a lot of my collection and got started. When it was finished it looked great. He gave me the menu and I suggested Elvis names that fit each meal. He didn't use all of them but he used most. I did the same with the cocktails, it was all very exciting. In the end it was like the Hard Rock Cafe only with Elvis Presley everywhere!

I did the opening night for him and it was a big smash. Dave wanted me on every week but I refused saying even if it was an Elvis restaurant it would be too much. Plus I couldn't do every week my diary was fairly full. He needed me on once a month and on both Elvis anniversary dates. My thought was it would give the punters something to look forward to and consequently would sell out. And so it proved right. In eight years we only didn't sell out twice!

I negotiated a fee with Dave of just £250 per show for Friday shows. A lot less than my usual fee but I saw it as an Elvis project and I had always wanted to be resident at an Elvis venue. Deep down I was buzzing I had all sorts of ideas. I had to put the ideas into Dave's head and let him think they were his ideas. It was quite funny he would call me and ask if I could do such a thing and I had spoke to him about the same thing a month or two before.

I decided he needed other tribute acts on every other Friday. He finally asked me to arrange it for him. He knew that I knew all the top tribute acts and I could get them for £400 nett (£500 less the agents cut). So in the end I called them all up and convinced them to do some gigs at The Kitchen. We had my mate Rob Leigh (Neil Diamond) Rod Stewart, Abba, Freddie Mercury, Frank Sinatra, Tina Turner, Adele and Robbie Williams. Every single act sold out.

I had Dave's trust so I came out with my best idea. I suggested he advertised himself as David Elliott The Elvis Chef! And he should come into the restaurant and mix with the punters etc. He already had a chefs Elvis Eagle whites that Jacqui had made him so he would come out and talk to everyone. As time went on Jacqui made him a black Elvis jacket with the high collar with a golden eagle on the front and back along with hundreds of studs. We gave this to him for Christmas and he was in tears. He really felt the part. As time went on we worked something out where when I was on stage half way through I would introduce The Elvis Chef and the crowd went wild. Especially when I got him to sing The Wonder Of You. We had such a laugh I used to tell the audience he was my brother and we were twins like the movie. I was five foot nine and Dave was six foot six, the audiences loved it plus it gave me a breather.

I offered to look after all the restaurants social media as well. I set up a Facebook page and I built my first website which I was quite pleased with. The only downside to the restaurant was it was upstairs which made it unviable for people in wheelchairs and some people with learning difficulties.

Although Dave did lift a few wheelchairs upstairs we did lose some custom because of the stairs. Unfortunately Elvis had quite a few fans that had severe handicaps and couldn't get upstairs which was a shame but there was nothing we could do about it. Dave had it measured for a stairlift but the logistics just didn't work.

In 2010 John and Breeda (The Dyers Landlords) asked if we would like to rent there house up the road. They themselves lived in a lovely apartment above the pub. We jumped at the idea, it was a little more expensive than Frederick Street but it wasn't far short of the size of Graceland. I think Breeda let us have it cheaper because of the work I had done for The Dyers (I had booked all the bands for the pub at no commission) I had also done cheaper shows there as well.

Anyway we had three bedrooms, a conservatory, a dining room and a downstairs office. We both loved the place and everyone said how pleased they were for us. Buddy especially liked more space he had and lying in the sun in the conservatory.

We still did the odd corporate solo shows like at Bush Hall in London for the BBC. Don't let the BBC tell you they have no money. At that particular show you could smell the money. Free bar, six top Tribute Acts, a Soul Band and a Corporate Karaoke/DJ who was being paid £2000. You can only imagine what the full cost of the day was, it was obscene.

The week after I was in a small pub in Liverpool on £350 half the price of the BBC. Our friends John and Norma came along for morale support. John had said it was a bit rough and it was! But the landlord was so nice and friendly and the locals were the same. I wasn't sure how to approach it. If I rock and rolled my way through and they wasn't bothered I would be shattered for no reason. So I decided to put on my theatre style show with all the big production numbers like Bridge Over Troubled Water and Just Pretend etc.

It proved the right decision, it brought the house down they were a fantastic audience. You could hear a pin drop when I did the quiet lyrics in Bridge. Not for the first time in my career it was a bit surreal. I don't think this little pub had had anything like me on before but they were brilliant.

From six hundred in London for the BBC to three fifty in a pub in Liverpool, I suppose that's showbiz!

Chapter 19

2010-2018....THE FINAL CURTAIN

I had been feeling more tired during and after the shows. I put it down to performing with my rock band which was very energetic. But when that finished I was still tired after the Lewis Gates shows. Maybe I was getting older I was forty seven now? I didn't know why but it was taking me longer to recover after shows. Earlier on in my career it took me a couple of hours the following morning to recuperate, now it was taking a couple of days. I spoke with my good friend Rob Leigh who was thirteen years my senior and he said it just gets harder to recover as you get older. However he also said I was too young to be taking that long to recover. There was nothing I could do so I just carried on.

I was finding I was getting more out of breath on the fast songs so I slowed it down a bit. But how could I not do songs like Jailhouse Rock, Suspicious Minds, Hound Dog and Blue Suede shoes? They were the staple of all Elvis shows. It was becoming harder and I knew there was something not right, I just didn't know what.

But we were still doing one nighters just not as many as before. One of them we did regularly was Hotel Smokie's Park in Oldham. It was the old Smokies Nightclub that me and my grave digger friend Rob Walker had frightened those girls off years ago. Anyway the tribute acts played in the bar area on a little stage. In the main club/function room they had guest celebrity DJs on Friday nights. This night it was Mike Sweeney from Piccadilly Radio. I was doing my show and going down well and had about four songs before I finished when up jumped this scruffy character in his ripped jeans shorts and said " give me the mic kid " I didn't recognise it was Mike Sweeney so I told him abruptly to get lost. He kept saying he wanted to let people know he would be starting in five minutes! If he had introduced himself and asked to borrow my mic it wouldn't have been a problem. I told him to get lost and in any case if he was starting in five minutes it would have clashed with my show.

There was an open door next to the stage and I would have been drowned out in sound. I told him if he's got a problem go see the management fully knowing the Asian management loved having me on, I brought people in early before the nightclub started and it was a bonus income for them. He returned with a face down to the ground giving me daggers, so Jacqui saw.

I finished my show and picked up my fee and was contracted for another repeat booking three months later!

It used to make Jacqui and I laugh at the initial crowd reactions as I walked on stage at some venues, especially when I was starting to gain weight. Of course I never claimed to look like Elvis but I wore the replica suits and dyed my hair and sideburns black to give the illusion of Elvis. Some really rude people would be shouting derogatory chants as I walked on stage. Society was changing. As I took the guitar off Jacqui we both jokingly copied there shouts so they could hear us because we knew what was coming next. Of course my show was based on my vocal similarity to the king and when I started singing the whole place would hush and then applaud in embarrassment. This happened quite a lot at new venues but I always won them over by merely singing. When I got a return booking the people that were rude in the first place were now sat at the front cheering me on. It just goes to show you should never judge a book by its cover!

My adopted ' Little Sister ' Debbie Fellows got married to Dave Pearshouse that year and I was a witness which I was honoured to be. Debbie had had an awful controlling first husband and I was glad she had married Dave who was the complete opposite and all round nice guy. It was a great day down in the midlands, they know how to party I can tell you. But later on when she sent me some wedding photo's I was shocked at my appearance. I hadn't realised how bad I looked. I decided no publicity photo's from then on, I looked awful.

We did many midweek solo gigs at Universities nationwide and one we did was Leeds. Fifteen minutes at midnight for a full nights wage, it was great I had to have my picture took with one of the bunny girls but I still looked awful. Another one was Warwick University in the midlands. It was really cool Jacqui was escorted to the mixing desk to work my sound and then I was escorted to the stage by two of the biggest security men id ever seen. I felt extremely small but appreciated. Again I was contracted to just fifteen minutes so I had to rock it up I had no choice. By now I found I wasn't able to sing from my diaphragm as I had done for years. So I sang from my throat which believe it or not is a lot harder, its like holding your breath while trying to get the notes right. I conquered Warwick by the skin of my teeth, the two thousand students loved it and couldn't tell I was struggling. I was escorted back to the dressing room and the students carried on the party.

Jacqui and I decided I wouldn't do any more weddings or private parties because they expected the full rock n roll experience, which was fair enough, I just couldn't cope with it. With the contracted hotel and restaurant shows we had I opted to do a more theatre style shows with more slower songs. I didn't seem to get out of breath with the big production songs so that was the game plan for now.

I was in the bath getting ready, we had to travel to Middlesborough for a show at The Sporting Lodge Hotel. Then right out of blue I felt a terrible sharp pain in my right eye. Instantly I knew it was what Mr Hamzi had spoke about a few months earlier. My Cornea had blistered and I couldn't even open my eye it was that painful. It felt like somebody had stabbed me in the eye with a knife. Against Jacqui's pleas I decided the show must go on. It was a nightmare though, even the two hour drive up there was bad. Every bump in the road was agony but I was so determined to do the show. Two hundred people had paid thirty pounds a head to see me so I couldn't let them down.

I finished the show and it went down great as usual even if I did have to wear my Elvis style sunglasses. I couldn't let everyone see what state my eye was in, it was constantly leaking but it looked like sweat to the audience.

We got in to see Mr Hamzi the following day as an emergency. He told me straight away I would definitely need a cornea transplant. He gave me pain killers and a black eye patch, I felt like Captain Jack Sparrow!!

On the day of my operation they gave me four injections around my eye to numb it then wheeled me in to theatre. I was awake all the time and Mr Hamzi talked with me all the way through. When he took my cornea off it was the most brilliant sight I had ever seen. Imagine a kaleidoscope image only ten times as vivid, it was wonderful. Then he put the new cornea on and I was back to seeing nothing. He stitched it in and told me not to do any shows or singing for at least six weeks. I went home bandaged up feeling very sorry for myself. Jacqui and Ben were so good they treated me with kid gloves. I thought I could get used to this being fetched and carried for every day!

I had to go back to Mr Hamzi every other day for him to check up on me. And eventually he told me I could leave the bandage off. Everything was a blur for two days then on the third day it was like WOW I can see. Not only that I could see far better than I had ever seen in my life, everything was now so very vivid and clear. Everything was how it should be at my check ups so I started taking bookings. I think I only had to cancel four or five shows.

Alas it was a false dawn. After a couple of months my eyesight slowly went back to what it was like before. I was gutted. I cant tell you how down I was.

Mr Hazmi was brilliant of course he told me all the different options I had. I chose to just carry on and hope nothing worse happened. The worst being having a false eye fitted or stitching up my eye up completely. I wouldn't wish that dilemma on my worst enemy. The only good thing was I still had my left eye, my right eye didn't look too bad and I could still carry on performing.

At this time Dave from Elvis Kitchen offered Jacqui the Front of House Managers job. He new we would be short of money for a while and it definitely helped us out.

Before too long Dave realized that Jacqui was a very important part of the restaurant. Of course she had been a restaurant manager in Rhyl years before and she just settled in nicely.

Elvis Kitchen was doing so well financially that Dave decided to open another Elvis Kitchen this time in Didsbury, Manchester. I went along with Jacqui to oversee the Elvis décor. She made an Elvis walk of life on the ceiling which was fantastic. When everything was finished Dave said he wanted me to do opening night. We timed it so it didn't clash with me eye recuperation period. I suggested we get an Elvis VIP to come along. I found out that Jerry Scheff (Elvis bass player in the 70s) was living in Scotland. I got in touch with him and he was very impressed with what we had created. We sorted out his fee which was very reasonable and he came to open the restaurant. My band had disbanded by then so Ben put a band together from his friends at University. We had done a few low key shows and they were very good.

On the actual night Big Jim White was there and he came up to me and apologised for being rude all those years ago. Now if someone is man enough to apologise in my book you have to accept it. I found out after the show that Dave had told him to apologise to me or he would throw him out. It was nice of Dave to do that but I would have much preferred it to have been genuine.

Jerry Scheff is a true gentleman and very humble too. I had spoken with his wife on the phone the day before and she said to make sure he gets up and plays some songs with me and the band. I explained he had only been booked to do a meet and greet but she just said to get him up to play its what he does best. I broached the subject with Jerry and he said he thought he was down for playing anyway. Half way through our set I got him up and he played Steamroller Blues with us. It was the highlight of my career. Even in his seventies he was superb. I couldn't believe

I was sharing the stage with this guy that had played with the King on The Aloha From Hawaii Show and Elvis On Tour. He took my microphone and spoke with the audience about his time with Elvis, the crowd were mesmerised. After Elvis died he had toured with John Denver every year and earlier in the late sixties he had recorded an album with Jim Morrison and The Doors, what a life he's had. Go and buy his book off his website " Way Down with Elvis " the list of stars he's played with is mind boggling. Yet again it was a magical moment that I'll never forget.

Ive kept in touch with Jerry and regularly speak to him on Facebook.

However, Elvis Kitchen 2 only lasted a few months. Dave had gone into business with some of Manchester's underworld, specifically the infamous Quality Street Gang! I met Jimmy Swords and his cronies, they all came in for a meal and to see my show. They just seemed like normal old men but I don't think I would cross any of them. I had a meeting with Jimmy Swords about supplying one of his other restaurants with tribute acts but I think the fees were to high and he decided to back out. He wanted the best for the cheapest price and as we all know you only get what you pay for. It took me ages to get it out of Dave why EK2 had to close. Even now I'm not sure but I have my suspicions.

It was a great shame, Jacqui had worked her socks off with the décor. It looked pretty amazing. But people with money had spoiled it for me yet again.

In 2013 Ben finished University with a 2.1 in Music Performance and Recording. As you can imagine Jacqui and I were so proud of him. We went to his graduation and I for one had a tear in my eye. Nobody on my side of the family had been to University let alone pass with flying colours.

It was his 21st birthday that year and he just wanted a party at home with our friends and his band mates from University. We set up the conservatory with his drums and guitar amps and we were all treated to a great jam session. Even though I wasn't supposed to sing because of my eye I got up and did two songs. I promised Jacqui I would stand still, probably the only time I ever did. People came from everywhere for Bens party, Debbie & Dave from Birmingham, Ken & Julie from Macclesfield, Eileen & Steve from Northwich and May & Jeff from Stoke. I was so pleased they had all come for Bens party! Almost all the locals from The Dyers were there also. The sun was shining and it couldn't have been a better day!

In 2017 we had to have Buddy put to sleep. The three of us were devastated. We were on the fields throwing sticks for him and when he turned we heard his cruciate in his knee snap. He didn't care he wanted to keep chasing the stick but we took him straight to the vets where they told us about the cruciate. The vet told us he could do an operation inserting wire into his knee and it probably would solve the problem. It cost us £1100 but I didn't care I wanted my best friend out of pain. It worked for about a year when we noticed him struggling to stand up and walk. The vet advised us the best option was to put him to sleep. We had a few days with him and then on the actual day I was a blubbering wreck. As the vet injected him he went to lie down to sleep so I held his head in my hands so his head wouldn't hit the floor. Jacqui and Ben were stroking him and I think he knew what was happening but never complained. He was in no pain now. The vet left us for a while and the three of us were all crying. I couldn't get my head around it and I still cant. Along with Blacky from when I was a kid, Buddy was the best companion I ever had. I could never own another dog, he was such an important part of our little family.

Back on the road and it was a Friday night at The Great Barr Hotel in Birmingham. We did it three times a year and it was always full, I had a decent following down there including all the Fellows family. Everything was going well until I got to Jailhouse Rock. I turned to Jacqui and said "my legs are shaking " of course she just said " they're supposed to you idiot your doing Elvis". I turned to her again and said " they're shaking on they're own I'm not doing it ". Then I saw a worried look on her face. I felt totally out of control of my body. I persevered and got to the end. When I did My Way it was very visible something was wrong. I had to hold the microphone with both hands, but even then my hands were shaking. I think my loyal audience could tell I wasn't well because they cheered even more, almost trying to help me get through. I was really worried about the Saturday and Sunday shows that were to follow. Jacqui said to cancel, we didn't need the money. I refused, there was two hundred people in Essex that had paid for tickets to see me and the Sunday was a wedding for a man that was in my fan club. I could never let anyone down, it just wasn't in my nature.

On the Saturday we were at Colchester Hotel and Golf Club in Essex. I had been booked to perform for an hour at their tribute night. I felt a little better than last night in Birmingham and I was going down really well, people were up dancing and singing along. Then came Jailhouse Rock again, and it hit me like a brick wall. I just couldn't catch my breath. Its a song with very fast lyrics which I hadn't had a problem with before but there was just nothing left in the tank. I sang when I could but I thought I was going to faint or something. I took a long breather after the song but the crowd were getting restless so I changed my set and did Its Now Or Never. It was an easier song and I knew the crowd would sing along, which they did. After that everything is pretty much a blur. I remember singing the last one, Cant Help Falling In Love and staggering back to our hotel room. As soon as I got in the door I collapsed on the bed. Jacqui used to deal with the guests that wanted to buy CDs or an autograph. That would usually take ten to fifteen minutes before she got to our room. She had to wake me, I had been out for ten minutes. We both decided to get to see the specialist as soon as possible. We had accommodation at the hotel so I just stayed in bed. I signed a few autographs and sent them back with Jacqui. They must have thought I was a real diva.

Sunday we were up in North Yorkshire to appear at at wedding for this guy who was in my fan club. Jacqui just really wanted to cancel I think she was scared I would collapse again and maybe it wouldn't be a good outcome.

Anyhow I decided I wasn't going to let the bride and groom down they had been to see my show dozens of times.

297

It was being held at the place where they filmed the TV series Heartbeat in the village of Goathland near Whitby. I had turned down a part in that series once they wanted me and my band to play a couple of songs in the hotel for £300! Obviously that was no where near enough especially for being on prime time TV on a Sunday evening. Anyway I digress, the show was going down well and I decided to leave out Jailhouse Rock after the last two nights debacle. Even so about half way through I could feel it happening again so I slowed it down and got the bride and groom up on the dance floor and I sang The Hawaiian Wedding Song, which brought the house down. I had to speed it up after that so I did Johnny B Goode and I just couldn't cope. I did some throw away songs (as Elvis called them) Teddy Bear/Don't Be Cruel/Hound Dog. All played a hundred miles an hour but more or less with spoken vocals so they were easier.

I just about finished the show but I had to sit down for a long time afterwards my legs felt like jelly and my breathing was hard. God bless Jacqui she pulled all the speakers, amps and lights down on her own. I have a guardian angel walking on earth with me.

Monday morning Jacqui got me in to see the specialist at Oldham Royal Hospital. Ironically she was called Jacqui as well, she was brilliant and very caring. She gave me some coping techniques but most importantly she got me referred to Mr Allen at North Manchester Hospital. He was running a clinic that specialized in asthma and breathing problems. After some tests he told me I had Acute Allergic Asthma and he put me on the strongest dose of steroids, 40mg a day. In less than a week I could feel the benefit already. I had to see him once a week where he did more tests on me and told me I was improving well.

I carried on doing shows now that I could breathe easier but I did alter the show, making it more of a theatre show with more big production numbers they weren't a problem it was the fast rock n roll I struggled with. So I cut out as many as I could and the audiences seem to love it even more.

298

Twelve months after first seeing Mr Allen, he told me I was very lucky. If I had waited another two weeks to get treatment it would have been too late for me. So I would publicly like to thank Mr Allen and his staff for saving my life.

I was still doing shows for the learning difficulties clubs and one we did was at The Village Hotel in Bury. I had done quite a few weddings at this venue and it was a decent size function suite. This particular event was for the learning difficulties from Bury and there was about two hundred there with their carers. Halfway through the show this lovely guy asked if he could get up on stage and dance like Elvis. I said sure and before I knew it there were around thirty on stage it was chaotic but beautiful. Not one of them asked to take my microphone and sing, they were so respectful. Unlike all the drunks on the Christmas party nights. I really enjoyed that show, money cant buy that feeling that your making people deliriously happy. The fact I was getting £500 off Bury Council made it all the more sweeter.

At the hospital they put me on two more inhalers as well as my Ventolin and my breathing seemed a lot better. Apart from the side effects the high dose of steroids was causing, they were awful. One of them made the front of my legs turn completely black. This went on for a few months but nobody knew why this had happened Gradually it went away.

Another one was the steroids had attacked my Adrenal gland and taken it over. It meant that my Adrenal gland was only working at 50% so I couldn't get enthusiastic about anything. Even at the shows I wasn't excited at all. I smiled at all the right times, I was programmed for that but my smiles were false. I just couldn't get into anything whatsoever. And it remains the same today, they told me I'll be like this permanently.

The next side effect was the weight issue. Everyone knows that steroids can put added weight on but I'd never been this weight before and it was embarrassing on stage. I'm sure the audiences thought I was overeating on cheeseburgers etc. just like Elvis. The trouble was I only had extra weight on my tummy and my neck, my arms, legs and everything else were the same as before. The neck problem created Sleep Apnoea. They tested me over night and found that I was stopping breathing thirty four times every hour. This was quite disturbing because I had no idea, well you don't when you're asleep. They gave me a C-Pap unit with a facemask. When i've got the mask on I feel like a second world war spitfire pilot! However it does give me pure oxygen so I can sleep alright.

I had not been sleeping properly for a while so to let Jacqui have a good nights sleep I went into Bens room. He was living away from home at that time. The first night in there I got this pain in my back, it felt like a knife. It settled down then it happened again and again in a different places. Then even more in my back all in different places, six in all. I felt paralysed, I couldn't move or go to sleep. Every time I tried six of these knives in my back twisted and paralysed me. I found out later they were back spasms like trapped nerves. Normal people get one trapped nerve but I just have to be more dramatic don't I. The doctor gave me yet more pain killers. The spasms rear up now and again but there's nothing can be done. I was beginning to think I had more tablets than Boots the chemists.

The next side effect was that all my body was hurting really badly. To cut a long story short the steroids had attacked my nervous system so my nerve ends were not working. This meant that just to touch my body anywhere was extremely painful. I tried to avoid touching everything but its almost impossible. I saw the specialist and he diagnosed this nerve end thing. He also diagnosed that my knees were not aligned properly, they were pointed outwards. By all accounts when I was doing the young Elvis years ago my legs got damaged. Trying to impress the audiences with the Shakin' Stevens movements, legs spread apart etc. had been a real negative effect now. You don't care or think about things like that when you're young you just live in the moment. That didn't help me now so the Doctor told me to try and lose some weight and he could then re-align my knees with physio.

That was great I could see some light at the end of the tunnel. Until I found out that the steroids had attacked my stomach muscles. So much so that where a man has his six pack my muscles were growing outwards. They thought it was an hernia at first but the specialist told me about the muscles. I've now got to wait to see a physio, God knows how long that will take. Great! So while the steroids were necessary, they were a necessary evil!

The final side effect was I developed Diabetes Type 2 through the steroids. I won't bore you with how this affected me we all know about Diabetes. It has changed my life in every way possible.

This seemed to be the final straw because depression hit me hard as you can imagine.

I want to explain something to you, I c all it The H.I.T. These are the three main topics that people get jealous and sometimes downright nasty about.

H....Honesty, for whatever reason a lot of people can't handle someone being honest. I've found this out countless times throughout my career in show-business.

I....Intelligence, people don't trust and are envious of intellect. This affects people that are control freaks and there are many of them.

T....Talent, in show-business there's a multitude of jealous cat fighting if someone is more talented than themselves. And I can tell you I've witnessed this a thousand times.

It's all a bit sad really and I really can't understand jealousy or back stabbing. If someone is talented we should all applaud them, no matter what business they are in. I've always said about other Elvis shows " They are all good in they're own ways they're all talented. If you can get up on stage and entertain people then you are talented end of.

That's why I loved working with other tribute artistes, I was fascinated how they worked and won an audience over with they're talents and little stage tricks. I suppose it's just a sign of the times we live in that some people will always be jealous of somebody.

Whilst all these changes in my body was happening we had some really raucous nights at Elvis Kitchen. Especially some New Years Eves. The restaurant was licensed for seventy five but I swear Dave squeezed around a hundred and thirty in sometimes. I did two sets on New Years Eve shows instead of one and Jacqui and I did a disco to close the night, sometimes around 2am. I don't know how I managed it, it must have been sheer determination.

One particular December party night warmed my heart. Remember Denis from the Elvis Fan Club all those years ago? Well we had been in touch for last few years and Denis said he was booking a table for him, Bev and their family. And if I could would I stop the show during "Love Me Tender" and say to Bev that Denis had something to say. He got down on one knee and proposed to Bev. She was speechless and the whole restaurant cheered when she said yes! These were the nights I cherished, when it was personal You couldn't wish to meet a nicer couple and we went to their wedding which was very special.

One New Years Eve everyone was up dancing, even dancing on their seats and the floor was bouncing that much I got worried it would fall into the chippy below. Its funny now but at the time it was a bit scary!

By that time I had started getting changed into my Elvis jumpsuit at home and travelling to Elvis Kitchen ready to go on stage. Dave agreed to leave my sound and lighting system set up permanently so I could just walk on stage. We got some funny looks at traffic lights but it made life so much easier not having to set the sound rig up in the afternoon. We timed it so we would arrive ten minutes before showtime. I would wait backstage while Jacqui would switch everything on. She would then come and check on me and tell me any special song requests and then we would start.

I had come full circle from when I started my career on Langley arriving in Tony's car ready dressed to Elvis Kitchen ready dressed, albeit five stone heavier!

One night at one of the December party nights Jacqui warned me backstage that there wasn't much room even to put my guitar on. When I walked out to a rapturous welcome I couldn't believe how Dyan had set the tables out. She had put a long table right in front of my little stage area. I turned to Jacqui and said " how am I supposed to perform like this ", she shrugged her shoulders and told me she had told Dyan that Pete wouldn't be able to perform properly. Dyan and Dave were adamant it had to be like that to fit more customers in!. I did the show I had no choice, they were all chanting my name afterwards. It went down extremely well due to my professionalism but afterwards I had a row with Dave. I told him that Jacqui would have set the tables out better instead of Dyan and still get the same numbers in. He took objection, he took it personally and slammed his fist on the table and stormed off. I'm sure Dyan thought I was some sort of karaoke singer, she had no respect for my show whatsoever.

We made up the following week, Dave backed down and after that Jacqui was designated to arranging the table plans from then on. I never had any more problems and everyone was happy.

In 2016 we received the awful news that Brian Fellows (Pauline's husband) had passed away. I was very upset he had always been great with us. He was a larger than life character who had been a bouncer at Birmingham NEC in his younger days. Unfortunately it had left him deaf being at stage front next to the huge speakers, but he never let it him affect him.

His daughter Debbie asked if I would sing Crying In The Chapel and The Wonder Of You at his funeral, it would be an honour!

We got through his funeral pretty much as hard as Pauline's was and I hoped I would never have to sing at a funeral ever again.

Debbie had become another of my adopted " Little Sister's" and we are like family nowadays.

Meanwhile my band gigs had been limited to about two or three a year until eventually one year I had none. It was such a shame they were a great band but they had all gone on to other projects which was understandable they were jobbing musicians.

I had one final gig with them but it was a small fee in a venue in Ashton, Manchester. Chris the drummer couldn't make it and the fee wasn't viable for Jonathan on keyboards. So Chris Williams said he would play some of the piano melodies on his guitar. My son Ben offered to help out on drums which he was more than capable of. However on stage the quality just wasn't there any more and Ben ended up carrying the band on his drums which was very intelligent of him but it must have been embarrassing for John and Chris. Afterwards Ben said he didn't want to play with them ever again, and these were the musicians he had looked up to for years. But I suppose age catches up with all of us. It was heartbreaking watching it die right there while I was singing on stage! After all we had been through from The New York Club in Southport to The Americana Festival and beyond. It was over!

In March 2018 I did what was to be my final show ever. Although I didn't know it at the time. Jacqui had said to me in January that something was in the air but she didn't know what it was.

So on Easter Friday thirty five years almost to the day I did my first show at Langley Labour Club, I came on stage for the very last time. It did feel strange, the atmosphere was weird. The audience were great though when I did Hurt and My Way they stood up applauding, It was as if they knew, and as I started singing the final song Cant Help Falling In Love I knew this would be the last time I would ever experience this wonderful experience of entertaining people. I couldn't call it a job because I had loved every second of it. But now I took my final applause and walked off with a lump in my throat and tears in my eyes. Thirty five years of a magical rollercoaster ride gone and Lewis Gates had finally " Left The Building "......

Then out of the blue Elvis Kitchen closed. After six years of success with the Elvis theme Dave had decided to go for a different theme. Robins Nest, as in the old TV show. He'd changed it into a French restaurant, it didn't work and they had to close within weeks. I have no idea why he would discard a winning formula like Elvis Kitchen but that was Dave all over.

304

When Jacqui came home and told me about it I was stunned, we both were. Even more strange was that on the actual last night he had booked Pure Magic (Freddie Mercury Tribute). I wasn't even there but it went down well apparently, Freddie was always the true pro. Later when Jacqui had tilled up Dave, Dyan and the staff were having a last drink. Jacqui wasn't even offered a drink, just thanks Jaks and that was it, she came home pretty upset. They could have sent her home with a bottle of something there was plenty left behind the bar. On that last night they took well into four figures behind the bar and ticket sales.

After everything she had done to make the restaurant a success I was disgusted in the way they had treated her. Six years and just thanks, see you! Without Jacqui the place would have shut down long before it did.

I worked it out, and over a full year I was saving Dave £12,500 with running all the media, Booking all the tribute acts without commission and doing cheaper shows for him. I felt like I had been taken for a fool.

They haven't contacted us ever since and its probably better that way. He was once my brother but in reality he was a charlatan.

The day after the closure Jacqui called Dyan to get my Elvis memorabilia back. She said it had all been put in the lock up behind the restaurant and she would see what she could do. A week later we found out it had all been sold on eBay! The absolute cheek of it. I had leant it to Dave in good faith and now he had sold my memorabilia. Jacqui was going to call the police but I told her to leave it we were much better off just cutting them off and have nothing to do with them ever again. Besides I had only leant him the cheap memorabilia, it wasn't worth a great deal apart from sentimental value.

So that was that, the end of my career. I always thought I would end up doing a farewell concert, but no it ended abruptly and I just couldn't get my head around it, still can't. Thirty five years and over five thousand shows gone in a flash. From Langley Labour Club to The Cannes Film Festival to Planet

Hollywood and The Dorchester Hotel in London, Lewis Gates had finally 'Left The Building'......

I was fifty four years old and the only trade I had was being Elvis. I wasn't capable of touring any more and everyone suggested I sign on to Universal Credit to get permanent sick pay, which I should have done a few years prior.

I went with Ben and when I walked in for my interview the guy said well I can see your obviously not well. He was really nice, he sympathised with my position and immediately signed me up. He also suggested I try for PIP (Personal Independence Payment) this was paid irrelevant of whatever I was awarded on Universal Credit. So I went for that interview in Manchester and there was no parking spaces nearby so we had to park a few miles away. Of course when my name got called I was struggling to breathe and again the guy was very sympathetic, he asked me a few questions and signed me up on PIP. This was great but I felt so embarrassed having to do this. I had worked all my life from being fifteen years old and never relied on handouts from the government. Jacqui and Ben both said I had paid taxes for all those years so I was entitled to it, but it just didn't sit well with me, still doesn't. But I was in a corner with no options so I put aside my pride and accepted it.

To my immense pride Jacqui rolled her sleeves up and got a job as a carer. She was qualified for this as she had done it years ago in Wales. Then one morning she called me from work and said her mum Avril was really poorly in hospital in Wales and she was coming home to travel to see her. Before she got home her dad had called her to tell her Avril had passed away. She phoned me from the side of the road and told me. She was in uncontrollable tears. I was in shock Avril was one of my closest friends and confidants years ago. She had helped me with the show when my mum was poorly. After the shows I had spoken to her way into the night about my dreams etc. she always had the right answer. Now I had her daughter, my wife, coming home heartbroken and I didn't know what to say. The house was so quiet then I heard Avril saying in my head just look after Jacqui, console her and love her. My feelings could come later, I wasn't twenty any more I was a grown man, as usual Avril was right and that's what I did when she walked through the door. She was inconsolable as you can imagine. She drove down to Wales and spent time down there with her dad, Pamela her younger sister and nieces. Her other younger sister Michelle was on a flight back to the UK from her home in Australia.

It was all very sad I thought Avril was going to live forever, all of us did! Jacqui came back to pick me up so I could go and see Avril in the chapel of rest. She looked just like herself with that dubious look on her face. She didn't want a funeral she wanted her ashes blasted into the sky in a rocket firework from the beach. So we all attended that and it seemed appropriate, she was a force of nature, you knew when she was in the room. I think I was one of just a few that wasn't wary of her personality. I thought she was funny especially when she got mad. I'm glad she went up in a rocket firework she had often told me I would skyrocket with my career one day. Of course she was right again I had hit heights I had only ever dreamed of, most of which she never got to see.
But in the cold light of day I had lost my best friend!

A month or so later I got a call from Joy Williams, my guitarist Chris's wife. He had died suddenly, he was sixty five and so full of life. Again I couldn't believe yet another loss. He had a dry sense of humour and it showed at his funeral he had Johnny B Goode coming in to the church then Route 66 played as the curtain closed. He had also played for a long time with the sixties band The Avengers, Steve and the band were there and were just as in shock as Jacqui and I. We'll miss you Chris "James" Burton R.I.P

Jacqui didn't feel she could carry on working as a carer so she got a job in a factory in Middleton. After that she moved to a job in Oldham as a shift supervisor where she still works today.

Ben for reasons known only to himself has ended his musical career. It broke my heart after all the work he had put in to it and the level he attained. A fantastic talent wasted in my opinion.

307

However he his happy riding his cruiser motorcycle in a bike MC. As long as he's happy that's all that matters to me.

Me, well I've always thought I would do a farewell show alas it was never to be. All my musicians are scattered around the globe or sadly passed away. It breaks my heart not being able to say farewell on stage one last time.

There are many people I miss like the kids I grew up with on Langley, my school friends, my football friends. And I miss my best friend Steve McKay "Macca" who lives in Brisbane, Australia. Were going to visit him and his lovely family at some point when my illness levels out.

But most of all I miss the heady days of summer seasons in North Wales. It seemed magical then and even more so now. I did my apprenticeship at those venues and I hold them and the people very dear, especially The Harbour. I miss the comradrie of performing with the different bands ive had. There's really no feeling like it when it all comes together on stage then afterwards in the dressing room the atmosphere was amazing! I miss my good friend Rob Leigh and the Vegas Nights show we did for fifteen years around the UK. He left us too soon.

The only thing I have left that works properly now is my voice, so i used my touring equipment to make a mini recording studio in my Elvis room at home. So I still release about four or five albums a year, either Lewis Gates or Pete Presley CDs. If I make just a few people happy with my music that makes it all worthwhile.

I hope you have enjoyed this Rock'n'Roller coaster of a life I've had. I achieved things I could only ever have dreamed of and not many people can say that.

I have been truly blessed.

So I'll close with a quote from a very special man......

" I learned very early in life that

Without a song the day would never end,
Without a song a man ain't got a friend,
Without a song the road would never bend,
So I'll just keep singing the song "

Elvis Presley 1971

Epilogue

In December 2019 I had my quarterly eye check up. I had been feeling a bit unwell with my eye aching up and leaking. When we went in to see the Doctor he knew straight away something was wrong. He gave me a thorough check over and said my diabetic sugar levels were through the roof in my eyes. He put me on a drip to get the levels down which they did after a few hours. He said he'd make an appointment to see Mr Musa the new top eye specialist at Rochdale Infirmary. I had to wait until February 2020 to see Mr Musa, who told me my optical lens was shot caused by Glaucoma and I had a hole in my pupil causing fluid to leak.

When you have Glaucoma its very painful but I hadn't felt anything at all. Mr Musa explained that because I was on very strong opiate based painkillers for other medical problems I hadn't felt anything. However he said if he could operate within two weeks he could perform another cornea transplant and plug the leak as well. This would give me some eyesight back.

From February I had to wait until October to have my operation. Jacqui had called lots of times but was rebuffed by the bookings department. She told them it was urgent but they just didn't care, once they even slammed the phone down on her. It was all very stressful. When we actually got to see Mr Musa in October we told him what had happened with the booking office and he concurred the same had happened with him when he had tried to get me in. He said the booking department was shambolic, he recommended I contact PALS for an apology. If the Doctors couldn't book a time slot for an operation what chance did we stand!

Meanwhile he said he might just be able to do another cornea transplant if it was done in the next few days. You guessed it I had to wait a further three weeks at which time it was too late to do anything for me apart from permanently surgically close my eye! I was devastated, I was going to be left with just my left eye.

After everything I had been through fate was now throwing this at me. Anyway I just got on with it and got in the right frame of mind for the operation on November 6th. When I checked in the following morning they did all the usual tests they have to do for a local anaesthetic. The nurse came back and told me I had had a silent heart attack and the operation would have to be put back twenty four hours or until my heart had settled down. I was stunned, I mean I'd had a few chest pains but I thought it was just stress. They monitored me overnight and in the morning they did another heart scan and it seemed alright so I was good to go.

Mr Musa did the operation successfully and now I'm left with no sight at all in my right eye! I can tell you it didn't help with my depression.

On July 6th 2021 I was admitted to hospital with yet more breathing problems. This time it was Covid. They kept me in for a week putting me on multi medications and 200% oxygen 24/7. My nurse was a little old lady called Mary, she had come out of retirement to help the NHS. A massive thanks to her she couldn't have looked after me any better. I was sent home with antibiotics and a blood sugar monitor. I felt alright when I got home but I wouldn't wish Covid on my worst enemy. I ended up with long Covid.

As I was coming out of hospital my best friend Rob Leigh was going in and on 19th July that year i lost my best friend. I was distraught. He'd had a triple heart bypass years ago and it seemed his body just gave up. We had been on the road for fifteen years together doing the Vegas Nights Live Show until I had to retire in 2018. We knew each other really well. I couldn't believe he was gone, after I had retired we still spoke every other week. He would tell me of the comical situations he found himself in. I would be crying with laughter. He was one of the good guys and it didn't seem fair. Of course he was the best Neil Diamond tribute artiste in Great Britain. He was old school like me and I miss him greatly. R.I.P Rob, we will sing together again in heaven.

Early 2022 I was told about my old sound engineer Gary Mac suddenly passing away. This was getting too much, he was younger than me, what was going on! Still cant believe he's not here, R.I.P Gaz.

As I look back at my thirty five year career performing as Elvis Presley. I often wonder how it was all possible. Lets be honest I have no resemblance to Elvis Presley at all. I suppose I got away with the illusion with my dyed black hair, sideburns and Elvis replica suits that my Mum and Jacqui had made. When I was a mime act early on I tried to match Elvis' vocals and timing with that dummy microphone that wasn't live. I was successful at this and I truly believe I had Elvis as my vocal coach without me actually realizing it at the time! He gifted me with his exact vocal range and timing and for that I am eternally grateful.

Whatever the reason I know Ive been lucky and blessed. After leaving The Co-op at fifteen I don't feel as if I have worked a day in my life. It's like a professional footballer, he would have played in a pub team on a Sunday morning if he hadn't made it as a pro. Its been an incredible experience that I wouldn't have missed for the world!

Today Jacqui, Ben and i went to see my bass player John. He's 78 now and in a care home. He has Parkinsons and Dementia and its just a matter of days before he goes to play bass with the real Elvis. It was extremely hard seeing him there although he did recognise us for a while then he drifted off into his own world. I don't know what I'm going to do knowing I can't call him up any more. He never ever said this but he treated me like a son, he never said no to any favours I would ask and gave me some great advice over the years. He was an excellent musician who knew music inside out. He was the base of the band so that we could all embellish our talents to produce an incredible authentic feel. Single handedly he taught Ben everything he needed to know to get him into Manchester Music College and later Salford University. For that I will be forever grateful and I'm going to miss John more than words can say.

John died on 3rd October 2022, the same date my mum died, we were devastated!

On 17th December 2022 I was on a night out with my old Road Manager Ricky at my local pub. When all of a sudden my only good eye went blind. When we got to A&E the doctor told me my cornea was swollen, I was really scared I didnt want to be totally blind. I was told to come back the following day to have a proper examination. Mr Altaan explained my cornea had perforated and he would need to glue it which took him an hour and half in theatre. He told me to come back after Christmas to be checked out.

It was an horrible Christmas being blind, Jacqui tried to make as special as she always did but I just couldnt get in the mood at all. Then on Christmas Day night I got up to use the toilet, got disorientated and plunged head first down the stairs. As I started to fall I tried to get my left leg to stop me on the newel post, I heard a big snap and a lot of pain. I knew straight away what it was, it was my cruciate ligament. What a great Christmas!

When we went back to see Mr Altaan he said the glue had not taken so he immediatley to theatre to glue it again it again. He also told me he would eventually do a cornea transplant when the swelling had gone down. The glue didnt take again so he had to do it for the third time. This time it stayed glued and he refered me to The Manchester Royal Eye Hospital for a transplant.

We got in at Manchester and saw Mr Au who explained it would be better to do a cornea graft then eventually have a transplant. At this point my head was spinning. I can't begin to tell you what Jacqui did for me at this time, she was my only light. She was doing absolutely everything for me even guiding me to the bathroom during the night, she was unbelievable. She took six weeks off work to look after me and i'll never be able to repay the care and love she showed me.

Eventually I had my cornea graft and instantly I could see again. Mr Au was surprised, he had told me I might get some vision but not like it was. Somebody was smiling down on me that day along with the exceptional skills of Mr Au. It was the worst six weeks of my life but all seems good now, fingers crossed.

Ive lost many people over the years like we all have but the one that shook me to my very core was my Mother. She was such a huge part of my life and I can still feel her presence today. My biggest regret was that she never got to hear me sing live in theatres, I think she would have been thrilled that her Peter had been given this talent. I owe everything that I am as a man to her and I hope she's looking down smiling and proud of me. Love you Mum!

But all is definitely not doom and gloom I'm very upbeat. I have my son Ben who never fails to amaze me with his different antics. I know he would walk through a brick wall for me and his mum and I love him with every fibre of my being. He's a very talented musician and chef and I'm extremely proud of him.

And finally I also have my beautiful wife Jacqui. She has taught me lots of things but mainly how to be patient. Ive been lucky enough to have a second chance with a soul mate and not many people get that chance. I'm looking forward to going on different adventures with her and spending the rest of my life with the strongest and most beautiful person I know, my wife!

I love you loads more Jacqui xxx

Just Remember In The Winter,
Far Beneath The Bitter Snow,
Lies The Seed, That With The Suns Love,
In The Spring,
Becomes The Rose.

Discography

Albums

Lewis Gates Band....The ELVIS Experience
All Shook up - The Essential 50s & 60s Collection
Hits Of The 70s
Songs From Tonight's Show
Old Friend
The Very Best Of Lewis Gates Vol.1
The Very Best Of Lewis Gates Vol.2
The Very Best Of Lewis Gates Vol.3
The Very Best Of Lewis Gates Vol.4
The Very Best Of Lewis Gates Vol.5
White Christmas
I'll Be Home For Christmas
Lewis Live
Tales From The Jungle Room
Elvis Duets Feat. Lewis Gates Vol.1
Elvis Duets Feat, Lewis Gates Vol.2
Elvis Duets Feat. Lewis Gates Vol.3
Legendary Star Duets Feat.Lewis Gates Vol.1
Mr Songman
Rocker Vol.1
Rocker Vol.2
Live At The Dyers
Walk A Mile In My Shoes
Live At Madison Square Garden – Fantasy Concert
From The Lewis Gates Vaults Vol.1
From The Lewis Gates Vaults Vol.2
From The Lewis Gates Vaults Vol.3

The Lewis Gates ELVIS Experience DVD
The Spirit Of Elvis Show DVD

Pete Presley's RAISED ON ROCK

Pete Presley's RAISED ON ROCK Double CD

Pete Presley – Fearless (Solo Album)
Pete Presley's RAISED ON ROCK DVD

Very Special Thanks To Denis and Bev for making this whole project successful, we cherish you're friendship TCB

Acknowledgements

My Mum Brenda Gow, My Wife Jacqui Gow, My Son Ben Gow, Little Sister Michelle & Nevekka, Little Sister Pamela...Jacob..Lydia & Sophie, Rob Leigh, Stephen McKay, Rob Walker, Little Sister Christine Roberts, My Showbiz Dad & Mum Alan & Louise Grayson, Jimmy & Marion Bond, Michael Rugerrio, Richard Kelly, Jerry Scheff, Mike & Sue Smith, Little Sister Debbie & Dave Pearshouse, Daniel Pearshouse, Gail Stockton, Cath Ward, Natalie Davies, Rachel Davies, Tracey Smith, Tracey Rowlands, Little Sister May Whitby, Lynn & Keith, Colin Barber, Rob Banks, Jimmy Bond Jr, Pete Bond, Carol & Tommy Price, John Tremayne, Guy Schalom, Neil Bowden, Alan Faulkner, Dave Faulkner, Jonathan Davies, Chris Williams, Chris Wharton, Paul Pinkham, Graham McGrotty, Johnny Ball, Testa Rosa Studio's, Plank Lemmy, Quo Iddon Stanley, Tommy Slash Roberts, Iain Angus Young, Stringbean, Trem Feighery, Trim Stanislaus, Simon Stanislaus, Gavin Law, Avril Henderson, John Clayton, Arthur Sheridan, Lawrence McGlaughlin, Ken & Julie, Steve & Eileen Sharman, TJ Slater, Betty & Joseph Wood, John Shirt, Brian & Pauline Fellows, John & Breeda Bene, Ray..Barbara & Mary, Paul & Clark Topham, Butch, Steve Grayson, John Clews, John & Norma, Hilary Brereton, Eddie & Maureen, Stan Price, Phil Hughes, Gary & Jackie Marriott, Johnny Peller, Paul Beardow, John Henderson, Gary Mac, Erica Crompton, Steve James, Bob Crossland, Jack Roach, Nigel Round, Betty Webster, Ann Armstrong, Daz Catlin, Wayne Catlin, Martin Witherford, Paul Hughes, Syd Edhouse, Mark Nuttall, Mark Ward, Pete & Gina Fanning, Dave & Cath Hughes, Tony Valenti, Tommy Price, Mr & Mrs Highfield, Chris Mannion, Mick Barker, Ged Philbin, Ian Corless, Christine Adams, Jackie Corless Gibson, Phil..Sharon & Brenda, Shoney, Lennie Capuano, Paul Tandy, Showtime Productions, Tony Reddin, The Dakotas, Bobby Ball, Robbie Williams, Steve Steinman, Les Hughes, Dave Leonard, Dr Allen, Karl Ballentine, Andy Wood, Gerry Trew, Kinisha, Steve & The Avengers, David Leacy, John Malloy, Mark Keely's Good Rockin Tonight, John O'Malley

Ingram Content Group UK Ltd.
Milton Keynes UK
UKHW020935020623
422771UK00014B/421